McILHENNY'S GOLD

Also by Jeffrey Rothfeder

Every Drop for Sale: Our Desperate Battle over Water

COLLINS BUSINESS

An Imprint of HarperCollins*Publishers*

McILHENNY'S GOLD

How a Louisiana Family Built the Tabasco Empire

JEFFREY ROTHFEDER

HarperCollins books may be purchased for educational, business, or sales promotional use. For information, please e-mail the Special Markets Department at SPsales@harpercollins.com.

First Collins paperback edition published 2009.

Library of Congress Cataloging-in-Publication Data is available upon request.

ISBN 978-0-06-072184-8
ISBN 978-0-06-072185-5 (pbk.)

20 21 22   LSC 10 9 8 7 6 5 4 3

To Claudia, my partner, my love

CONTENTS

McILHENNY'S GOLD

TABASCO ROAD

In a plant shed nearly leveled by arson, its once elegant lattice-work reduced to burned shards, Edmund McIlhenny pondered the miracles that he held in his hands. The Civil War had just ended, allowing McIlhenny, his wife and in-laws, the Averys, to return to their island in Louisiana's Gulf of Mexico after a two-year exile in Brenham, Texas, that began when they fled in 1863 as Union troops bore down on their home.

Trudging back, much had changed. The Confederacy was no more. The Averys, previously one of the wealthiest plantation owners in Louisiana, were destitute, their Dixie dollars valueless and their slaves emancipated. Edmund McIlhenny, who had made millions as a celebrated banker in New Orleans before the war, was fifty years old, out of work with no prospects. He and Mary Avery, Judge Daniel Dudley Avery's daughter, had been married for seven years and still did not have a home of their own.

And if the family was surely disconsolate, what they encountered on Petit Anse (today known as Avery Island)—a salty, swampy, isolated corner of south-central Louisiana, a mere ten miles in diameter—did nothing to buoy their spirits. The island was their sole remaining possession of any value. But crossing the narrow bayou, they found it, too, had been despoiled. With the exception of a few slave cabins, all of the homes—some palatial, others more humble—were ransacked by Union soldiers. The salt mines were ravaged. The once fertile sugar fields were scorched to bare earth. Avery Island appeared virtually devoid of life, but for a handful of former slaves who had refused to leave, unsure of where to go and what to do with their freedom.

The returning family moved into the old plantation house, although it was in disrepair. Much of the Averys' cherished period furniture had been chopped up by Northern troops and used for firewood; priceless finials and balustrades as well as family objets d'art had been looted. But the roof wasn't leaking, and the house provided shelter. Judge Avery and his sons hired the ex-slaves to help restore the fields in hopes of growing sugar again. Absent other options, they agreed to work for nothing for a short period, assuming they would receive a salary when revenue began to come in.

Judge Avery was not particularly fond of Edmund McIlhenny; he believed him to be uncouth, undereducated and lacking in sophistication. So he was determined to keep his son-in-law as far away from family plantation operations as he could. Instead, McIlhenny was given the more menial task of tending to the vegetable garden—a relatively small plot of artichokes, lettuce, tomatoes, watermelon and Irish potatoes.

While working in this garden, McIlhenny stumbled upon his miraculous discovery. As McIlhenny recounted later, he had just begun to clear the weeds, windborne rubbish and ashen debris in preparation for planting when he was stunned to find a dozen or so stunted red pepper plants, bearing fruit, poking up out of the undergrowth and tangle.

McIlhenny had to think a moment to recall how these plants came to be in Avery Island soil in the first place. In the early days of the Civil War, McIlhenny had met a Confederate soldier with the mysterious name of Friend Gleason, who had given him a handful of chilies just brought back from the Tabasco region of southern

Mexico. "You will find that these will add exceptional flavor to your food," Gleason told McIlhenny. Intrigued, McIlhenny had planted the seeds from these peppers on the island, just as the Union soldiers were poised to invade. Astonishingly, McIlhenny thought, Gleason's chilies had survived—and thrived—despite the sacking of the island.

McIlhenny remembered stripping a few of the peppers from their stalks and taking them into the plant shed to study them more closely. They were exquisite—deep bloodred in color and perfectly shaped. Although not a religious man, McIlhenny found it impossible to deny the divine qualities of plants that had stood up to hellish destruction, according to family legend. It seemed certain to McIlhenny that these scrawny vines with the picture-postcard peppers were omens pointing to some as yet unclear direction he should take. So he tinkered with the peppers, planting their seeds for future crops and using their juice in recipes, especially for pepper sauces.

The ex-slaves on Avery Island were familiar with hot flavors from their native African and Caribbean cuisines. McIlhenny asked them for advice. Some of them said the pepper juice had to breathe over time before its full taste and character could be brought out. Let it mature and ferment, they told him. Others offered suggestions for ingredients that taste best with peppers. Based on their recommendations, McIlhenny added salt and vinegar to pepper mash and aged the mixture for twenty, thirty, forty days.

When he finally unveiled his concoction, McIlhenny feared the worst. This mishmash, full of disparate flavors, could never have a pleasing taste, he thought. Upon sampling it, though, his concerns were immediately allayed. He was overjoyed by the pungent but rewarding recipe he had cooked up virtually by accident. McIlhenny's pepper sauce, he would soon learn, perfectly seasoned fish and meats and superbly fit in with the growing Louisiana hunger for spicy dishes.

McIlhenny shared the sauce with friends, who liked it as well. So he poured the thick wine-red liquid into discarded cologne bottles with narrow necks, added sprinkler fitments so only a drop of the piquant sauce could be dispensed at a time, labeled them E. McIlhenny Tabasco Pepper Sauce and offered them for sale. In the initial shipment in 1869, wholesalers were so excited about the prospects for this fresh and entirely original condiment that they purchased nearly 700 bottles for national distribution at $1 each, equal to about $15 per bottle in today's money. And thus, what we now know as Tabasco sauce was born.

McIlhenny's story is an engaging, uplifting narrative of a providential pepper plant that saved the fortune of a once wealthy but now humbled man and his family. The trouble is, large parts of it are false, nothing more than marketing fables Edmund McIlhenny fabricated to promote his new product as one that had risen up out of the depths of the Civil War. This much is known to be true: his ex-slaves did help develop the recipe for Tabasco sauce after the Averys and McIlhenny returned from exile; the dates are correct; and McIlhenny did combine vinegar, salt and pepper mash to produce an instantly profitable product with a novel taste and texture. But virtually all of the most memorable and inexplicable aspects of the story—the appearance of the shadowy soldier who handed McIlhenny the peppers, the plants' ability to survive a conflict that in the South primarily produced only victims—are as much invention as Tabasco sauce itself.

Edmund McIlhenny told and retold this tall tale so often that even those closest to him who should have known better, his wife among them, believed it. And the story became so woven into the historical thread of McIlhenny's 140-year-old family business that it, or something quite similar, has been repeated without suspicion in virtually every article written about McIlhenny Co. or Tabasco sauce, including an entertaining investigation of life on Avery Island by the respected journalist John McNulty in a 1953 issue of the *New Yorker*. Indeed, until very recently the credulous saga of Friend Gleason and his stunningly prodigious peppers was the official version of Tabasco's origins posted on the product's Web site, a factual lapse corrected only grudgingly after indisputable evidence came to light proving that the real story was something a bit less, well, saucy—although exactly what the real story is even Edmund McIlhenny's heirs are unable to say for sure.

It would be difficult to find another company so mysterious (and uncertain) about the genesis of its flagship product. But then McIlhenny Co., one of the most profitable and oldest family businesses in U.S. history, has made a habit of being out of sync with the rest of corporate America. Since Tabasco sauce was invented, four generations of McIlhennys have overseen the making of this international staple from the seclusion of Avery Island, an Acadian Gothic landscape enveloped by thick, grassy marsh and dark, antediluvian woods. Protected in this insular environment, the McIlhennys have operated unaffected by voguish business trends and untouched by modernity. In the process, the company (and the family) has remained anonymous, while its product, Tabasco sauce, has taken its place among the best-known brands in the world, a category killer whose name *is* its market classification, like globe-straddling goliaths Coke, Kodak and Kleenex.

McIlhenny's Tabasco sauce was a cult hit when occupying Union soldiers in the years right after the Civil War first shipped the product north from Louisiana. And during the initial decades of its existence, as word of the new flavor sensation slowly spread throughout the states, Tabasco grew to be a lucrative product with a loyal following. But Tabasco's popularity didn't soar internationally until around the 1930s, when the pepper sauce was included in the recipe for Bloody Mary, a drink favored by flapper-era hipsters introduced at the King Cole Bar in New York City's St. Regis Hotel. Or did the Bloody Mary—a combination of vodka and Tabasco sauce (along with ingredients like tomato juice, lemon, salt and Worcestershire sauce)—originate at Harry's New York Bar in Paris a decade earlier? Accounts differ.

Since the Bloody Mary first delighted trendsetters, Tabasco sauce has become nothing short of a ubiquitous product worldwide and it remains so today. It was seen in a photo on a mess table during the excavation of Tutankhamen. Just before World War II, a furor arose in the House of Commons when the U.K. government tried (and failed) to remove Tabasco from the Parliament's dining room tables as part of a "buy British products" campaign. Tabasco traveled with mountaineers on some of the earliest Himalayan expeditions. The pepper sauce was a part of the U.S. soldier's mess kit during the Vietnamese conflict and the first and second Gulf wars. And both Hillary Clinton and George H.W. Bush have proudly boasted they always carry a bottle of Tabasco.

From Avery Island, the McIlhennys distribute the pepper sauce to 120 countries. There are few foods that Tabasco doesn't go with (it's even poured on pizza and chop suey), few people that don't have a bottle in their pantries and few restaurants that don't offer it with other basic condiments. Craig Claiborne, former *New York Times* food critic, pronounced Tabasco sauce "as basic as mother's milk."

It's little surprise that McIlhenny Co. has risen to be a $250 million a year family business, including royalties from oil, salt and product licensing. As many as 600,000 of the recognizable, long-necked two-ounce bottles with the signature green-and-white diamond label are produced on Avery Island every day, where at the company's peak more than 200,000 Tabasco plants grew on about eighty acres of humid, loamy fields. For much of the company's existence, McIlhenny's profit margins have hovered at stratospheric levels of 25 percent or more. And this performance has produced vast wealth for the secretive McIlhenny clan, who retain 100 percent ownership in the business.

Primarily on the strength of Tabasco sales, the McIlhennys have become the richest family in Iberia Parish, where Avery Island is located, and the largest landowners. Dozens and dozens of separate Tabasco fortunes of upwards of $1 million, and in some cases well beyond, have been spread among Edmund McIlhenny's nearly 200 descendants both in Louisiana and across the country. Indeed, to avoid sharing even a tiny portion of the company with outside investors, McIlhenny has never in its history sold shares to the public. Over the years, many larger consumer goods companies have sought to purchase McIlhenny. One recent offering was for well over $1 billion. But the family has steadfastly refused to part with the company that is so conjoined with its destiny.

Except for a tumultuous twenty-four months in the late 1990s, every McIlhenny CEO since Edmund has been a direct descendant of the company's patriarch. Outsiders have been mostly unwelcome among the company's brain trust. Blessed with the slightly off-kilter McIlhenny personality, each chief has been more eccentric than the previous. There was John Avery McIlhenny, a diffident Rough Rider who took San Juan Hill with Theodore Roosevelt and later became his hunting partner. Outwardly a man's man, John also had an effete, artistic side, hidden during his lifetime but revealed recently: he was a closet collector of netsuke and other tiny, precious, rare and sometimes erotic Asian porcelain trinkets.

John was succeeded by Edward Avery McIlhenny—more commonly known as Mr. Ned. A fearlessly charismatic adventurer and naturalist, he traveled alone to unmapped regions of the world and, according to McIlhenny lore, used his powerful physique to kill Avery Island alligators with his bare hands for dinner. For nearly a half a century Mr. Ned so towered above the company and its employees, so treated Avery Island as his personal fiefdom, that he would be mourned as the "Great White Father" in his obituary.

Later the family business was managed by renowned World War II Marine sharpshooter Walter Stauffer "Tabasco Mac" McIlhenny. Stiff-necked and comically formal, Walter is remembered for the life-sized, cardboard-mounted color cutout of a Marine in full-dress uniform—his "business partner," he would tell people—that stood sentry in the entryway to his office at the Tabasco factory.

The current CEO, Paul McIlhenny, is a large man with outsized tastes in food and liquor. Some of the older, more discreet family members recalled with some embarrassment New Year's Day 2000, when Paul offered revelers in New Orleans's French Quarter a drink from a ten-foot vat he called "the world's biggest Bloody Mary for people with the world's largest hangovers." Through spigots, McIlhenny employees poured samples into large cups and handed them out to the city's postparty crowd. The recipe contained 800 gallons of V8 vegetable juice, 12 gallons of Tabasco sauce and 220 gallons of vodka.

One common thread links all of McIlhenny's CEOs: they are inextricably wedded to the company's past. The recipe for Tabasco sauce hasn't changed a bit since Edmund devised it. The company's business model—three ingredients, locally available; one factory; extremely low overhead, especially raw materials and labor costs; a demanding level of employee loyalty; and a jealously guarded brand—is as it always was. And McIlhenny's management approach—inbred and baronial—has barely advanced, even as other centuries-old companies have experienced a revolution in labor rights. For better or worse, McIlhenny Co. is an undiluted family business; save for a few unavoidable bows to innovation and size, the company today is a mirror image of Edmund's vision.

A choice made by Edmund in the latter half of the nineteenth century set the tone for the unconventional conservatism practiced ever since by the McIlhennys. Before the Civil War, Avery Island was a thriving sugar plantation, managed by McIlhenny's in-laws. Although he watched from a distance, in time McIlhenny was struck by the economic advantages of plantation life—principally, a captive, inexpensive labor force beholden to landowners. So when the war was over and the Tabasco business launched, McIlhenny sought to reclaim these bygone benefits for his own company. Hence, in the early 1880s, he began the process of transforming Avery Island into a company town, a worker's village that would in essence replicate plantation life. By the early 1900s, Avery Island was alive with free housing for hundreds of Tabasco factory and salt mine employees, a church, schools, social clubs, stores and a post office—as well as, of course, jobs for everybody that lived there.

Within years of Edmund McIlhenny's labor experiment, the coal industry also established company towns. Since most of the mines in the deep hollows of West Virginia, the Carolinas and Kentucky were located far from established communities, many coal companies built villages around the mines to provide food, clothing and shelter for their workers. Soon after, industrialists in the steel industry and auto manufacturer Henry Ford created somewhat altered models of company towns, in which the businesses would often own many of the employees' homes and generally charge rent that approached going rates. But while these industrial giants controlled aspects of the commerce and social structure of the villages, they tended to be less involved with day-to-day life than the coal companies; their primary interest was to reap profits as developers by turning these communities into thriving cities, as Ford did with Detroit.

McIlhenny's model was similar to the coal industry's, but with one vital distinction. Mine owners didn't live in the company towns. Avery Island, by contrast, *was* the McIlhennys' home; they were simply sharing it with their workers. That produced a self-sufficient community on the island composed of a small number of landowners—the McIlhenny family—and many dependent laborers; in short, a postbellum plantation. Like the pre–Civil War model, the workers were obligated to the McIlhennys for their jobs, their homes, their social lives, their environment, their safety and their spouses' and children's well-being.

Remarkably, this system survived intact on Avery Island until just a decade or so ago, well after company towns elsewhere were long gone. And although Avery Island's company town has shrunk in recent years, tangible vestiges of it—notably evident in the relationship between the McIlhennys and their workers—remain.

It's impossible to exaggerate the uniqueness of this social structure in a corporate setting or to find another example of a major company that has had an equally archaic compact with its employees for such a significant length of time. And anachronistic though it may be, McIlhenny's company town—its blend of low overhead and high productivity and the way these advantages dovetailed perfectly with the family's secluded lifestyle on Avery Island—is among the primary reasons for the success of the Tabasco business. Edmund's decision to adopt what he considered to be the best features of plantation life colored his company's culture and performance well into the future. Without it, McIlhenny would not have been able to maintain its provincial business model while competing against global condiment makers, whose multiple factories, products and business units afford them a level of cost-saving efficiency that the McIlhennys' relatively tiny operation on Avery Island cannot otherwise match.

Yet, despite the company town's paramount importance to them, the McIlhennys have hardly uttered a public word about it. Its existence is not included in any family histories. And when pressed to talk about the company town, McIlhenny Co. executives have consistently downplayed its value, possibly embarrassed by the antebellum texture of the village—even though its role in the family business's survival is obvious with a minimal amount of exploration.

This desire to sugarcoat the truth is a recurring motif in the story of McIlhenny Co. The family has historically relied on half-lies and legend to embellish the image of its pepper sauce, generate increased sales, eliminate rivals and adorn the McIlhenny myth in southern Louisiana.

However, during my many conversations with McIlhenny family members (mostly those who live outside of Louisiana, because the Avery Island group was opposed to my writing this book), their friends and current and former McIlhenny Co. employees, I learned that every family story is a blend of facts and what family members, past and present, wish the facts to be. By embroidering on the achievements of those who preceded us we make the quotidian heroic and the mythical real, perhaps in an effort to bestow larger meaning on the lives we lead today. For that reason, in recounting the story of a family—any family—verifiable memories only provide a kernel of the picture. The truth matters, to be sure, but so do the many versions of the truth, which can offer just as much insight about the family—its personality, its aspirations, its self-image—as what actually occurred.

The McIlhennys were a particularly slippery subject to explore. Consequently, I tried to unearth multiple sources of information, and I concede that in some cases people's inherited recollections of decades- or centuries-old incidents were all I had to work with. And so reality, as I suppose it always will be, is laced with imagination.

The saga of the McIlhennys and the Tabasco sauce they created is an extraordinary narrative touching three centuries of economic, social and cultural life. It returns again and again to the classic American themes of mobility and perseverance, of ingenuity and innovation, of clannishness and individualism, of arrogance and humility, of self-confidence and self-doubt and—most of all—in virtually every generation, of accomplishment.

At times, it's an unbelievable story; at least, that is, when the truth is told.

Chapter 1
THE FOREBEARS

The celebration of the marriage of Edmund McIlhenny and Mary Eliza Avery in June 1859 on Petit Anse Island was a highlight of the social season that year in southern Louisiana.

The groom, forty-four at the time, was one of New Orleans's wealthiest bachelors, a banker whose earnings were at the top rung of his profession. His young bride, more than twenty years his junior, had even more money than McIlhenny. The vast Avery fortune engineered by her father, Judge Daniel Dudley Avery, and the family's influence in Iberia Parish—tied to landholdings, the South's most cherished commodity—placed her in economic strata that McIlhenny couldn't hope to equal alone. Mary Eliza was a glowing bride; coquettish, if plump and a bit severe looking. As was the case with all of the weddings of the wealthy in the area when a man married up, these nuptials were well covered in the book *How to Get a Rich Wife,* a gossipy tome issued periodically, eagerly devoured by the hoi polloi of the day.

Judge Avery's servants and slaves prepared the wedding feast, set the tables and trimmed the lush gardens skirting the main house. Horses and carriages were draped in family colors. Just a half century before, Petit Anse Island had been virtually untouched, a primitive wilderness. But in that short time, the island, mostly during Avery's control, had been tamed and transformed into a model farming community with roads, mansions and huts—and customers in all parts of the world. With that type of metamorphosis possible, the prospects in southern Louisiana for families like the Averys, even with war on the horizon, seemed boundless.

On his wedding day, Edmund McIlhenny felt like an intruder on Petit Anse. He had never farmed in his life; urban areas were more to his liking. And while in time he came to appreciate the value of the plantation, when he first met Mary Eliza he hadn't yet given this much thought. McIlhenny could not have imagined that in a few decades the island would be his, and he would be amassing a treasure from a product whose primary ingredient grew out of its soil. Equally unlikely was the course that brought McIlhenny to Petit Anse.

Born in 1815 in Hagerstown, Maryland, Edmund was the second oldest of nine sons raised by John and Ann McIlhenny. His birthplace was a tiny apartment in the town square above what is now the Square Cup Cafe, but which then housed McIlhenny's Tavern, owned by his father.

Edmund's father was a swaggering Scottish immigrant with a rebellious streak. He had abducted his wife-to-be Ann Newcomer from a female seminary, where she had been sent to keep away from men like him. They married hours later, and for the next decade had children, one after another. Though John had been a woodsman, a bartender and a carpenter, among other things, to support his instantly large family, he became a doctor. He died suddenly in 1832 after contracting a fatal disease from a patient.

With his family short a breadwinner and facing financial ruin, Edmund discontinued his schooling at seventeen and went to work to help his mother care for and educate his seven younger brothers. He took a position as a messenger in one of the dozens of banks in Baltimore.

By mid-1837, the twenty-two-year-old McIlhenny had lost his job after the nation's economic panic that year decimated Baltimore's banks. Desperate for money, McIlhenny begged his bank contacts to help him find work anywhere. Obviously, Baltimore wasn't an option anymore. But an associate who had powerful friends in New Orleans offered McIlhenny a letter of introduction to a manager of the Bank of Louisiana, the state's third-largest bank with $4 million in capital at the time. McIlhenny's youthful willingness to dive into the most difficult or menial tasks and his sober, scholarly face— intensified by his thick, dark beard, itself made even more prominent by the absence of a mustache—particularly impressed the bank executives in Louisiana. McIlhenny was hired on the spot.

The crash of 1837 hadn't spared the South. The region was dependent on agriculture, especially cotton and sugar, and the rising number of unemployed around the country led to a sharp downturn in clothing and fabric sales, sending the price of cotton tumbling. Moreover, a succession of weak British grain harvests had induced a growing foreign-exchange deficit with the United States. To repair this imbalance, the United Kingdom restricted American imports, primarily textiles and other cotton goods. This, of course, only made cotton prices drop even further.

And the South's slave economy, a bounty of cheap labor in good times, was a liability in bad times. As the economic historian George Green described it in *Finance and Economic Development in the Old South*, a survey of Louisiana banking in the early 1800s, "In the South, labor was a fixed expense and excess field hands could not be laid off" to reduce output. The planter would only "shut down his plant when market prices for cotton fell so far that he could not even cover the relatively small variable costs of harvesting his crop."

But New Orleans wasn't like the rest of the South. Nestled on the mouth of the Mississippi River, it was, at least to a degree, immunized from the worst of the fiscal crisis and, in some important ways, able to take advantage of it. The city Edmund McIlhenny found when he arrived there in the late 1830s didn't resemble in any fashion the depressing, semilifeless, homogeneous streets of abandoned shops, beggars and petty gangsters that he had left behind in Baltimore. Instead, New Orleans was a revelation to him.

The nation's fifth-largest urban area and second-leading port, nearly 30 percent of Louisiana's population lived there. Unlike any other city in the United States, New Orleans was a cosmopolitan blend of all of the ethnic and cultural groups that had put down roots in the New World: Spanish, French, Anglos, Indians, free blacks (often from the Caribbean) and African slaves. To comprehend the full scope of this mix, consider that in 1840, 20,000 people out of a total population in New Orleans of slightly over 100,000 were free blacks—a racial amalgam unimaginable even in the North—and about 10 percent were Spanish and French. It was the first real melting pot in the nation, and this produced an intellectual and artistic golden age that with its music, painting and architecture distinguished as pure New Orleans survived intact until Hurricane Katrina ravaged the old city. Even then, the nightlife—dancing, gambling, drinking, theater, opera, cockfights, concerts and circuses—was heady.

Edmund McIlhenny, however, saw New Orleans in a different light: he was drawn to the money in town—and there was plenty of it. To McIlhenny, money was the electric undercurrent that made the city buzz, the magnet that attracted the city's unique culture and gave it its uncommon personality, not the other way around.

New Orleans was the gateway to the Mississippi Valley region. Wheat, corn, lard, pork, furs and hides, whiskey, hemp and lead from the upper Midwest and cotton, sugar, molasses and tobacco from the South were shipped to the Northeast, Europe and the Caribbean through New Orleans. And luxury goods, salt, coffee, West Indian and Brazilian sugar, gold and silver from foreign ports entered the United States through the city.

The American economy before the Civil War was a network of separate regional markets—roughly, the South, the West, the Southeast, the Northeast, the Mid-Atlantic and the Midwest—each of them with independent systems of money and credit. As a result, the idea of international trade was a much more parochial notion than it is today, involving any transactions outside of the local region, even though they were within the United States. "To the cotton planter, the rural storekeepers and the New Orleans retailer, exports to Charleston and New York or imports from Boston and Cincinnati were almost as truly 'foreign' trade as dealing with Liverpool, Paris or Havana," wrote historian Green.

Even in the midst of an economic collapse in the rest of the country, New Orleans had enough trade to support an elite cadre of bankers, insurance companies, factors, attorneys and middlemen, who cut themselves in on all the capital flowing through the city as regularly as the Mississippi itself. It was among this strata of the city, not the artistes and the intelligentsia, that McIlhenny felt most at home.

Financial services companies in New Orleans were, in effect, downturn-proof businesses. They flourished during periods of expansion by providing loans for capital projects and handling the numerous details of the great number of commercial endeavors. And when the economy struggled, they were an indispensable lifeline for Southern manufacturers, merchants and plantation owners who, lacking diversification of any kind to fall back on, could not afford to shutter poorly performing operations while waiting for the fiscal picture to improve, even with prices plummeting. Thanks to the ability of financial services firms to provide working capital as a bridge until the economy turned around, many of the businesses that traded through New Orleans during that period survived.

McIlhenny's work put him at the dead center of the action. He started out as a bookkeeper at the Bank of Louisiana, but it was only a short time before he was named the agent in charge of paper money. This was a coveted position. In the decades before the U.S. Treasury produced the first United States note, the greenback, in 1862, there were as many as 30,000 different varieties of paper currency in circulation around the country, issued by 1,600 state banks, Each of the banks had agents, essentially loan officers, to allocate their institution's paper notes to businesses needing an infusion of cash for day-to-day operations or longer-term capital expenditures. The agents' compensation was tied to commissions on transactions they backed that paid off.

And while McIlhenny was in competition for clients with the other agents in the South, he and his New Orleans counterparts had a significant leg up: Louisiana's paper notes were considered among the safest in the nation, primarily because the state had the most advanced banking laws in the country. In fact, there was so much confidence in Louisiana's money and lending policies that the state's banknotes became a de facto currency in the surrounding states and even in areas outside of the region. The use of the term *Dixie* as a nickname for the South was inspired by the popularity throughout the United States of the Louisiana "Dix", or $10 banknote, issued by New Orleans firms.

McIlhenny made the most of his tenure at the Bank of Louisiana—a two-decade run during which he accrued a personal fortune of well over $100,000 (more than $2 million in today's money). But what stands out about his success is the strategy he used to achieve it: a personal marketing campaign unheard of in financial services then and, except for rare exceptions, now. In this effort, McIlhenny made himself the star and his financial talent and access to money and powerful people the irresistible product. This spin was the first display of the sales and marketing skills McIlhenny would eventually hone to near perfection as the purveyor of his famous sauce.

It started with the notion that the sole way to profitably separate oneself from the pack is to be more desirable than the other wolves, certainly an apt metaphor for the financial services specialists in money-crazed New Orleans at the time. Edmund McIlhenny may have been sitting on a cache of Louisiana's prized paper money, but he knew that any transaction offered him was simultaneously dangled before agents at other banks in town as well.

This gave too much power to the borrowers, McIlhenny believed. It assumed that one bank agent was just like another and that the deal makers were nothing but a commodity, while the deals themselves were the only thing of value. Unchanged, the job of being an agent was destined to be a business of shrinking margins and high risk as loan officers fought over potential business, offering lower and lower interest rates without properly assessing whether the deal was worth the cost—and, as importantly, whether the transaction would result in compensation for the loan officers.

So McIlhenny differentiated himself from the other agents by imposing two rules that had to be met for him to fund a deal: first, he would exclusively do business with companies that were pitching their projects solely to him; and second, the companies he worked with had to have produced solid recent results or be able to provide unassailably convincing evidence that the project would succeed.

This proved to be an uncanny strategy in a community of quick-buck artists where the agents were usually in no position to call the shots. McIlhenny promoted himself as a premium agent who might be a bit more expensive to woo, but well worth the effort. In exchange for meeting McIlhenny's demands—and sometimes even accepting banknotes at somewhat higher interest rates—companies received a series of perks from McIlhenny: financial advice; a favored position for future funding; and the chance to meet the widening group of local business graybeards who were drawing closer to McIlhenny as his influence in the commercial activities of the city grew.

As one competitor was said to recall some years later: "Edmund McIlhenny understood money and he understood that people of business wanted to be around people that understood money. He would sit across the desk from someone applying to borrow notes from his bank and stare at you with that serious, humorless expression. He would ask a lot of questions, sometimes for an hour or more, and then never say if he was approving the transaction immediately. That would happen in another day or two. But if he found out that you were talking to some other agent about your project, he would go to your office, unannounced, and tell you to your face that you have wasted his time and that he will not let you approach him again. He kept his word about that."

McIlhenny keenly appreciated the aphrodisiac-like qualities of knowledge and wealth, and, to further attract clients, he pursued both. He was secretary of Louisiana's Board of Currency, a state agency that supervised banknote activity. From that position, he received reports about virtually every new project or business plan that had been funded, extremely valuable information for making his own financing decisions and advising would-be clients about their commercial activities. As well, McIlhenny was a regular at some of the city's most exclusive clubs. He was on the governing committee of the Orleans Club, famous for lunches of seven courses of wild game, and he was vice commodore of the prestigious Southern Yacht Club. McIlhenny mostly used his time at these venues to pursue personal real estate and business partnerships, distinct from his banking activities—deals that as much as his day job were responsible for the significant amount of money he amassed before he was even thirty.

McIlhenny traveled quite a bit to Bank of Louisiana branches as far north as Baton Rouge. And it was there, sometime in the early 1840s, that he unexpectedly met Daniel Dudley Avery, an attorney and businessman whose plantation on the island of Petit Anse in Iberia Parish would in time play a stunningly pivotal role in McIlhenny's life.

Like McIlhenny's fortuitous encounter with Avey, the history of Petit Anse up until then had been shaped by a series of chance meetings. Elizabeth Triett was the first white settler to set foot on the island. A mother with five children, by no means an adventurer, she was an unwitting pioneer. In 1780, Triett, her husband, Malachy Hayes, and hundreds of other Catholics from Fort Pitt (currently Pittsburgh), Pennsylvania, sojourned west to escape British religious persecution. After months of wandering, they found shelter in Opelousas Post, a Louisiana village of 2,000 people near Iberia Parish. Ten years later, Hayes deserted his family, leaving Elizabeth

Triett and their children, ages one to fifteen, to fend for themselves. A single, abandoned mother, Triett and her offspring were cast out by the Opelousas colony.

The trail they were forced to take was in hostile frontier territory, but salvation came deep in the southland, at the Gulf of Mexico, in the form of a much-weakened Indian tribe known as the Attakapas. At one point, this stocky, dark-skinned, tattooed people were warriors—Attakapas means "Eaters of Human Flesh." By the time Triett was lucky enough to bump into them, they were docile, vanquished by their greatest enemies, the Choctaw, the Opelousa, and the Alibamon.

The Attakapas offered Triett an empty island—a giant hill— that their tribe had relinquished many years earlier after some unspeakable event had befallen them. Since the catastrophe, the Attakapas had refused to set foot on this island's soil or to speak in specific detail about it. With no other options, Triett gladly took the Attakapas up on their offer.

When Elizabeth Triett and her family forded the muddy bayou to reach the high ground of Petit Anse, they found a primeval forest—to the naked eye, unspoiled. The ground was wet in parts; unformed quaggy ponds drew water from the Gulf of Mexico or the tepid swampland surrounding the island. The air was hot and humid and felt even more tropical than the Louisiana mainland.

To generate income, she opened trading posts on the island for fur, meats and other goods, some of it indigenous and some of it brought by merchants, and built small footbridges over the thin bog separating the property from the mainland to give locals access to the concessions. By 1812, the same year Louisiana was admitted to the union, Eliza, as she was known to the locals, had a spacious house on the 400 acres of land she owned in Petit Anse Island's uppermost quadrant, her own cattle brand and seven slaves.

Yet, despite Triett's role in founding the island, she is hardly remembered. In fact, when she is recalled, it's often as the mother of her oldest son, John Hayes, who made an extraordinary discovery not long after arriving on the island that provided a tiny hint of how valuable the property really was and opened a small window into what the future held for Edmund McIlhenny. One day in 1790, the fifteen-year-old Hayes happened upon a clear pool of water and kneeled down to take a drink. Much to his surprise, it was salty—extremely so. He had unexpectedly found a brine spring.

Although it would be years before anyone realized how deep the reserve was, this was the first sign, at least for white settlers, that the island was sitting quite literally on a mountain of salt. Hayes and his mother immediately saw the profit potential in his discovery. Salt was a precious item at the time, treasured as a food preservative, a spice and an ingredient in medicinal tonics. So Triett and her son devised a series of crude evaporation schemes to extract salt crystals from the water percolating out of the ground and then commercialized the operation. These brine works were a lucrative venture for Triett and Hayes until about 1815, when large-scale, modern European suppliers underpriced the fledgling business.

Elizabeth Triett died in 1815, at sixty-six years old. There are no records of her funeral and no extant descriptions of it. It is said that Eliza is buried on Petit Anse somewhere, but her grave has never been found. Soon after her death, John Hayes built a sprawling plantation on her 400-acre estate combined with adjacent property purchased from local authorities. He imported dozens of African slaves, horses, mules and oxen to clear the land, plant sugar and thrash the cane. And after just a few plentiful harvests his Petit Anse plantation had become one of the more profitable in the Iberia region. Hayes wouldn't have the island to himself for long, though. Nor would the future of Petit Anse include Hayes or his descendants.

Indeed, the events that would decide the immediate fate of the property were already unwinding many miles away on a dairy and vegetable farm in Rahway, New Jersey. There, in 1810, John Craig Marsh had begun to grow deeply concerned about the impact that the rising support for state legislation to ban slavery in New Jersey was having on the price of his slaves. Merely the passage of a weak-kneed bill intended to eventually outlaw human bondage in New Jersey had sent the price of an able-bodied male in his late teens tumbling to as low as $225 in the state, nearly half of what he would cost elsewhere in the United States.

Unwilling to idly watch the value of his black workers decline, John Marsh decided to move them out of New Jersey and start a new farm in a location—the South—where there was still a dollar premium on African slaves. Marsh's associates convinced him that Louisiana, with plenty of inexpensive, high-yield land available in its relatively unsettled rural areas, offered the best agricultural opportunities for a newcomer to the South. As he prepared for this journey, Marsh was struck by a potential bonus opportunity. By purchasing additional low-cost slaves in New Jersey to take South with those he already owned, Marsh figured that he could realize a tidy profit by selling some of these discounted slaves at slightly lower prices than they typically commanded in Louisiana.

However, first he had to hatch another unsavory scheme. To avoid the appearance that he was transporting slaves to the South to sidestep New Jersey's emancipation law or to traffic in slaves—both of which, of course, were precisely what Marsh had in mind—he chose to get the blessing of the state courts for moving his slaves. Consequently, he instructed his indentured men and women to sign agreements stating that they were traveling to Louisiana on their own volition. In effect, Marsh made them declare under oath that they wished to go south with Marsh, with no prospects of ever being anything but slaves, instead of taking the chance of winning their freedom before long in New Jersey.

In all, John Marsh transported about 200 slaves to Louisiana beginning in 1810. During his initial years in the state, he planted his entourage in Baton Rouge and looked for a place to settle. Then, in 1818, he picked up a book that finally put an end to his indecision. Reading William Darby's highly regarded *Immigrant's Guide to the Western and Southwestern States and Territories*, Marsh came across an enchanting description of Petit Anse Island and its environs, a short distance from New Iberia. Darby wrote of the five domes of salt protruding out of the Gulf of Mexico like thick arms buried wrist to shoulder in the sea: "It is the most curious phenomena that the country affords to see these elevations arising of the deep morass and exhibiting features in common with the [high woods of Louisiana]." Upon Petit Anse Island the author enumerated upwards of forty different species of trees and shrubs, "amongst the most agreeable of which were live oak, walnut, white and black hickory and sweet gum. The land is excellent and consists of about 3,000 acres of highly productive soil."

Soon after reading this, Marsh visited Petit Anse. One look at the output of John Hayes's plantation persuaded Marsh that Darby's description of the prolific soil was apt; he had found the site for his farm. All of Iberia Parish was awash in rich earth, but Petit Anse, surrounded as it was by a febrile, slowly flowing bayou, seemed to produce a sugar crop more fertile than anything he had seen on the mainland.

Over the next two decades, Marsh purchased nearly the entire undeveloped southern parcel of Petit Anse Island. Obviously, Marsh couldn't have known it then, but whatever he paid for this tract— the records have long been lost—was a bargain. South Petit Anse was the most resource-rich section of the island, with huge reserves of salt and oil concealed alongside the abundant farmland. Indeed, Marsh's huge stake—on which he developed one of the region's greatest sugar plantations with hundreds of slaves and thousands of acres planted dwarfed John Hayes's property and would in time be the centerpiece of Edmund McIlhenny's holdings, the land that to this day is so critical to the McIlhenny Co. business.

Not long before he became the predominant landowner on Petit Anse, Marsh grudgingly accepted an invitation to meet Daniel Dudley Avery, recently admitted to the state bar in 1832, who was traveling throughout the region handling legal cases as circuit prosecutor out of Baton Rouge. Primarily at Avery's behest, local Iberia Parish politicians introduced the pair. The neophyte attorney had political aspirations; Marsh had money, prominence in Iberia Parish and contacts that Avery felt might be able to help him in subsequent campaigns.

Over many months, Avery visited Marsh on Petit Anse often. It's not certain what year Daniel Avery had his first introduction to the island that would one day be named after him, but it was likely around 1834. At first, he was drawn primarily to the plantation. Land poor and never having farmed, Avery viewed Marsh's large-scale operation as an ideal business: self-contained, self-sustaining, a simple manual operation not affected by the demands of workers or industrial tariffs. With inexpensive labor and the earth itself as the factory, much of it was pure profit.

But farming wasn't the sole thing that caught Avery's attention. He also fell in love with Marsh's daughter, Sarah. There is no indication in Avery's correspondence that his feelings for Sarah were anything but genuine. But considering Avery's subsequent aggressive acquisition of the Marsh family's property, his writing to the young woman of yearning for the day "when I shall claim you as irrevocably mine and mine only" carries at least the hint that he viewed her as the entrée to property and money he would not be able to amass any other way.

Just months after that note, Sarah Marsh and Daniel Avery married. By 1839, John Marsh, turning sixty, had tired of life on Petit Anse and decided to return home to his farm and the relatives and friends that he missed in New Jersey. Shedding his Petit Anse holdings, Marsh divided them in a way that he believed would ensure that his descendants would maintain ownership of the property. He split the land equally in thirds among his son George, Daniel Avery, and a second son-in-law, Ashbel Henshaw.

This arrangement was unacceptable to Avery, who was convinced that both George Marsh and Ashbel Henshaw weren't viable partners for the plantation. They had shown very little business aptitude in the past, usually preferring to stay in the shadow of the much more shrewd and tough-minded John Marsh, whom Avery successfully emulated. In Avery's view, George and Ashbel had neither the fearlessness nor the instincts to take risks and not fold in the face of losses. Acting on this presumption, Avery took advantage of the smallest financial weaknesses of his fellow Petit Anse landowners to swoop in and snatch their land out from under them. Piece by piece, he acquired swatches of the former Marsh parcels at pennies on the dollar, frequently to save his erstwhile associates from a horrendously onerous debt they had incurred in some poorly executed transaction. Avery also wrestled John Hayes's property just before Hayes's death in 1869. In a single generation, this young itinerant lawyer and frontier judge had methodically seized the coveted Marsh sugar plantation on Petit Anse, and much of the rich land around it, for the Avery name.

Upon meeting in the 1840s during one of Edmund McIlhenny's business trips to Baton Rouge, McIlhenny and Daniel Avery began what was to be a somewhat frosty relationship. They shared so few similarities. It is true that like Avery, Edmund McIlhenny was a success in commerce; the value of his banking practice couldn't be downplayed. But although Avery was only five years older than McIlhenny, the Judge, as he was known by this time, was already a family man, with a wife and three children (and three more to come during the ensuing years). And Avery considered McIlhenny's bachelorhood a sign of immaturity.

Moreover, there were other aspects of McIlhenny's life and personality that Avery didn't quite know what to make of. McIlhenny never attended college, while Avery (and later his sons) excelled at Ivy League schools. McIlhenny was a bit uncouth and even unmanly; he didn't have either the Protestant manners or rugged outdoorsman's skills that Avery prided himself on. McIlhenny's marketing acumen was highly respected, but the way he sold himself to would-be clients lacked humility. McIlhenny was a thinker, almost scientific in his approach to solving problems, while Avery was more impulsive and impatient.

But if the two men didn't quite hit it off, their mutual commercial interests would keep them in touch with each other. Avery's plantation was almost always in need of a financial benefactor like McIlhenny, and McIlhenny was drawn to thriving businesses led by honest businessmen like Avery who could be counted on the repay their loans. And there was something else that would bind the two men through the years: Avery's child. Just as Judge Avery met his future wife on Petit Anse when he happened upon John Marsh's daughter, this time McIlhenny was the landless outsider who encountered his soon-to-be spouse—Mary Eliza Avery—on the island. There was a sharp distinction, though, between the two relationships. While Daniel and his wife, Sarah Marsh, were contemporaries, Mary was probably not yet in elementary school when she and McIlhenny first met.

Despite their twenty-three-year age difference, Mary developed a crush on McIlhenny and would tell friends she was going to marry him someday. When she was sent to boarding school on the Gulf Coast near New Orleans in the 1850s, still a teenager, she and McIlhenny saw a lot of each other. He would take her out on his yachts and they would spend hours discussing her schoolwork, books and current political issues.

At first, McIlhenny viewed Mary as nothing more than the youthful offspring of a business acquaintance, someone whom he could mentor. But before long, McIlhenny, who was fixated on his commercial pursuits and went out on few dates, began to warm to the young girl's rapt interest in him. Although they courted through her preadult years, the pair kept their intentions quiet until Mary came of age. Finally, in 1859, when Mary turned twenty-one and Judge Avery thought it proper, the couple got married, among the arrowhead and longleaf pine, the sugar and salt, the alligators and waterfowl in the fairytale landscape of Petit Anse.

The newlywed McIlhennys lived on North Rampart Street in New Orleans, near the trendy Storyville district, which by the turn of the next century would become the home of jazz and legalized prostitution. They visited Petit Anse regularly but had little to do with the family plantation business.

It's extremely possible that the couple would have remained in New Orleans, pillars of the business community, and raised a family there. But the Civil War intervened. In January 1861, Louisiana seceded from the Union. New Orleans was too great a prize for the North to leave in enemy hands. It was the gateway to the Mississippi River, a supply line to the interior United States clear up to Minnesota, and it was a sentry point for the Gulf of Mexico.

With these strategic considerations, in the spring of 1862, a fleet of fifty U.S. Navy ships led by Captain David G. Farragut entered the Mississippi from the south and retook New Orleans. The McIlhennys fled to Petit Anse, taking whatever valuables they could claim quickly. In their haste, though, they were forced to leave behind a king's ransom in personal items, including Edmund's collection of precious uncut gems and bronze and silver pieces.

More than likely, the couple expected to return to their home in the city before long. But it was the last time they would live there. Surrendering a lucrative banking portfolio, Edmund took with him hard-earned and invaluable lessons about creating, promoting and managing a decidedly competitive business, which he would use again to his advantage later.

Chapter 2
WHITE HOT

Petit Anse was no place to hide during the Civil War—a fact that Edmund McIlhenny and his wife, Mary, learned to their dismay all too quickly. Although the island is a mere ten miles in diameter, an isolated dollop on the Gulf, leagues from the strategic heartland fanned by the Mississippi River, its importance to Union forces was just a touch below that of New Orleans. Thus, the McIlhennys had barely arrived at Petit Anse when they were hounded again by U.S. soldiers, compelled to retreat deeper into the Confederacy. Ironically, Mary's father, Daniel Avery, was chiefly at fault for alerting the Union to how valuable his relatively unknown island was, thereby turning it into a target.

Although Louisiana seceded from the Union in early 1861, placing it among the first six states to do so, there were no battles fought on Louisiana soil until Farragut's invasion the next year. In the intervening months, as in the years leading up to the war, many of Louisiana's wealthiest farmers remained confident that the bloodshed occurring elsewhere would be a temporary aberration and that it would end soon with the Confederacy's way of life intact. But a year later, with New Orleans taken and Baton Rouge soon to follow, even Judge Avery, an inveterate optimist, expressed despair about the war, realizing finally that his livelihood was in danger.

Some of this resignation is contained in a letter that Avery wrote in 1862 to his son Dudley, serving in the Confederacy's Delta Rifles brigade. In the letter, described by a family member recently, Avery displayed none of his usual bravado and conviction that he and his clan would flourish; instead, he betrayed a sense of imminent loss. He began by saying that he had "hoped and believed" the war would be short and "we would not be affected by it very greatly." Avery now knew that he was wrong and for the first time, he admitted, he felt "a deep foreboding, maybe because you are in harm's way, that we may have met a turning point from which there is no coming back to what was before." Because of this, Avery believed that he and his family had no choice but to support the Confederacy, the South's last hope.

To do his bit, Avery reopened the brine works on Petit Anse. These spring-fed wells of salt water, originally unearthed by the island's founders, Elizabeth Triett and her son John Hayes, had been shuttered since the end of the War of 1812. Avery felt, though, that since Petit Anse had a ready supply of untapped salt, his duty was to share it with the Confederate military, which had been cut off from its overseas salt sources by a naval blockade.

While appreciative of Avery's gesture, Confederate officials nonetheless told the judge it was insufficient. The need for salt as a preservative and for medicinal purposes among the hundreds of thousands of men fighting the war was so great that these tiny springs, they said, would hardly make a dent in the shortfall. In response, Avery was determined to increase the volume of salt he produced. He ordered the workers to try to sink additional springs at a site where the ground was more elevated.

Seventeen feet below the surface, the workmen's shovels struck what appeared to be a buried tree stump or a clot of roots that they were unable to dig around. They cleared the earth to see what they were up against. The bottom of the open pit revealed a mysterious smooth and dark material, too hard to be fractured by a spade. An ax was tried next. The initial blow produced a fragment of pure white salt. More swings of the ax and more salt chips. No matter how far down the laborers descended and regardless of where they struck the gigantic block, there was only salt.

This was the first sighting of rock salt anywhere in North America. Another equally remarkable discovery followed quickly. As Avery and his team dug into the hard, flaky crystal, they found that a mere five yards down, it was 99 percent sodium chloride. Only Petit Anse and its sister salt domes in the Gulf so easily yield such an unadulterated form of the mineral. In most other salt-producing sections of the United States, the pure mineral is buried hundreds of feet below the earth's surface and must be mined in deep seams or veins, much the same as coal is. Judge Avery told Confederate officials about his cache and offered them a seemingly boundless supply of salt to the war effort.

Major General Richard Taylor, a commander of Confederate forces west of the Mississippi, was ecstatic about this development. In his memoirs, he wrote: "The want of salt was severely felt in the Confederacy. . . . Intelligence of [Avery's discovery] reached me at New Iberia and induced me to visit the Island. The salt was from 15 to 20 feet below the surface and the underlying soil was soft and friable. Devoted to our cause, Judge Avery placed his mine at my disposition for the use of the government. Many Negroes were assembled to get out salt and a packing establishment was orga-nized at New Iberia to cure beef. During succeeding months large quantities of salt, salt beef, sugar and molasses were transported by steamers to Vicksburg, Port Hudson and other points East of the Mississippi. Two companies of infantry and a section of artillery were posted on the island to preserve order among the workmen and secure it against a sudden raid of the enemy."

Taylor's enthusiasm would promptly be crushed. No sooner had he learned about the vast and easily accessible salt deposit than the Union found out about it as well and immediately marked the island for attack. The prospect of a vast supply of precious salt in enemy territory was too rich for the North to pass up, a turn of events that Daniel Avery likely never expected when he initially offered his brine wells to the Confederacy. It's virtually certain that had Avery not let on at all about what he thought was a mere limited supply of salt on Petit Anse—a move that inevitably led to the discovery of deep pockets of salt—the island would have been useless (if even known) to the Union and left untouched during the war. Had that been the case, it's also likely that Tabasco sauce would not have been invented, at least in its present form, because, besides pepper, salt is the most important ingredient in the product.

But with news of the evidently bottomless wells of pure salt, annexing Petit Anse indeed became a priority for Northern forces. And on May 21, 1863, in a pincer attack involving troops stationed in Baton Rouge and New Orleans, Union general N.P. Banks invaded the island and easily overwhelmed Confederate forces there, claiming the salt mine for the North.

The Averys and McIlhennys escaped just in time. Edmund McIlhenny's brother Marshall lived in Brenham, Texas, a remote German community near Houston. And only days before the Petit Anse offensive, as word of the approaching Union forces reached the two families, the Averys and McIlhennys fled in a caravan, accompanied by dozens of their slaves, to join Marshall at his home hundreds of miles to the west.

The families stayed in Brenham, in exile, for two years. Little is known about them during this period. Because the two families were together, there was no correspondence among them that could offer details about their day-to-day existence in Texas. And family members alive today are at a loss to recall stories passed down through the generations describing this unusual period when the Averys and McIlhennys were displaced. In fact, few even remember that Edmund McIlhenny had a brother in Texas. Marshall McIlhenny, like the exile itself, occupies a forgotten corner in the family's long chronology.

Unforgettable, though, was the shocking condition of Petit Anse in the summer of 1865 after the war had ended and the Averys and McIlhennys had returned. The Union devastation—the torched properties and farmland—was heartbreaking to a family that no longer had anything else.

The post–Civil War period was disorienting for the Averys, who strained to come to grips with the dissolution of their vast fortune. They seemed shell-shocked and listless, incapable of responding imaginatively to the hard times. Lacking the wherewithal to produce any other plan, they simply endeavored to rebuild their life as it had existed before the war—to re-create the plantation with as few departures from the way it had been run in the past as possible—even in the face of every indication this was foolhardy.

In a letter written in 1866 that demonstrates the severe pinch the Averys were in, Dudley Avery, the judge's son, told his father, who was away visiting relatives, of his difficulties coming up with compensation for the workers. After much discussion, he had worked out a deal and staved off a revolt, Dudley wrote: "I payed [*sic*] off the hands on Saturday their pay, house servants and field hands, amounting to four hundred and forty dollars. . . . They all seemed perfectly happy with the settlement."

And later in the correspondence, Dudley asked his father to buy him seventy yards of leather for his boots. In the past, of course, this would have been a routine request. The judge would have complied at whatever price the leather cost without giving it much thought. But this time Dudley added, in a sentence succinctly summing up his family's embarrassingly fragile financial condition, "Only get it in case you can spare the money, as I can do without it very well."

Nothing seemed to work for the Averys. They tried to place the salt mine back into operation, but they couldn't restore it to anything near full capacity. The family lacked the backing to support the expense of labor and equipment. Meanwhile, the farm stumbled from bad year to good, but was not consistently profitable again.

One reason for this, of course, was the added cost of now having to pay workers. But the Averys were facing another challenge as well. To survive as a plantation in the postwar period, it was essential to implement modern yield techniques, such as newly developed crop rotation programs. By diversifying in this way, farmers could take advantage of more efficient, mechanized production technologies and were less vulnerable to market crashes in their primary crops. However, the Averys were too financially hamstrung to consider buying more equipment and expanding beyond a relatively one-dimensional farm.

The Averys weren't the only ones in southern Louisiana to believe that possibly some version of the past could be resurrected for their profit. Most of the region's elite families were similarly tempted. Giving up the privileged lifestyle they led before the war was hard indeed. An examination of a map of Iberia Parish in the first half of the nineteenth century shows a pattern of large rectangular properties that in their nearly flawless symmetry seemed to reflect the orderly grace and gentility of antebellum days. The names of the plantation owners are preserved now only in street signs that dot the district: Segura, Weeks, Duperier, Darby and Bayard. Each had their rectangle, side by side, and within these rectangles each was, to a great measure, a self-sufficient community. But these plantations were unmoored, their perfect boundaries engulfed, by the Civil War, primarily because the master-slave social compact that provided their ballast was set adrift.

Although everything had clearly changed, the Louisiana plantation owners clung to the hope that nothing had. And they chased that illogical fantasy to its logical conclusion—a cycle of financial ruin, bitterness, disillusionment, personal failure and racial hatred that colored the lives of many white descendants of plantation owners.

Emma T., an eighty-year-old heiress of a family that had a plantation north of New Iberia (and who requested that her family name not be used because she didn't want to publicly denigrate her living relatives), recalled the stories she heard from her grandparents about coming back to the farm after the Civil War. "They were angry," she said. "They wanted what they had before the war and they were too stubborn to accept that it was over. My family never recovered financially and in many other ways, too. It had been a proud, upstanding family and suddenly we had relatives that were drunks and wife-beaters and people getting divorced.

"Everything broke down when the plantation, which was the center of their lives, was taken away. Now my relatives are spread all over the South. I don't know where half of them are. They mostly blamed Negroes for the war and for what happened afterwards. Rather than just forget it and move on, when they could, they took it out on the Negroes."

Or as journalist Edward King described it in a *Scribner's Monthly* article published in the postbellum years: "It was a grand and lordly life, that of the owner of a sugar plantation; filled with culture, pleasure, and the refinement of living;— but now!"

Seen in this light, Edmund McIlhenny was fortunate that Judge Avery thought so little of him to keep him at a distance from the plantation. Given the job of tending the family's vegetable garden instead, McIlhenny could safely avoid becoming a partner in his in-laws' losing venture on Petit Anse, and it afforded him plenty of time to consider what to do next. His most fervent desire was to return to New Orleans with his wife, Mary, where they could resume their interrupted life there.

In February 1866, McIlhenny traveled to New Orleans on a job-hunting trip, his first time back in four years. He was reasonably confident that his prewar reputation as a money wunderkind would land him a position in the city's financial services industry. He thought maybe he could prove again that his ideas about the premium inherent in uniqueness were still valid even in this postwar environment.

But New Orleans was stunningly different than McIlhenny remembered it; it had become shadowy, with darker impulses. An occupied city, New Orleans no longer had the soaring spirit that emblemized it during the antebellum period. Its wealth and unparalleled delight in multiculturalism had dissolved in defeat.

Now New Orleans was in lockdown. Union forces patrolled the streets, their spanking blue uniforms, swaggering gait and menacing bayonets a constant reminder to the residents that they had been vanquished. And in the process, the city had become an intolerant place. Where once it celebrated its large free black population—almost

20 percent of the community at one point before the war—and its Caribbean, African and Haitian influences, New Orleans was now no different than more provincial, less-tolerant southern cities, such as Natchez, Mississippi, or Birmingham, Alabama. Like everywhere else in the Deep South, the whites hated blacks for the war and its aftermath. Postwar whites felt like aliens in the rugged country their families had settled and tamed. They blamed blacks for placing them in that position and for the punitive era of Reconstruction.

This anger was so palpable in New Orleans that in July 1866—just months after McIlhenny visited the city in search of employment— a riot broke out during a constitutional convention called to give blacks voting rights. A cadre of Confederate sympathizers backed by the local police attacked the attendees with sticks, rocks and guns, killing about 35 blacks and injuring another 100. "An absolute massacre," observers termed it, among the most shameful and violent racial incidents of the period. It would take New Orleans until well into the civil rights movement of the 1960s before it began to shed the worst of its racist image. And as Hurricane Katrina exposed in 2005, the city's racial divide—the gap between the conditions of the city's poor, who are overwhelming black, and the more bountiful lives led in the white communities—still persists.

Indeed, the landscape in New Orleans had changed radically by the time McIlhenny returned in 1866, and many of his former colleagues had left the city. Those still there were desperate to find jobs themselves, or, if working, had little power anymore to offer him something worthwhile. For McIlhenny, the trip was frustrating and demoralizing, holding out no hope.

Until, that is, something abruptly altered his prospects. Here the details get hazy, but it appears that while McIlhenny was in New Orleans, he at once conceived what his next venture would be. Attempting to resurrect his prior life as a banker, he realized, was folly; it's impossible to repeat even a flourishing past if the conditions that contributed to it don't exist anymore. That, in essence, was also what the Averys and many of the other plantation owners were trying in vain to do.

McIlhenny grew excited about what he was considering: to become an entrepreneur with his own product—specifically, a new pepper sauce; to market a manufactured brand instead of himself; and to run his own company, which could be passed along to his yet to be born children so they would never have to beg for a job the way he had during this trip.

Precisely how McIlhenny arrived at the idea to build a business around pepper sauce is not clear. It is known that McIlhenny loved spicy foods. It could be, some historians conjecture, that McIlhenny was mulling over recently successful products—chiefly, new condiments like ketchup and Worcestershire sauce—when he realized there was an opportunity for a more piquant seasoning. And perhaps that daydream drew closer to reality during a walk by the farmers' market or the old city's quays, where he could see the crates of burgundy red peppers just arrived from the Tabasco region of Mexico.

But there is another, more plausible explanation. Contrary to the McIlhenny family's claims, it is increasingly evident that Edmund did not invent pepper sauce. Rather, most likely McIlhenny adopted the basic concept from Maunsel White, a New Orleans businessman and politician who, until his death in 1862, had run a large plantation on the outskirts of the city known as Deer Range. An orphan from Limerick, Ireland, White became a fixture in New Orleans society in the early 1800s after marrying the daughter of the extravagantly wealthy Pierre Denis de la Ronde III, the owner of the Versailles Plantation in southeast Louisiana, a site envisioned to become a full-fledged city that would one day outgrow New Orleans and rival France's Versailles.

Maunsel White was gregarious, dashing and a lover of fine wine, high living, silks and beautiful women. Among the city's elite, he was known for his late-night soirees at Deer Range, where he would charm guests and flatter the New Orleans influential with the latest in gourmet foods and regional taste trends.

White made a wise decision in choosing to use epicurean skills to reinforce his place on the social ladder in New Orleans. In the antebellum period, the city was nothing short of a gastronome's delight. The remarkably successful melding of so many distinct cultures in New Orleans had a direct analog in the delicious dishes made from the combination of ethnic flavors and foods derived from these cultures—an amalgam of culinary styles that became known as Creole, Cajun or just plain Louisiana cuisine.

Every immigrant culture in the region contributed the best-loved items from their country's menus to this stew. As described in an article titled "Louisiana Food—Cajun and Creole," by Maida Owens, in the *Smithsonian Folklife Cookbook,* the French brought breads, sweets and bisque; the Spanish added jambalaya (a rice dish probably from the Spanish paella); the Germans provided sausages and hot-brown mustard; Africans contributed okra, barbecue and deep-fat frying; the Caribbean influence is seen in the bean and rice dishes; and from the West Indies and Haitian smoke pots came exotic vegetables and new cooking methods, such as braising.

All of these cultures had one thing in common: they had fallen in love with spices—the hotter, the better. And among the spices, chili peppers were singularly prized. Ever since Columbus had brought chilies from the Caribbean to Spain in 1493, recipes in Europe had taken a distinct tilt toward the piquant. In the southern Basque region of France, for example, sauces with a base of olive oil, hot pepper and garlic became popular. And in Spain, paella turned markedly pungent. In time, hot peppers were introduced into Africa by Portuguese and Spanish traders.

There were hundreds of different types of chilies, and they could grow in numerous types of soil. As a result, once they were brought to a region, peppers were easily and rapidly spread to nearby areas by pollinating birds. "By the year 1600," said Dave DeWitt, the author of *The Chili Pepper Encyclopedia* and president of the Web site www.fiery-foods.com, "chili peppers were established virtually everywhere in the world."

DeWitt, a chili industry expert who calls himself the Pope of

Peppers, attributed the enduring popularity of hot spices around the world to two factors: they make foods taste strikingly better, especially bland vegetable dishes, and they have extraordinary antibacterial properties.

Moreover, said DeWitt, these factors curiously appear to be linked. He pointed to a 1998 study by Cornell University scientists Jennifer Billing and Paul Sherman published in the *Quarterly Review of Biology* that explored why people use spices. After examining nearly 5,000 traditional recipes from thirty-six countries, the pair found that "countries with hotter climates used spices more frequently than countries with cooler climates. . . . Indeed, in hot countries nearly every meat-based recipe calls for at least one spice, and most include many spices, especially the potent spices, whereas in cooler countries substantial fractions of dishes are prepared without spices, or with just a few."

In addition, Billing and Sherman tested various spices for their ability to kill germs. Chili peppers, they found, destroy 75 percent of the bacteria with which they come in contact. From this the researchers concluded that in warmer regions people who put more spices on their foods—that is, those individuals who most enjoyed the taste of hot dishes—tended to get sick less often and live longer. Hence, the taste for spicy foods became an evolutionary imperative. "Traits that are beneficial are transmitted both culturally and genetically, and that includes taste receptors in our mouths and our taste for certain flavors," said Sherman, now a leading evolutionary biologist and professor of neurobiology and behavior. "One way we reduce food-borne illnesses is to add another spice to the recipe. Of course that makes the food taste different, and the people who learn to like the new taste are healthier for it."

Although the elite in New Orleans in the late eighteenth and early nineteenth centuries—mostly descendants of Spanish and French aristocrats and entrepreneurs—were drawn to diets rich in chili peppers and other available pungent spices, initially very little experimentation to combine individual recipes and produce new dishes occurred. For example, the wealthy Europeans were fond of Caribbean dishes like mirlitons—a vegetable pear stuffed with shrimp, conch, ham and spices—and African piquant soups prepared by slaves. But they wouldn't eat either of them at the same table with traditional French or Spanish fare. Indeed, it took the more democratic lower classes—specifically, the Cajuns—to mix the numerous culinary styles and tastes of New Orleans.

The Cajuns were French colonists from Normandy and Brittany who settled during the early 1700s in Nova Scotia and New Brunswick, an area in the Canadian Maritimes known then as Acadia. A mere half a century later, they were forcibly evicted from the region by the British, who by then controlled it and feared that the French-descended Acadians would side with their homeland against England in the French and Indian War. The Cajuns (the word is in fact a southern U.S. corruption of Acadians) were exiled at gunpoint in two waves of what has become known as Le Grand Derangement. The men were sent first and the women and children some months later.

More than half of the Cajuns—upwards of 10,000—died in the first year of diaspora, mostly from hunger. Survivors who reached Massachusetts, Maryland, the Carolinas and Virginia were robbed and then forced to move on because of anti-Catholic sentiment. In Georgia, some Cajuns were even sold into slavery. Finally, in about 1755, surviving Cajun men began arriving in New Orleans, where a Catholic Spanish regime and the many French who had settled there grudgingly welcomed them. To avoid conflict with the aristocrats of the city, the Cajuns moved west into Louisiana's unsettled territory—roughly from Lafayette to the modern-day Acadian parishes of Iberia, St. Martin, Acadia, Vermilion and St. Mary.

Meanwhile, many of the Cajun women and children returned alone to their ancestral homes in the coastal seaports of France. When they got word that their husbands and fathers had resettled in the bayous of Louisiana, they traveled again to North America to reunite with them. The Cajun families were destitute and set up homesteads in the deep marsh where they could fish, hunt and, to avoid a repeat of their experience in Canada, remain out of the way of political and military authorities. But despite their relative isolation, the Cajuns had a great deal of commercial interaction with local plantations and businesses, mostly to sell hides, fish, meat, leather, crafts, candles and household goods. Living a hard-luck existence, the Cajuns were outliers in a society built on an expanding pool of wealth with strict social castes that limited their partaking of it.

To survive, the Cajuns had to stretch every provision they had. To feed their families, Cajun women made stews and soups, "sweeping the kitchen," as they called it, to toss everything they could find into the pot. Among the ingredients were plants and animals found in the fields, woods and bayous, or leftovers that the Cajun men were given by their customers in the Spanish, French and Caribbean communities. Recipes, such as they existed, were highly eclectic. A Cajun jambalaya, for example, could include any combination of beef, pork, fowl, smoked sausage, ham and seafood, celery and tomatoes. Or a seafood gumbo, the West African word for okra, could consist of shrimp, crab or oysters topped with filé (ground sassafras leaves) and whatever vegetables were locally available. Held together by broth or rice, these recipes were a mélange of diverse tastes. And all of them were embellished with a heavy dose of hot peppers and other spices to bring out a pungent flavor.

These one-pot dishes were the first manifestation of a distinct, homegrown Louisiana style of food. Indeed, it's an odd twist of fate that the emergence of Louisiana cuisine at the turn of the nineteenth century was in great measure impelled by the tragedy of the Cajuns—a group of people who, upon emigrating to the cold crevasses of the Canadian Maritimes from France, could scarcely have considered that their predominant impact would be on the cuisine and culture of the dank southernmost region of the United States.

Not surprisingly, taking into account the rich melting pot that typified the region, it wasn't long before the Cajun recipes were tinkered with, refined by adding still more ethnic touches. In the homes of the wealthy, chief cooks, usually the best-paid and most respected servants, were encouraged to mimic Cajun creativity and freely fuse recipes from different nationalities. These dishes became known as Creole cuisine, which initially was in effect an urbanized, upscale version of Cajun food—full-flavored, with generous amounts of high-quality butter and exotic herbs as well as more commonly found peppers and salt.

Both styles of food became extraordinarily popular at restaurants, exclusive clubs, plantation dinners and celebrations. Today, little distinction remains between Creole and Cajun cooking. The names are used synonomously to characterize Louisiana cuisine, a feast of flavors, textures and, most of all, hot spices. A devil's blend, in which, as noted Cajun chef Paul Prudhomme described it, "the taste changes with every bite."

Against this colorful culinary renaissance, New Orleans plantation owner Maunsel White threw his famous gourmet-themed dinner parties at Deer Range in the 1840s. A Francophile, White was especially enthusiastic about experimenting with sauces, which have always been at the heart of French cooking, changing their texture and flavor with different herbs and spices. And among his original recipes, White's greatest and most popular chef d'oeuvre was his pepper sauce, primarily a simple blend of chilies and vinegar.

White's friends invariably asked him to serve the pepper sauce at his dinners—it was a suitable topping for fish, oysters, beans, rice and even soup—and guests always left with a bottle or two. White called his sauce Maunsel White's Concentrated Essence of Tabasco Peppers. Although he never tried to market it nationally or even bottle it, once a year, White would deliver the product to local grocers and druggists in big containers. The storeowners would pour the sauce into small bottles and put White's label on them before placing them on the shelves. As more and more people requested it, White's pepper sauce was soon available in most distinctive New Orleans eateries as a spicy adjunct to Cajun and Creole offerings. In a region where chili peppers were the rage, the thought of conveniently dripping a squirt of pepper on a dish—any dish—instead of having to chop, sprinkle and cook the pepper, was a godsend.

White's hot sauce itself was a unique idea, but its uncommon taste garnered the most attention. The recipe's main ingredient was the recently arrived Tabasco chili, a more pungent pepper than any previously found in southern Louisiana and perfect for the area's spicy palate. A member of the species *Capsicum frutescens*, the Tabasco was at least twice as hot as the chilies routinely grown in North America—jalapeño, paprika, cayenne and bell, to name a few, all varieties of *Capsicum annuum*.

Although the McIlhennys have tried to dismiss the possibility, it seems clear now that in 1849, a full two decades before Edmund McIlhenny professed to discover the Tabasco pepper, White was already growing Tabasco chilies on his plantation. A letter that year to the *New Orleans Daily Delta* newspaper, written by a visitor to Deer Range, confirms this: "I must not omit to notice the Colonel's pepper patch, which is two acres in extent, all planted with a new species of red pepper, which Colonel White has introduced into this country, called Tobasco [*sic*] red pepper. The Colonel attributes the admirable health of his farmhands to the free use of this pepper."

The year of this letter is noteworthy. In 1849, the Mexican War had just ended, and many U.S. servicemen were returning to the States through New Orleans. With a large contingent of these men in the city, it's likely Maunsel White was given Tabasco chilies by a soldier who had brought them back from southern Mexico. In other words, the fable of Friend Gleason in McIlhenny family tradition is more probably a tale that grew out of Maunsel White's life, which Edmund McIlhenny adopted as his own.

The Tabasco chili has a rare characteristic among peppers: it's juicy—squeeze it and a dozen drops of liquid pour out. This attribute made it impractical for White to apply it to most recipes; it would be too wet to be used as a seasoning or a sautéed vegetable. But this strange facet of the chili piqued White's interest in it even more. He found this piquant fruit to be so unpredictable and tasty that he was determined to unearth another culinary role for it. A January 26, 1850, article in the *Daily Delta* explained how White's invention of pepper sauce grew out of this resolve: "Owing to its oleaginous character, Col. White found it impossible to preserve it by drying; but by pouring strong vinegar on it after boiling, he has made a sauce or pepper decoction of it, which possesses in a most concentrated form all the qualities of the vegetable. A single drop of the sauce will flavor a whole plate of soup or other food. The use of a decoction like this, particularly in preparing the food for laboring persons, would be found exceedingly beneficial in a relaxing climate like this. Col. White has not had a single case of cholera among his large gang of negroes since the disease appeared in the south."

Edmund McIlhenny likely knew Maunsel White personally, or if he didn't, he surely knew of him. When White was making a name for himself and his pepper sauce in New Orleans, McIlhenny was a top-tier investment banker there. McIlhenny's business demanded that he befriend the city's wealthiest residents, and the rich were eager to make the acquaintance of a man who could get his hands on a great deal of capital quickly. Considering those motivations, it would have been improbable for McIlhenny and White to not cross paths. In addition, the social aspects of McIlhenny's job required him to frequent the best restaurants and men's clubs, places that carried on their tables Maunsel White's Concentrated Essence of Tabasco Peppers.

With White's passing in 1862, his pepper sauce died as well. Some people close to the McIlhennys surmise now that the mysterious post–Civil War epiphany experienced by Edmund in New Orleans, which led to his decision to make pepper sauce, may have occurred while he was having dinner at one of his old haunts, upon realizing that something familiar and essential—Maunsel White's hot sauce—was missing from the meal.

Whether it occurred that way or not, the history of the period strongly suggests that McIlhenny's Tabasco sauce was, if nothing else, inspired by White's recipe. But being perceived as a brilliant entrepreneur—a successful adopter, if not an innovator—held little value for McIlhenny. It was more important to promote the originality of his product and the myth that gave birth to it, not his own talents. Consequently, McIlhenny couldn't let on that he knew White or his sauce.

Nonetheless, the relationship between McIlhenny and White would percolate to the surface from time to time, as rumor more than fact. And in the early 1900s, some years after her husband's death, Mary McIlhenny approached Maunsel White's widow to clear this matter up. According to the sworn testimony of Sallie Huling, a friend of the White family, Mrs. McIlhenny asked Mrs. White to tell her what she recalled about who had been the first to ascribe the name Tabasco to the pepper and the sauce. The women were quite old; they were discussing fifty-year-old history, striving to rekindle dim recollections. Near the end of her life, Mary McIlhenny was walking on emotionally fragile ground.

She was trying to rediscover whether the legend Edmund McIlhenny had left her had completely obscured real events, of which she had no memory anymore. As Huling described it, "When Mrs. White told her the truth"—that the pepper and the sauce were, indeed, originally named by Maunsel White, nearly twenty years before McIlhenny—"she cried."

Mary McIlhenny never told her children what she had learned.

Chapter 3

E. McILHENNY'S TABASCO PEPPER SAUCE

However McIlhenny came up with the idea for Tabasco sauce, his future at once didn't appear so dim. He was eager to execute his plan. While still in New Orleans, he purchased some Tabasco peppers from local sellers and brought them back to Petit Anse, where he excitedly planted next year's crop and dove into tinkering with recipes for his new sauce.

McIlhenny's vividly crimson and compact pepper fields were in sharp contrast to the overgrown monotonous green stalks of sugar Petit Anse Island had been famous for. A short, stubby fruit, about three inches long, the Tabasco faces the sky in bushes that can grow as high as five feet, but are more commonly no taller than three feet.

By 1869, McIlhenny had finished fine-tuning his pepper sauce—mixing salt, vinegar and pepper mash age in carefully calibrated amounts and then letting the blend age for forty days before uncovering the jar and pronouncing the product ready.

McIlhenny developed the pepper sauce in a cramped, two-story brick-and-clapboard laboratory across the lawn from Petit Anse's main house, where the Avery family lived. His laboratory had originally been the plantation's *pigeonnier,* the name for the coop where the wealthy in Louisiana housed training birds. At the start of the Civil War, a watchtower was added to the building, so Confederate soldiers guarding the island's valuable salt could monitor the approach of Union forces. The building had been ransacked by Union troops, but working mostly alone, McIlhenny renovated it, turning the somewhat dingy structure into a utilitarian research laboratory and, eventually, the first Tabasco sauce factory.

The facility was abandoned in 1905, when McIlhenny's sons constructed a new, much bigger plant to handle the exploding demand for Tabasco sauce, and was subsequently razed some fifteen years later. Recently, archaeologists from the University of Alabama spent six weeks unearthing artifacts and ruins from the laboratory's site in an effort to better understand, as the project's field director said, "the history of American rural cottage industry." Some relics of the early days of the Tabasco business were found—among them, shards of a stoneware churn probably used at some point to pulverize peppers and an olive green glass bottle that may have stored early versions of the sauce.

Dug up also was McIlhenny's collection of bones from giant extinct mammals—ten-foot-tall mastodons, mammoths and sloths—that populated Petit Anse Island 10,000 years ago. McIlhenny searched for these fossils in his spare time, delicately exploring the island's wooded terrain and loamy soil with large shovels and tiny spades, while holding a cardboard box to carry his ancient skeletal findings.

McIlhenny claimed that the first batches of his newly minted sauce were distributed in discarded cologne bottles, probably out of a desire to have his company be perceived as a plucky start-up operating on a shoestring. He, in fact, used containers designed for him by a New Orleans glassworks. Not surprisingly, considering the McIlhenny family's love of tradition, these bottles were very similar to the distinctive rounded-body, thin-topped ones used today, except the shoulders were sharper. (He switched to rounded shoulders when he learned the initial bottles broke too easily.) McIlhenny had wanted to call the product Petit Anse Sauce, but the Averys wouldn't let him use the island's name in a commercial product. He chose E. McIlhenny Tabasco Pepper Sauce in its place.

In 1870, with fewer than 2,000 bottles of E. McIlhenny's Tabasco sauce in circulation, McIlhenny patented his recipe. It's clear from the description in the patent application that McIlhenny had invented a remarkably intricate, extremely efficient, small-scale manufacturing process. Every last drop was squeezed out of the raw materials; waste was minimal. Although this was his first attempt at manufacturing, McIlhenny undoubtedly had excellent instincts: an engineer's sense of the way each action in a manu-facturing plan affects the next step, and a businessman's intuitive grasp of the importance of lean and simple systems in generating the highest profit margins.

The mashed pulp of Tabasco peppers was first mixed with fine vinegar and rock salt, McIlhenny said in the patent application. Then the combination was covered for six weeks. When the con-tainer of pulp was opened, according to the patent, the mash was "worked through a sieve," after which "about one drop of bisul-phate of lime is then added to every ounce of mixture" to prevent additional fermentation. "The skins and suds" that failed to pass through the sieve, wrote McIlhenny, "are potted for about twenty-four hours, with an ounce of alcohol to each pound of the residue. This mixture is thoroughly agitated and then placed under a press, by which the remaining pulp and juice are forced out.

"A drop of bisulphate of lime is added to every ounce received from the press. The two mixtures thus prepared are now put together, and the whole compound worked through a fine flour sieve. The sauce is thus completely prepared and ready for use."

McIlhenny had two reasons for patenting his formula. First, a patent would enable him to boast, particularly in a period before there were regulators to police truth in advertising, that this product was one of a kind, created by techniques so original they were even endorsed by the U.S. government. And with classic McIlhenny guile, his second reason for obtaining the patent somewhat obvi-ated the first. McIlhenny wanted the patent to thwart would-be imitators. So he applied for it with a recipe that wasn't precisely the actual formula for making Tabasco sauce. In other words, the patent McIlhenny received—the foundation of his claims to distributors and customers that his sauce was exceptional, it was akin to an invention—was based on a false recipe, just misleading enough to sabotage anyone who attempted to use the patent as a crib sheet to copy the product. The detail that appears to be made up is the use of bisulfate of lime to retard fermentation. According to McIlhenny historian Shane Bernard, "There are no records of his purchasing bisulphate of lime."

Much of the rest of McIlhenny's recipe for Tabasco sauce was accurate when he wrote it in the patent application, but obsolete before very long. A priority for McIlhenny was to continually streamline the production process for Tabasco sauce while improving the product's quality. Hence, within a few years of the 1870 patent, McIlhenny had eliminated the need for two sieves to reduce the mash to a moderately thick but smooth, saucelike consistency. Instead, he had implemented a manufacturing process much closer to what the company still uses today: he fermented the pepper mash in casks for longer and longer periods—up to three years—adding salt during fermentation and vinegar after the cask was opened; and he improved the efficiency and performance of the filters so that the mixture only had to be strained once to produce a texture that was perfectly identical from one bottle to the next.

In fact, in short order McIlhenny's production methods and recipe became so sophisticated and so difficult to mimic—and so identified with him, similar to his approach to banking in New Orleans before the war—that he let his patent expire in the late 1870s. He never applied for another one for his manufacturing techniques.

Joseph Dubois, who ran McIlhenny Co.'s Tabasco factory for thirty years, explained that "nobody was making any condiment that was consistent from batch to batch the way McIlhenny was. It was too hard to do. It required too much supervision, and most companies didn't have the equipment or the stamina or the know-how to figure out how to do this. That is really what Edmund McIlhenny started, I believe: the idea of a hot sauce that is so carefully produced that every bottle you buy is the same as the one before." Indeed, this distinction, this perfect uniformity that still exists today, enabled McIlhenny to market Tabasco sauce as a premium brand, not a commodity—and charge top dollar for it in groceries around the country.

Some of the very first bottles of Tabasco sauce were purchased by Union soldiers in Louisiana. They so enjoyed the unusual product that many of them told their friends and relatives in the North about it. McIlhenny wisely piggybacked on this word-of-mouth network before approaching distributors to sell the new condiment in their regions. He encouraged the soldiers to recommend Tabasco sauce to people they knew back home in hopes of building interest in the brand in areas of the United States where it wasn't yet being offered, thus making it impossible for wholesalers to ignore him when he called on them. Indeed, this premarketing campaign enabled McIlhenny to persuade E.C. Hazard, one of the nation's largest food wholesalers, to carry Tabasco sauce in the Northeast. Even before McIlhenny's contact, Hazard had sufficiently heard about the product to be at least positively disposed toward distributing it.

McIlhenny was initially so desperate for national distribution of Tabasco sauce that he offered Hazard a 50 percent stake in his fledgling company in exchange for managing the brand's rollout throughout the country. But Hazard wasn't convinced that Tabasco would be a roaring success, a miscalculation he came to regret. Hazard liked Tabasco sauce—its purity, flavor and novelty—and he admired McIlhenny's marketing and manufacturing skills, but he didn't want to tie his hugely successful food distributorship so closely with any one product, especially one with uncertain prospects. He turned McIlhenny down, agreeing only to become the exclusive agent for Tabasco sauce from Maryland to Maine. This was itself a lucrative arrangement, but a far cry from what he would have earned had he taken McIlhenny up on his original proposal.

For McIlhenny's part, Hazard's rejection was fortuitous. Offering

Hazard such a sizable stake in the company was an uncharacteristic mistake by McIlhenny, who usually had superb business instincts and seldom acted out of fear or precipitously. But, frantic to regain his prior wealth, he momentarily lost the distinctive confidence that had guided his commercial efforts in the past.

On the heels of the Hazard distribution agreement, signed in the early 1870s, Tabasco sauce sales soared. Orders for thousands of bottles poured in and requests for Tabasco sauce came from farther and farther away. In 1872, in only his third year in business, McIlhenny opened a small office in London to handle the growing appetite for the product in Europe. And international sales got a big lift when Tabasco was cited for its unique taste and quality in winning the prestigious gold medal at the World's Industrial and Cotton Centennial Exposition in New Orleans in 1884.

By that time, less than two decades after making his very first batch of Tabasco sauce, McIlhenny was selling upwards of 20,000 bottles a year, about as much as he could produce. Soon, though, with a limited pepper crop and labor pool and the difficulty of coordinating efficient shipping arrangements from Louisiana to the rest of the world, McIlhenny was unable to keep up with demand. This shortfall was a blessing in disguise. It ensured that the wholesale price of $1 a bottle—an astounding $15 each in today's money— would hold for much of the company's early history.

Two recent discoveries demonstrate how quickly Tabasco sauce caught on in far-flung niche markets soon after its debut, despite its high price—an unexpected achievement for a product that relied primarily on word of mouth and mainstream distributors for promotion. The first occurred in 2001 when archaeologists digging at the site of the Boston Saloon, a black-owned bar and restaurant in Virginia City, Nevada, during the gold and silver boom of the mid-nineteenth century, excavated a Tabasco bottle from around 1870.

At its heyday, from 1859 to 1880, Virginia City and its nearby sister village, Gold Hill, were international mining capitals. Rabidly pro-Union, this large settlement was a preferred destination for freed blacks who sought to avoid indentured servitude in the urban centers of the East and instead chose to work more independently as barbers, cooks, waiters and even entrepreneurs in this flourishing region.

The proprietor of the Boston Saloon was William A.G. Brown, a prominent black businessman from Massachusetts. The presence of Tabasco sauce, so exclusive at the time that only a few thousand bottles were in existence, as well as prime cuts of meat buried in the ruins, indicate that the Boston Saloon was an upscale eatery.

"The people at Boston Saloon ate high on the hog, not pigs feet as they did in Irish bars," said Ronald James of the Nevada State Historic Preservation Office. "Tabasco was a premium product, an expensive, high-quality new product at the time, and one that matched the spicy tastes of African Americans."

The second recently uncovered odd and remote placement of Tabasco sauce concerned a location far removed from the rough-and-tumble West. Not long ago, the McIlhennys found a letter written in 1888 from a British soldier in India to his mother. In it, Arthur A.S. Barnes, a lieutenant in the 2nd Battalion of the Duke of Edinburgh's Wiltshire Regiment, said: "I want to call your attention to a certain sauce. It's called 'Tabasco Pepper Sauce' and seemingly emanates from a man, E. McIlhenny, New Iberia, Louisiana. A drop or two in soup, stew or mixed around with mashed potatoes gives one a great appetite. Here it costs 1/12 rupee or what you would call 3s. [shillings] 6d. [pence]. It seems dear, but should last as long as 12 of the ordinary sauce at 6d. a bottle. Try it. I can recommend it."

Edmund McIlhenny's unforeseen and rapid global success with Tabasco sauce paralleled a period of steadily falling fortunes for the Averys and the Petit Anse plantation, both of which were increasingly deeper in debt with minimal cash flow to cover expenses. In fact, in the early 1870s, a judgment was rendered against Daniel Avery after he failed to come up with the money to cover expiring mortgage notes for a tiny portion of the island belonging to the estate of David Hayes, a descendant of the Triett clan that first settled Petit Anse eighty years earlier. An awkward episode followed in which Avery's wife was forced to sue him to safeguard her share of the property from being seized to pay the debt. In the end, financial and legal moves such as this one didn't help protect Avery's land from creditors and litigators. As more loans came due from old mortgages and former business associates, Petit Anse was confiscated by the local authorities and set to be auctioned off at a sheriff's sale. In a desperate effort to hold on to his property, Avery cut a deal with a local bank, which agreed to purchase the island at the public auction and then sell it back to Avery, who would repay a series of new mortgages little by little.

McIlhenny saw an opportunity in Avery's misfortune. McIlhenny needed additional property to extend his pepper fields, which were confined to the small slices of cropland where sugar wasn't grown. So as his cash flow from Tabasco sauce became increasingly dependable, McIlhenny acquired more and more of the island from Avery to cover the judge's spiraling debts—a strategy not unlike the one Avery had used to wrest the island from the Marshes, his in-laws, many years earlier. At other times, Avery scions sold McIlhenny parts of their holdings simply because they needed pocket change.

In the midst of their deep financial crisis, McIlhenny's in-laws died within twelve months of each other. Sarah Craig Marsh Avery passed away first, in 1878 at sixty years old. Heartbroken at her death, Daniel Avery followed her the next year. He was sixty-nine.

The passing of the Avery parents only hastened the sell-off of the island by five of their six children, as well as the end of the plantation. Only Mary Eliza, McIlhenny's wife, maintained her stake. As the Avery family's circumstances changed, the island became less and less of an anchor for them. Some of Judge Avery's children left to seek work elsewhere, in Baton Rouge, New Orleans and other cities, and other children got into trouble, unable to ever find their way to an honest living. A son, Dudley Avery, was arrested in 1889 during a racial incident in New Iberia "for conspiring to drive certain Negroes from the Parish," as he described the charges in a letter to a relative. He admitted that he was "standing in the courthouse hall with the group of men" who had come there to forcibly expel black people from the community for vagrancy after they demanded jobs and education. But Dudley claimed he was innocent, among the crowd "to use my influence against violence and disorder."

Such episodes served as an indelicate coda for the Averys in Iberia Parish, where the family that once was one of the wealthiest plantation owners is barely represented now. During this period, in honor of his in-laws, Edmund McIlhenny renamed Petit Anse; he called it Avery Island. That stands as one of the enduring ironies of the McIlhenny story: just as the Averys were ceding the island to Edmund, their name was finally ascribed to it.

Chapter 4
THE BUSINESS MODEL

Tabasco sauce debuted in the midst of the Industrial Revolution, whose extraordinary advances made it possible for Edmund McIlhenny's new brand to quickly become a national best seller.

With the invention of the telegraph and railroad, retailers and manufacturers could unlike before routinely order products and raw materials from thousands of miles away and be reasonably certain to receive shipments on an as-needed schedule. No longer was it necessary for rural or western urban merchants to make tortuous annual pilgrimages to wholesalers and manufacturers on the eastern seaboard to buy and then haul back many of the provisions they would sell in their shops over the next twelve months. Instead, they could periodically make purchases via telegraph, replenishing inventory as supply dwindled, adding lines that they never carried before and ensuring that throughout the year they had enough stock to serve growing local populations. Alternately, because of increased mobility, storeowners could await the monthly visits of wholesalers—or jobbers, as they had become known—who frequently journeyed to even the most outlying venues, offering familiar as well as untried items from large networks of suppliers.

As modern communications and distribution channels snaked

farther and deeper into every corner of the country, markets for consumer goods expanded furiously. Consequently, a Louisiana brand like McIlhenny's Tabasco sauce, little more than a regional favorite when Maunsel White originated the idea, could readily be found on store shelves in California, Nevada, Maine and Florida—in short, any place with telegraph lines, paved roads and train depots.

The economic activity stirred up by this unparalleled wave of consumer activity generated hundreds of thousands of jobs. Standards of living rose faster in the United States than in any other part of the world. Their pockets full of money, Americans in turn clamored for ever more novel products. To feed this appetite, mass retailers emerged—department stores like Marshall Field's in Chicago, Macy's in New York, Strawbridge & Clothier in Philadelphia and the Emporium in San Francisco, all of which sold scores of items purchased directly from manufacturers, eliminating the cost of the middleman. Interest in the diverse range of brands in these freshly minted shopping bazaars was so high that Macy's turned over its inventory about twelve times in 1887, a performance the best retailers today are unable to match.

Responding to the bubbling demand for their goods, most manufacturers embraced mass production technologies, which enabled them to output a greater volume and variety of items more rapidly, efficiently and on schedule. An array of canning, bottling, mixing, blending, picking, labeling, sorting, stitching and preserving machines took center stage on factory floors and in the fields of the nation's largest farms. For the first time, consumers were treated to prerolled, packaged cigarettes; condensed milk; cans of preserved meat; boxes of oatmeal and cornflakes; fruits out of season; affordable bars of soap; and national brands of beer.

Edmund McIlhenny considered mass production a dangerous, ultimately unsatisfying, temptation. Automation was too expensive and too risky to undertake lightly, he believed; yet many companies were lured by the false promise of an ever-increasing customer base to do just that. As a result, McIlhenny stubbornly resisted the squall around him and continued to manufacture

Tabasco sauce by hand, using his basic recipe consisting of a long aging process for the mixed ingredients followed by manual straining and bottling.

Barely under way, McIlhenny's family business was already out of step with most other manufacturers in the United States. Numerous prepackaged food companies, some of which are still name brands today, inaugurated operations within a few decades or so of Tabasco's introduction. Before long, those that would survive into the late twentieth century had implemented a raft of new technologies to speed up their production lines, improve the quality of their products and initiate economies of scale.

Typical was the company created by James L. Kraft, who moved to Chicago from Ontario, Canada, in 1903 and invested $65 in a horse and wagon from which he hoped to peddle cheese to midwestern grocers. Prior to Kraft's efforts, cheese was a meager market. Consumers generally purchased the item directly from farms, primarily because it spoiled so quickly and storeowners refused to carry it. To overcome this resistance, Kraft designed an automated heat sterilizing manufacturing method that halted the aging process in cheese by killing off the mold and bacteria and then added sodium phosphate as an emulsifier, keeping fats and solids from separating. The resulting product was a mass-produced version of cheddar cheese stored in cans. As a measure of how briskly Kraft's production line mushroomed, the U.S. military bought as many as 6 million pounds of his cheese during World War I.

H.J. Heinz provides a more suitable contrast with McIlhenny Co., because the two companies were formed within a year of each other, and they manufactured parallel products. In 1869, Pittsburgh-based Henry J. Heinz and a partner, L. Clarence Noble, launched their company by introducing grated horseradish in a bottle. The condiment, traditionally made at home by rural housewives, was popularly used to enhance mundane meals or food not particularly well preserved. In an era when processed foods were unregulated, the safety of packaged goods was a significant concern; it was impossible to know whether tainted additives had been blended into the product.

Consequently, Heinz and Noble distinguished their horseradish from lesser brands by placing it in clear glass to prove its purity—a simple look inside would convince a consumer that it contained no mice droppings or wood shavings.

Heinz immediately followed the successful rollout of horseradish with high-grade lines of mustard, vinegar, sauerkraut, pickles and, of course, ketchup. Henry, the marketing genius of the company, traveled from city to city and store to store throughout the country, tirelessly tapping growing urban markets where prepackaged foods were increasingly a necessity. By the early 1870s, Heinz had established large sales operations in such emerging cities as St. Louis, Chicago, Omaha and Detroit.

His partner, Noble, oversaw much of the plant expansion to satisfy this demand, locating new automated processing, canning and bottling facilities in regional sites near metropolitan centers. Growth in output was immediate and rapid: in 1871, Heinz made 60 barrels of pickles; four years later it produced over 15,000. During that period, annual vinegar production rose from about 20,000 barrels to over 50,000. McIlhenny Co., it should be remembered, was manufacturing only 20,000 bottles of Tabasco sauce a year at peak capacity a decade hence.

Indeed, companies in virtually every manufacturing sector purchased automation equipment as quickly as it was produced. Sales of the McCormick reaper—a machine capable of harvesting in a few hours as much grain as two or three field hands could cut in a day—grew from 450 in 1847, not long after it was invented, to roughly 10,000 in 1870. The sewing machine had a similar trajectory. More than 85,000 were sold in 1870, up from about 4,000 fifteen years earlier, as owners of textile sweatshops strove to pump up their output. The popularity of Industrial Revolution machines was all the more remarkable when their price is considered. Reapers cost about $71,000 (more than $1 million in today's money) and sewing machines nearly $100,000. For farmers and factory owners, these were expensive purchases.

Which was precisely the problem, in McIlhenny's view. Companies were tying up precious capital and overextending themselves through costly bank loans in a headlong rush into innovation without considering the chances they were taking, he believed. Spending money they didn't have, these manufacturers presumed with no evidence that machines would generate sufficient additional revenue and profit to cover the costs of this new equipment, including the exorbitant interest expenses.

Perhaps worst of all, McIlhenny thought, many organizations were reinventing themselves to indulge the requirements of new technology. They were increasing output, extending factories and launching new lines of products, while attempting to cut back on labor costs. In the process, McIlhenny lamented, they were deserting the fundamental attributes that fueled their commercial triumphs in the first place.

In an apparent early 1870s letter to his wife, Mary—noteworthy because it would be one of the few notes written by the usually close-lipped McIlhenny that included a reference to business matters—he commented on this seemingly misguided behavior of his comtemporaries. As recounted by a McIlhenny heir, Edmund wrote: "We live in a period that desires only to eradicate the past. While I believe as much as anyone that improving and perfecting manufacturing systems are essential for consistent profits, this should be accomplished without taking on so much debt that you will drown if you have one bad year and without completely ridding yourself of the ideas that your company was built upon." McIlhenny continued by explaining that if businesses are "built on the good concepts that you make just enough products that the market can digest or never allow your brand to be anything but a distinguished product or don't introduce new brands unless older ones are established," then machines must never replace these ideas, as he believed some contemporary companies were doing. "Instead, machines may simplify the efforts to carry the ideas out," McIlhenny wrote, according to the family member. "A good business is the right mixture of people and processes. There shouldn't be more of either than are needed and neither should cost too much to make the business unprofitable."

McIlhenny's implied warning of imminent trouble for companies so blinded by the Industrial Revolution as to have lost sight of their business fundamentals was borne out in late 1873 when the giant banking firm Jay Cooke and Company suddenly went bankrupt. Jay Cooke, a national hero who won acclaim as the financier of the Civil War after floating more than $1 billion in bonds to support the Union military effort, had invested heavily in a planned second transcontinental railroad that was to run from Duluth, Minnesota, to the Puget Sound and be called the Northern Pacific.

But the project ran out of money in Bismarck, North Dakota. Inexplicably, for a businessman with a reputation for sound, even conservative, fiscal judgment, Cooke had tied up almost all of his capital in this venture. When construction on the railroad ceased, he was overextended in an undertaking that was generating no revenue to cover his debts. Cooke and his firm became the first significant victims of industrial exuberance.

Within months, 89 of the country's 364 railroads failed, as investors panicked and pulled their money out of the transportation sector. More than 18,000 companies that relied on the railroads to inexpensively carry their goods to new, distant markets collapsed as well. Many of these companies had only recently finished installing expensive machinery to increase their output and meet what they had forecast would be rising demand. Now they were drowning in excess inventory and interest payments.

Among the companies that went under was Heinz. Unable to cover banknotes linked to equipment and raw material purchases, the six-year-old business filed for bankruptcy in 1875. Heinz was low on cash, because consumer activity had fallen in the wake of the nation's economic collapse while shipping costs had risen steadily, a result of the troubled railroads. Worse yet, Heinz had a bumper crop in cucumbers and other vegetables that year. Before the produce spoiled, Heinz had to bottle and can it, leaving its factories operating at full bore and its warehouses brimming when the company could least afford this. Henry Heinz would restart his business a year later with his brother Frank, but not before his personal financial condition had so declined that in January 1876, he was too penniless to pay for groceries.

The financial crisis that began in 1873—there would be many others during the Industrial Revolution—occurred just as Edmund McIlhenny's Tabasco business was hitting its stride, and he was becoming a wealthy man again. From that perch, he viewed the business turmoil across the nation with some alarm, but also with some satisfaction. McIlhenny's decision to forgo automation often made it difficult for him to satiate the growing demand for Tabasco sauce. But what he lost in revenue due to his inability to produce products speedily enough, McIlhenny more than made up in inventory control—he was never saddled with unsold bottles—and steady cash flow, which invariably rose and was not vulnerable to exaggerated dips during periods of economic weakness. And he took solace in the fact that, as he put it, "his company was not so foolish as to only look forward."

Such unambiguously conservative sentiments—for their go-go time, unusual among family business owners—found its most idiosyncratic expression in McIlhenny's nostalgia for plantation life.

After his marriage to Mary Eliza Avery, McIlhenny had a unencumbered view of rural life in the antebellum South. And although he never expected to run an agricultural company or leave his lucrative New Orleans banking post, McIlhenny grew sufficiently curious about the unique management of big farms in the southern states that he studied the structure of the Averys' operations on the island.

Of particular interest was the relationship between the workers and the plantation owners. The postwar antislavery fervor, especially in the victorious North, condemned plantation owners by association and made it taboo to credit them with even the smallest achievements as businessmen. But this attitude, McIlhenny thought, completely ignored the fact that plantation owners had accomplished something quite extraordinary: they had established small, self-sufficient communities—towns dedicated to nothing else but the farm's output—where workers, not all of them slaves, lived in close proximity to their bosses.

Under this system, plantation owners enjoyed captive, cheap labor. In exchange, workers had jobs for life as long as they behaved; food, shelter and medical care; paternal overseers (in many cases); and a close-knit neighborhood of friends and relatives. Often, owners and workers shopped at the same stores, sent their children to the same schools, belonged to the same church and participated in collegial weekend picnics and sporting events on the property; in the process, class barriers were grudgingly lowered and labor-management tension, while not eliminated, was lessened.

Dispassionate about the very serious moral questions raised by the existence of plantations, McIlhenny viewed these communities as a shrewd business strategy that should not be cast aside lightly. If reviving them without slavery was possible, company-owned villages offered the prospect of a sizable degree of employee loyalty—the natural result of the relative intimacy between owners and workers who share a single plot of land. Such loyalty would translate into high productivity and low overhead; employees were more likely to work harder for—and less prone to demand more money from—managers who doubled as neighbors. Moreover, quitting their jobs would be an undesirable choice for workers. To do so, they would have to move.

Of course, a prime reason that plantations thrived was, in fact, the presence of slaves. But like most white southerners, McIlhenny was unable to recognize the enormity of the institution. Southern businessmen at the time commonly held that the quality of plantation life was more desirable than the Dickensian conditions in soulless nineteenth-century New England textile plants and towns. Instead of urban anonymity and financial insecurity, the plantation provided a predictable, familial stability, they believed. With home and place of employment interchangeable, owners and workers had an equal interest in the survival of the business.

Slavery was erased, regrettably to some landowners. Yet postwar Southern realities—the poverty, the itinerancy among all classes of people, the freed blacks seeking employment and housing at any price, the hundreds of thousands dead and the traditions that died with them, the vanquished and occupied homeland—combined to produce ideal circumstances for a restored version of a worker's village, a concept McIlhenny had become so drawn to that he was eager to implement it as the foundation of the Tabasco business.

Initially, however, McIlhenny had to be patient. While Tabasco was catching on around the world, in the early 1870s, McIlhenny Co. was still too immature and its performance too unpredictable to confidently forecast orders from year to year. Hiring a permanent labor force, even a small one, to live on Avery Island and work for the Tabasco company was overly risky to consider. In the first stages of this business, McIlhenny preferred a flexible workforce—generally, ex-slaves, who were mostly transients.

Resigned to waiting until his company grew large enough before establishing a company village, McIlhenny worried that this would not occur in his lifetime. Soon, though, a surprising opportunity proved his pessimism unwarranted. In 1880, McIlhenny was offered a lucrative deal to produce and distribute salt, the second of three ingredients in Tabasco sauce and the primary resource on Avery Island. This bit of unexpected good fortune would have two significant repercussions: it would greatly expand McIlhenny's business operations in the Gulf region and it would lead directly to the beginning phase of his worker's community.

The initial salt-production ventures on Petit Anse—during the War of 1812 by the island's founders, Elizabeth Triett and John Hayes, and during the Civil War under McIlhenny's father-in-law, Daniel Dudley Avery—barely made a dent in the island's reserves. Avery Island, it should be noted, is a geological oddity.

Distinct from most of the thousands of landmasses around the globe, the island is a huge column of salt, one of only a few salt domes large enough to protrude above the water. Because of Avery Island's immense height—from its visible tip to its bottommost grain of salt deep in the Gulf, it stands taller than Mount Everest—if 7,000 tons of salt were mined a day (approximately the current pace), the Earth would probably be extinct well before the salt on Avery Island ran out.

Avery Island was produced by a series of violent disruptions. Some 250 million years ago, the Earth was composed of a single supercontinent, known as Pangaea. But as the thick tectonic plates in the upper crust of the planet ground against each other like mismatched gears straining to mesh, rifts grew in Pangaea's surface. Over time, the supercontinent began to rend and drift apart.

It would take another 200 million years before the fragmenting of Pangaea produced the configuration of the Earth we're familiar with today—seven continents divided by vast oceans and narrow land bridges. During this upheaval, some of the planet's smaller seas became landlocked for short periods, surrounded by giant slabs of earth that had separated from the supercontinent. Thus choked, these seas evaporated, leaving behind large beds of salt. When the landmasses retreated, the seas refilled and flowed freely again, burying the salt on the ocean's floor.

The prehistory of the Gulf of Mexico is a rhythmic succession of dry, salt-producing epochs followed by equally productive millennia during which the Gulf would reconstitute, its fresh belly of water filling with layers of sediment from rivers emptying into it. Under the weight of 50,000 feet of sediment, the bottom-lying salt, which when pressured is plastic and rises, jackhammered its way upward through the rocks above it. Out of this geological Sturm und Drang arose Avery Island and four other salt domes observable off of Louisiana's Gulf coast—Jefferson, Weeks, Cote Blanche and Belle islands. At 152 feet above sea level, Avery is by far the largest.

(One fortuitous by-product of salt's ascent out of the Gulf was the development of mushroom-head-like seams in the rock—known as isoclinal folds—that were perfect storehouses for fossil fuel. Indeed, oil and gas production on Avery Island has been a pleasant revenue bonus for the McIlhennys since the mid-twentieth century.)

In 1867, two years after the Avery and McIlhenny families returned penniless to a demolished Petit Anse, the federal government commissioned an investigation into what could be done with the valuable salt mine on the island. The Union had made good work of the salt, deep in enemy territory, during the war. Now, in peacetime, with rock salt at a premium, a trade tariff imposed on imports and Petit Anse the sole domestic source, the government estimated that the remarkably pure product on Avery Island could underprice foreign competitors by as much as 50 percent. At the time, rock salt was primarily used as a spice as well as for food preserving and packaging.

The government's report, issued by the Bureau of Mines, called for a technique to extract the salt reminiscent of the way coal was drawn out from underground but not yet attempted in the United States: "There remains but one method of permanent mining; namely, that by well-constructed shafts and protected galleries in the salt itself. The extraction of the salt will be carried [out in] so-called compartments or squares supported by walls and pillars, as in the mines of the Wieliczka in Poland and of Vic and Dieuze in the east of France."

Two entrepreneurs, Charles Chouteau of St. Louis and a partner known only now as Mr. Price, immediately seized on this study to approach Judge Avery with an offer to cover the costs of sinking the mine and share a portion of the proceeds. Originally, the pair proposed to pay Avery $2 per ton of salt sold, a pittance with salt priced at upwards of $80 a ton on the open market at the time. But Avery needed the money badly and was in no financial position to negotiate. He accepted.

However, in 1869, before excavation of the mine began, the postwar tariff on salt imports was lifted and prices plunged. Chouteau and Price told Avery that they wanted to renegotiate the arrangement and pay him less for the salt. Avery was livid. What nerve they had to squeeze his tiny royalty when their profit margins were so outsized, even with salt prices on the decline. This is my island, Avery angrily thought, and Chouteau and Price were nothing but carpetbaggers, like all other northerners taking advantage of the South. He threw the pair off his property, secretly hoping they would soon realize the great deal they initially had and would eventually beg to restore the original agreement, at which point Avery planned to turn the tables on them and demand more money.

That never occurred. In 1870, Price, apparently the money man in the endeavor, died. Discussions between Chouteau and Avery to open the mine were never revived. Ironically, that project may have been Daniel Avery's only hope to resurrect his family's life on the island and rebuild his plantation. At a conservative figure of $1.50 per ton of salt, with no investment of his own, Avery could have generated about three-quarters of a million dollars a year in today's money. That would have been more than enough to buy machinery for the farm, hire labor to rejuvenate the dormant fields and ensure the island remained in his hands.

About ten years later, with Judge Avery dead and Edmund McIlhenny controlling the island, a similar opportunity cropped up—another salt venture with almost identical terms. McIlhenny instantly recognized the long-range benefits of an offer requiring little sweat or money on his part and a virtually guaranteed dependable cash flow, even if the royalty was paltry. If nothing else, he could count on consistent salt revenue to further expand his Tabasco business, and he would have free salt for manufacturing the product. Unlike Avery, McIlhenny only had one question for his suitors: Where do I sign?

McIlhenny's new partner, American Salt Company, drilled out the first mine shafts in 1880 and simultaneously installed modern machinery, such as tramways to carry the salt from the breaker building (where the salt was chopped into tiny rock crystals) to schooners at the docks. To ease the transportation bottleneck between Avery Island's shallow bayous and the much deeper Gulf port in nearby New Iberia, construction began on a barge and steamship canal linking the two sites.

The salt mining operation was an immediate sensation, well beyond McIlhenny's wildest expectations. For five years, until 1885, when the nation's second rock salt mine opened in Retsof, New York, American Salt was the sole supplier to the highly lucrative artificial soda (or sodium carbonate) industry. Although it had been available for a century, artificial soda—chiefly composed of salt and sulfuric acid and trace amounts of chalk and charcoal—became an industrial workhorse in the early 1880s as a raw material in paper, soap, glass and textiles. By 1900, artificial soda consumed about half the total salt produced in the United States.

In its early years, the mine employed about 100 workers, including 50 who actually descended into the pit. Many of these men took lodging in boardinghouses and provisional tent cities in New Iberia, about ten miles away down a pinched dirt road, with no easy transportation link to Avery Island. Absenteeism was rampant, and some workers would show up at the mine drunk or hung over, having spent their salary of $1.75 for a ten-hour shift at the bars and brothels of lower Louisiana.

The lack of a dependable workforce was a costly problem for McIlhenny and American Salt's management. On some days, there weren't enough laborers to operate the mine, which was especially vexing as the need for rock salt was growing rapidly and the amount of revenue the venture yielded seemed limited only by the amount of salt it could produce. Determined to find stable, responsible employees, McIlhenny realized that the conditions at the salt operation were ideal for a company village: It was a labor-intensive operation that required reliable, trained and skilled employees—in other words, a fairly permanent workforce with few transients—and was blessed with a large revenue base, which logically could be expected to deliver growth.

Excited by the prospect of creating a worker community on Avery Island, the postbellum plantation he had been pondering for nearly a decade, McIlhenny funded the project on his own. He began by constructing six houses built close to each other on a high ridge at the south end of the island, within hearing distance of the mine's imposing breaker building, where the salt was crushed day and night by steam-driven machines in loud, belching thunderclaps. A sole note remains containing McIlhenny's thoughts about how the homes should look: "They should be better than slave homes, but still fundamental lodging; plain and simple," he wrote.

That they were. The homes were modest—about 500 to 700 square feet (a typical slave dwelling was closer to 300 square feet)—one-story wood frames. Designed in no-frills Cajun style, they had steep-pitched, fifteen-foot gable roofs that covered the rectangular structure, including a porch, which was often used in the summertime as an open living area when it was stifling indoors. To suit the high water table in the bayou, the homes were elevated off the ground two to three feet on cypress blocks. The ceilings were about ten feet high with a storage attic above them.

McIlhenny built one-, two-, and three-bedroom models. A husband, wife and baby might live in a home with a single ten-foot-by-twelve-foot bedroom; the three-bedroom homes were generally reserved for families of six children or more, not an uncommon occurrence because many of the workers were Cajuns who were predominantly Catholic. Even the largest of the houses had only one bathroom and, in most cases, no dining room. Meals were usually eaten in nooks in the kitchen or in the living room.

Plain and simple, but the price was right. McIlhenny charged no rent, or merely pennies a month; otherwise, he reasoned, the workers would be more willing to leave—if they have to pay to live on Avery Island, they could just as well be in New Iberia or Lafayette or any other community with available jobs—and then they wouldn't be truly captive labor, an essential component of his plan.

Dozens of other homes, a church, a general store and a social club were on the drawing board for the next phase of development. Though this village was constrained in scope initially, it was enough to give Edmund McIlhenny a distinction that his family today prefers to not claim, perhaps because it now carries connotations of worker intimidation: The Avery Island company town was among the first ever in the United States. It would be a few years before the concept was widely embraced by manufacturing legends like George Pullman, Andrew Carnegie and Henry Ford, as well as the coal outfits in the threadbare hollers of West Virginia, Kentucky and Tennessee.

If McIlhenny's goal was to create an environment in which the difference between job and home was eliminated, he—and, more so, his son Edward, who took his idea and some decades later brought it to fruition—achieved that aim. Although conditions were crowded in Salt Village, as it became known—not only was the inside of the homes meager, but also no more than 100 feet separated one house from another—people who lived on Avery Island in the early decades of the company town recalled a period of rural idyll, a place where the troubles of the rest of the region were scarcely felt.

New Iberia, and Louisiana as a whole, faced inestimable difficulties in the aftermath of the Civil War: black-white relations were a tinderbox as the Ku Klux Klan, lynching, segregation and race riots strangled the region; jobs with decent salaries were scarce; quality health care was nonexistent for the underclasses; the overleveraged Industrial Revolution economy was constantly tumbling into and out of recession; and banks were dispossessing the poor from their homes with the slightest hint that they might default on their mortgage payments.

In this charged and unstable atmosphere, Avery Island was a bucolic oasis. Certainly, the pay wasn't particularly good in the salt mines or Tabasco fields and factory. In the 1880s, the salt miners and pepper sauce factory hands were making about half the national average salary of $16 a week, a disparity that remains even now on Avery Island. But for the workers residing there, there was all the alligator, coon and deer meat they could eat and all the fish they could catch. And there was the security of a job and a home for life; for most, it was well worth any economic trade-offs.

A more recent resident of Avery Island described the sanctuary and seclusion of the island in this way: "Living here for so long, I've paid very little attention to many of the things that go on off of the island," said Joseph Dubois, in his late eighties and a resident of Avery Island since birth. "I didn't have to because everything we needed was here. The rules on the island were pretty easy: as long as you work hard and don't do anything too stupid, you'll be taken care of. I was in World War II, fought in Germany and I came right back to the island. There's no other place in the world to be."

While McIlhenny became a salt entrepreneur only as an afterthought, the emergence of the company town made him appreciate the salt mining operation more and more. Indeed, given the opportunity to consider it, he realized that he was attracted to salt mining because it had the feature he esteemed most in a business: simplicity. Salt mining held few surprises; and it didn't require complex designs or complex strategies to make money from it. That type of operation suited McIlhenny perfectly.

Similar to the Tabasco business, salt mining involved a single product; it had a straightforward manufacturing process—workers were dispatched to chop and blast away at the walls of a vast underground cavern; it enjoyed an endless supply of raw material; and it had loyal customers.

What's more, the slow pace of change in the mining industry paralleled the quaint conservation of the past that McIlhenny treasured. Diesel engines have replaced steam-driven machines and new tools such as hoists and rigs have been automated, but basic mining techniques today are unaltered from those practiced when Edmund McIlhenny signed the deal with American Salt. Like Avery Island, like the Tabasco company, McIlhenny's salt mining business now is to a large degree a reflection of what it was.

This becomes strikingly clear at first glance inside Avery Island's salt mine. The mine is a series of sparsely lit gigantic rooms, or galleries—each of them 6,000 square feet with 70-foot-tall ceilings. It has a haunting, underworld pallor, a chiaroscuro of pure white crystals and bottomless shadows, creating an illusion of ripples on the walls like folds in the fabric of a curtain. It's surprisingly beautiful, hallucinogenic, as the color of the glistening salt seems to turn slowly in the darkness—from brown to gray to blue and then white again. What minimal lighting there is comes mostly from bulbs primitively strung on exposed wires, miners' headlamps and flashlights.

To mine the salt, workers (there are usually dozens of them in the mine at any one time) drill a string of six-inch holes at the base of a gallery's twenty-foot-thick walls and gingerly pack the holes with dynamite. The dynamite detonates sequentially in millisecond delays, a chain of blasts that produces 7,000 tons of rock salt. This sets off a storm of glittering rocks and powder as weightless as a fantail's feather. When the earth stops shuddering, some miners scrape loose chunks of salt from the walls and ceilings with pickaxes and sledges, others shovel the salt into a convoy of dump trucks, and earthmoving machines scoop up nineteen tons of salt per swallow. The salt is then poured into a grinding machine, which gnaws the larger rocks down to size and, subsequently, places the cargo on old wooden trams and in crates hauled by conveyor belts to carry the salt out of the mine.

Above ground, the salt is transferred into a breaker building, where it is further crushed, graded and ferried out of the mine directly to barges lining the Intercoastal canal to transport it to the Mississippi River. Until the mid-1990s, Avery Island's breaker building, built in 1899, was the oldest of any mine in the country. But after its wood and concrete foundation decayed, the structure was torn down. It has since been replaced with a new building that, while quite a bit more modern in design, essentially follows the original—and still somewhat novel—idea of using gravity-driven pulleys and hoists to convey the salt.

When a gallery in the mine is played out, a fresh one is blasted open. The galleries are separated from one another by two enormous columns of salt, left there to support the ceiling. After a level is exhausted, the miners drive farther into the earth. Currently, Avery Island's mine has ten levels—the lowest is about 1,500 feet under the surface—and more than 100 miles of roads and caverns.

At about 900 feet into the mine, there is a makeshift workshop. Because it wasn't possible to construct an elevator large or strong enough to carry into the pit the enormous hulking rigs that do the bulk of the grunt work, all of the heavy machinery, even the most complicated, is constructed in the mine itself. Parts—crankcases, chassis, spark plugs, tires and all other components large and small—are sent down to the workshop by shaft and the finished equipment is pieced together and precisioned in laborious, old-fashioned, non-assembly-line efforts. And when equipment is damaged or becomes obsolete, it's simply discarded in abandoned portions of the mine, rather than disassembled. Old trams without wheels, misshapen conveyor cars, heavy equipment that looks like it has been in a head-on collision—all sit idly in the pitch black.

There's a strict limit to how much salt can be taken out of the mine. At its current depth, the mine's climate is a pleasantly dry 72 degrees, compared to an uncomfortably humid 90 degrees plus during many months of the year on the tropical surface of Avery Island. But the further one descends into the mine, the hotter it gets. At 2,500 feet, it's as much as 110 degrees, intolerable for miners (at 40,000 feet, it's upwards of 800 degrees).

According to Greg Border, an Avery Island mining engineer, "We're only going to be able to extract about one percent of what's in the dome before we can't descend anymore. That means, within this century, we'll have to close the mine."

That is a difference between salt mining and making Tabasco sauce that Edmund McIlhenny could not have possibly guessed; one of them, it turns out, is not a perpetual business.

The McIlhennys were extremely fortunate that the American Salt deal came along when it did. At the turn of the twentieth century, American Salt was shipping upwards of 40,000 tons of rock salt a year. The McIlhenny family's cut of the revenue was 50 percent. At $3.80 per ton of salt on the open market, the McIlhennys cleared nearly $80,000 annually from the salt operation ($1.4 million in today's money), or about the same amount that Tabasco sauce was generating. Indeed, American Salt was a welcome safety net, at the time a stable and reliable business for the McIlhennys to fall back on in the event that the more inchoate and risky Tabasco business foundered.

On November 25, 1890, Edmund McIlhenny died. Family members can recite with some degree of unanimity, if not accuracy, even the minutest details of much of McIlhenny's life—especially following the development of Tabasco sauce. But none could remember the facts surrounding Edmund's death. Indeed, many of his heirs were themselves surprised by how little was recalled about Edmund's last days. They could offer no explanation for this, except to say that outside of his business activities, Edmund was diffident and shy.

This much family members assume: Edmund passed away a contented man. After a life that took an unlikely course—a journey of more than a thousand miles from Baltimore to New Orleans and finally to Avery Island, during which he staggered from poverty to fortune to privation and then wealth again—Edmund could die knowing he left the legacy he strove hardest for. Presuming that the success of his family business was enshrined, Edmund could take comfort at his death in the belief that his wife, Mary Eliza, would have enough money to live comfortably for the rest of her days and that his children would never be dependent on others for a livelihood, as he had been in Baltimore during the panic of 1837 and in post–Civil War New Orleans. Events would prove McIlhenny right on both counts. But the next few years—the years that many family businesses are unable to weather, when the company is passed from the founder to his or her offspring—would nearly destroy the Tabasco brand, and with it the gift that Edmund McIlhenny desired most to pass on.

Chapter 5
ROUGH RIDER

One statistic about family businesses has remained unchanged since Edmund McIlhenny made Tabasco sauce: only about 30 percent outlive the founder's death, and of those that do, a mere 12 percent are still around to see a third generation of family management.

In some cases, this meager survival rate can best be explained by external and arbitrary events, the result of one or more macroeconomic misfortunes that unhinge the company at the worst possible moment—when it is distracted, slowed by the loss of its framer and unprepared to respond nimbly. In the latter part of the nineteenth century, there were numerous such "episodes," which McIlhenny Co. and many other family businesses had to navigate gingerly.

These economic setbacks were primarily the consequences of indecision by federal fiscal managers in the late 1800s. From one administration to the next—and, indeed, one treasury secretary to the next—policy makers vacillated between silver and gold as the nation's monetary standard. And they interminably debated whether induced inflation or alternately deflation was the correct approach for propelling long-term expansion—ultimately trying one and then the other as popular opinion dictated.

Not surprisingly, such flip-flops produced little else than a period of poorly planned and purposeless fiscal performance in the United States. The value of the dollar spiked and slumped constantly, speculators effectively took control of stock and specie markets and onerous tariffs drove global trade, not supply and demand. At Edmund's death in 1890, the wholesale price of Tabasco sauce had dropped to about 35 cents a bottle from $1 on the day the first batch of the product was sold. This startling two-thirds decrease in revenue per bottle, almost all of it the outcome of inept national economic policy, cut McIlhenny's once-generous profit margins to the bone.

When Edmund died, a dozen or so brands were attempting to go head-to-head with Tabasco sauce. Among the memorable efforts were Chace and Duncan's Peppersauce from New York City, Bergman's Diablo Pepper Sauce from California and Popie's Hotter 'n Hell Sauce from New Orleans. Even Henry Heinz, his business barely out of bankruptcy, got into the fray with a product he had the temerity to call, simply, Tabasco Pepper Sauce.

A blatant Tabasco imitator was Chili Colorow Sauce, an early 1880s product backed by Chicago businessman William Railton. To sow confusion with the well-known diamond label that McIlhenny had already begun to use on Tabasco bottles, Chili Colorow had a Maltese cross–shaped label, which said it was "prepared from a Mexican formula." In an obvious swipe at McIlhenny, Railton claimed his product "is expressly suitable for family dining, possessing a fine, rich body of exquisite flavor and has neither the fiery nor nauseous taste which characterizes most sauces." According to its ad copy, Chili Colorow also "relieves indigestion and cures dyspepsia. Physicians recommend it."

Although Tabasco sauce remained preeminent in hot sauce sales, the presence of these rivals—and the relatively small inroads they made into Tabasco's market share—nonetheless raised alarms at McIlhenny Co., which was compelled for the first time to address the thorny question of how to maintain revenue growth in the face of intense competition.

Edmund McIlhenny had not equipped any of his six children

who survived to adulthood to manage the Tabasco company after his death. One reason was that he could not envision the company operating without him—a common conceit of family business founders. But of greater weight was McIlhenny's belief that successful people are self-made and that business education is to its detriment a survey of how others have succeeded, but not how to succeed. McIlhenny's unlikely prosperity as both a banker and a hot sauce maker overseeing a Louisiana farm, though he had never been formally taught the skills for either of these trades, was proof enough to him that instinct, not instruction, informed most business achievements. McIlhenny's two daughters and four sons heard about the virtues of common sense and resourcefulness so often from him that he felt confident they appreciated the inherent ingenuity it took to run a family business. He could only hope one of them had the intuitive talent to manage the Tabasco company as well as he did.

In the aftermath of McIlhenny's death, that task fell to Edmund and Mary's eldest son, John Avery. He was handed the job not after demonstrating any innate skills, but because at twenty-three he was the only McIlhenny boy to have reached the legal age to sign contracts and other binding business documents. In short order, it became evident that John was unfit for the task. The twin difficulties facing McIlhenny Co.—a troubled, erratic economic environment combined with the emergence of opportunistic competitors—were foreign to John's limited experiences. He was incapable of offering a suitable strategic response.

In appearance and, to a large degree, temperament, John McIlhenny didn't fit neatly into the McIlhenny mold. Most of the McIlhenny men—from the founder, Edmund, to the present CEO, Paul—are recognizable by soft, burnished, ruddy features, which have grown doughier through the generations. John, by contrast, was dark, pointy-nosed, handsome, thin and brooding. His eyes had a distant, liquid glare, the type loners often evince.

It wasn't that John lacked the intelligence to manage the family business. A bright man, immensely curious about world affairs and politics, he studied law at Harvard, although apparently didn't graduate. Nor did he lack charisma. John was well spoken with regal bearing, even if quiet and frequently shy. People often viewed his diffidence as a sign of inward strength, not social ineptness.

But none of this could help John overcome the sole shortcoming that really mattered in 1890: he knew very little—and had few native thoughts—about inspiring growth in a company whose profit margins had shrunk from obese to slender. And growth was, indeed, the only option. Cutting costs to increase earnings, a very familiar method in modern corporate settings, was out of the question. The family business John inherited was so streamlined—its labor, manufacturing and raw material expenses were minuscule, just as Edmund McIlhenny had planned it—that there was no fat in the operation to eliminate.

Uncertain about how to stanch the plunging profits before the company went into the red, John McIlhenny chose a strange path, one that telegraphed his callowness: he asked Tabasco sauce retailers and distributors—his direct customers, in other words—for assistance. "When my father died he left his books showing the customers that he then had," John said some years later during a trademark dispute. "I immediately wrote to all of those customers and acquainted them with the fact of my father's death and with the fact that I had assumed control of the business. . . . Then as soon as I could get my business organized I started out on a trip through the United States and visited these different people. . . . . [I] talked to them of the possibilities of the business and I advised with them as to the best method of developing it because I was very young and inexperienced. I knew that these men were of wide experience and that they were good people and knew they would be willing to assist me with their advice."

Advice was not in scant supply; genuine help, however, was. Sensing that John was out of his depth, many of McIlhenny's distributors took advantage of him. Some middlemen raised the price of Tabasco sauce to retailers, when inflation allowed them to, but didn't notify McIlhenny or pass along the increased revenue to the company. And together they encouraged McIlhenny to take on a string of revenue-building activities that would help sales in the short run, but that were clearly contrary to Edmund McIlhenny's attempts to imbue his brand with an aura of foggy, moss-drenched Louisiana mystery. These promotional schemes in great measure cheapened the Tabasco brand, threatening to turn it into a commodity and to dilute its image as an unorthodox product with an exclusive taste and lineage.

John was desperate, though, and wrongfully believed his distributors had the company's interests at heart. So he began what was then and still is now for McIlhenny Co. an unprecedented marketing offensive. Door-to-door salesmen—so-called drummers—tried to sell Tabasco sauce directly to Americans out of suitcases; the name *Tabasco* (along with a life-sized replica of the product) appeared in an operetta; a supermarket lottery offered a $3,000 prize to purchasers of Tabasco sauce; and reproductions of famous paintings were offered in exchange for a Tabasco coupon and a 10-cent handling charge.

There was more. "I had bill posters prepared and had large wooden signs in the outside, in the fields, near the cities," John said. "I had exhibits at food expositions with demonstrators attached. I gave away many thousands of circulars and folders and miniature bottles of Tabasco sauce."

Mass-marketing efforts like these had never before (and few times since) been undertaken in McIlhenny's history. In general, the company has avoided billboards, discounts and prizes to consumers because such untargeted promotional programs implicitly regard customers as part of a large, indistinguishable group, instead of an exclusive club sufficiently discerning to discover the value of a premium product.

John McIlhenny missed this point completely with his scatter-shot advertising. Not surprisingly, his sales strategy created more problems for the business than it solved. The cost of the campaigns was quite high and they didn't entice enough new customers to cover the expense. Moreover, the company's already burdened profit margins were stressed further by the discounts and freebies. Then John compounded the company's deepening problems by introducing two new products: specialty foods oysters and shrimp in a container.

This move wasn't entirely irrational. At the turn of the twentieth century, the nation's wealthiest people were drawn to delicacies that could be shipped around the country in recently invented refrigerated railcars. Prices of mollusks and crustaceans of all kinds, as well as such items as turtle and rabbit for soup, stews and hors d'oeuvres, were escalating rapidly. McIlhenny hoped that the increasingly well-regarded Tabasco brand name on shrimp and oysters from Louisiana's exotic Gulf Coast would attract a high-class clientele in the fast-growing cities.

Perhaps at another time in McIlhenny Co.'s history—when the company was not so cash poor—this product expansion might have had a chance to succeed. But John McIlhenny greatly underestimated the expense of producing and distributing oysters and shrimp, and he failed to consider that he and other McIlhenny managers were woefully ill trained to take on this new line.

Agreements had to be struck with fishermen, a group that McIlhenny had never dealt with before and wielded no influence over. Additionally, because of refrigeration, shipping costs for oysters and shrimp were much higher than for sending crates of sauces. And many of the distributors handling Tabasco sauce represented condiments and other foods, but not delicacies. So McIlhenny had to find new middlemen to manage the sales and shipments of these products. The amount of money that McIlhenny had to invest in this new venture and the negotiations he had to navigate just to get it off the ground were so significant that its fate was actually sealed quite early on.

Nonetheless, McIlhenny continued to fund the new line year upon year banking on a turnaround. But he never succeeded in developing an adequate national market for the products. Nor could he hammer out beneficial contracts with the Gulf Coast fishermen or compete against more sizeable delicacy purveyors, whose operations were set up to ship bulk food economically from numerous locations throughout the country.

In the end, John McIlhenny's ill-fated product extension was viewed as such folly that until recently McIlhenny management assiduously refrained from putting the family's name or the Tabasco brand on any items other than pepper sauce. Indeed, just two decades ago, McIlhenny executives characterized John's foray as possibly the biggest mistake in the company's history, "a disastrous push into specialty food products."

It could be argued that this hapless venture would never have been attempted had John heeded his father's advice. Edmund McIlhenny had pointedly warned that it was a fatal error for companies to put themselves deep into debt or tie up the little capital they had to chase innovation, whether in the form of new products, services, markets or business models. Innovation, he contended, should be used to improve the performance of a company's core business, not replace or alter it; but above all, it was not an effective response to desperation.

By the latter part of the 1890s, under John's leadership, McIlhenny Co. was in danger of becoming one of those family businesses unable to survive the loss of its founder. And despite its privileged position as the best-selling pepper sauce, Tabasco was in peril of becoming a forgotten product, like Del Monte coffee, Libby's mustard and Campbell's salad dressing from the same period. McIlhenny Co.'s deliberately small-scale operations and the lack of a strategy to continually expand the distribution network for its popular product placed the family business in the same bind that choked many one-hit wonders in U.S. commercial history. If John McIlhenny's company was still profitable then, it was by the slimmest amount, and neither he nor anyone around him had any promising ideas for improving its fortunes.

Frustrated and not a little embarrassed, John began to spend more and more time off of Avery Island, involved in pursuits that drew him closer to his deepest interests: politics, adventure and world travel. While retaining the title of McIlhenny Co. president, in 1898, John impulsively joined the Rough Riders, the eclectic group of volunteer fighters led by Theodore Roosevelt, and immediately left for Cuba to fight in the Battle of San Juan Hill, during which U.S. forces captured the island from Spain.

As McIlhenny told it, slogging through a Rough Rider campaign, he saved the future president from a sniper's bullet by pushing Roosevelt out of the way at the last moment and covering up TR's body with his own. That may be apocryphal, because like all of the McIlhennys, John was prone to exaggeration about his exploits. It is known, though, that McIlhenny and Roosevelt became lifelong friends while fighting alongside each other in the Spanish-American War. Moreover, Roosevelt considered McIlhenny sufficiently courageous in battle to promote him to second lieutenant for gallantry.

In 1900, upon returning to the United States from Cuba, John McIlhenny was elected first to the Louisiana House of Representatives and then to the state senate. In between sessions of the legislature, John claimed to call on Tabasco distributors and retailers across the country, but often, we now know, he would escape to barely charted locales as far away from Avery Island as he could get, such as Japan, China, the Philippines and eastern Russia.

In 1998, the extent of John's wanderings and passions during that time was laid bare following the death of his only child (at eighty-seven). An auction of John's collected items was held. It was telling, even to his family, who thought they knew of McIlhenny's travels reasonably well, to see among his holdings rare, effete treasures—in all, hundreds of works of folk art that were striking in how strange and foreign they must have been to most people in Louisiana at the time that McIlhenny lived: such things as a carved ivory netsuke of two chickens mating; tiny cloisonné vases with painted flowers; elaborately embroidered kimonos; and a Chinese ceramic pillow. To some who attended the auction, it portrayed a man much more disconnected from his family and home than had been known or guessed.

During John's extended absences, McIlhenny Co. was virtually leaderless, although at times his younger brothers Edward Avery and Rufus would step in and run the operation. Even non-family members remarked on how neglected the Tabasco business and the island appeared to be. Lucy Matthews Chambers, the socialite daughter of an influential St. Louis stockbroker and the cousin of Edward Avery McIlhenny's wife-to-be, Mary, visited Avery Island in the early 1900s and observed in her never-published autobiography: "The salt mine, most important during the War Between the States, was just dragging along. There was very little growing of the small red peppers for Tabasco sauce. This pepper sauce was being produced in an old barn in a large old-fashioned churn with a hand plunger to mash the peppers. The island was covered with every kind of growth from various mosses and palmettos to great live oak, willow, and cypress hung with the weird-locking Spanish moss."

Yet even with the Tabasco business in tatters, the McIlhennys were one of the wealthiest families in the region. Their property holdings and conservatively managed vast monetary portfolio, accumulated by Edmund, assured the family's preeminence in a backwoods, hard-luck, agrestic region that to this day has never truly recovered from the economic fallout of the Civil War and the end of the plantation.

Edmund's heirs, though, were not satisfied with simply being grandees on an anonymous patch of Southern soil. They had hopes that the popularity of the Tabasco brand would translate into global acclaim for the family, placing them on par with new captains of industry and finance like the Carnegies, the Mellons and the Rockefellers. That never happened, in part because of the equally strong xenophobic character of the family, which prized isolation and was guarded around most outsiders. Nonetheless, in the midst of the worst of the company's troubles, when he had all but abandoned the family business, John McIlhenny sought to combine the beauty of the salt mine and the glitz of celebrity to gild the McIlhenny family's national reputation. It may not have achieved its aim and it was foolishly spendthrift, but it was an evening so unusual that old-timers in southern Louisiana still say it emblemizes the McIlhennys' extraordinary distinctiveness in the region.

The affair took place in February 1903. It was a debutante's ball of sorts, but with a twist that no one in the United States—and only kings and a few other nobles in Europe centuries before—had ever attempted: The party was held underground, deep in the salt mine on Avery Island. To get to the event, invited guests, dressed in formal tuxedos and evening gowns, rode a dusty, cramped elevator in darkness, hundreds of feet into the pit.

When the elevator stopped, the wooden cage opened onto one of the mine's galleries, a massive, blindingly white room, 60 by 100 feet, with 60-foot ceilings. Unlike the semidarkness the miners work in, the gallery was brightly illuminated. Shimmers of lacy coruscating light glinted off of French candelabras onto the crystalline walls, ceilings and floors. Even the tables and chairs glimmered; they were made out of pure salt, constructed by a New Orleans tombstone cutter who also sculpted a statue of Lot's wife that perched in the middle of the room. The atmosphere was so charged by the sparkle of the surroundings, the splendor of the bejeweled guests, the strangeness of the location and the thrumming harmonic echo of black servants standing in the corners singing that it dazzled the senses, like driving into a snowstorm at midnight.

The honored guests—the debutantes—were about as A-list as you could get: Alice Roosevelt, the daughter of Theodore Roosevelt, who was president at the time, and Edith Root, whose father was secretary of war and would become secretary of state in the Roosevelt administration.

The two women were in their twenties and enjoyed each other's company, although their personalities couldn't have been more dissimilar. Edith was reserved and self-effacing. In 1907, she would marry Major General Ulysses S. Grant III, the grandson of the former president and Civil War commander, and live a life of quiet public service. Alice, by contrast, was saucy and provocative; she was the president's unruly child, who smoked cigarettes on the White House grounds in full view of the press and famously uttered, "If you can't say something good about someone, sit right here by me." In the early years of the 1900s, she and Edith Root, the children of the most powerful men in the United States, were the nearest thing to American royalty. Their presence at a party redounded well on the host.

Alice Roosevelt had met John McIlhenny, who was nearly twenty years her senior, through her father. Soon after TR and McIlhenny had finished their stint in the Rough Riders, John gave Roosevelt and his daughter an open invitation to Avery Island. Theodore visited a few times over many years, mostly to hunt. It is believed Alice showed up just once.

The days leading up to the soiree in the salt mine produced a flurry of publicity for the McIlhennys, which only heightened the anticipation for the party, especially among the less well-to-do in Iberia Parish. On their way to Avery Island, the two young women, along with McIlhenny, his mother and other family members, spent a whirlwind week in New Orleans taking in the Carnival—and virtually every step was captured by the local newspaper, the *New Orleans Daily Picayune*. The entourage toured the city in private streetcars, hopped from one party to another, attended cotillions, watched processions from VIP boxes, was introduced to the king and queen of the Krewe of the Atlanteans and rode at the head of an exclusive flotilla with war heroes and dignitaries on the yacht *Pansy*.

The *Picayune* covered the parade of boats this way: "The Pansy had among her Carnival visitors Miss Alice Roosevelt, Miss Root, Mr. and Mrs. Edward McIlhenny [Edmund's and Mary's son and daughter-in-law], Mrs. Mary Eliza McIlhenny and John McIlhenny. Miss Roosevelt and the little party with her drove to the landing quietly, hoping to escape the usual demonstration to be looked for from curious crowds, but she was received with quite a greeting from the assembled crowd."

Back home in New Iberia, stories like these were entrancing

and provoked a mixture of envy and respect for the McIlhennys. Gossipy articles about celebrities bathing in the high life in New Orleans were not unusual, but these celebrities were en route to Avery Island, to Iberia Parish—and some of them, the McIlhennys, even lived there. That simply didn't happen.

John McIlhenny was determined not to disturb the perception that the McIlhennys were anything but equals to the Roosevelts, deserved of a place in their social circle. In fact, an odd incident during the Carnival showed just how far McIlhenny was willing to go to protect this image.

According to John McIlhenny's son, Jack, his father was admiring a large fountain in a New Orleans public square when Alice Roosevelt, overtaken by mischief, snuck up behind him and shoved him into the water. "He was wet right up to his shoulders," Jack McIlhenny said.

John's mother, Mary, was outraged by the young woman's behavior and yelled, "You little twit! What do you mean pushing my son into the water and ruining his clothes?"

Jumping out of the fountain, John quickly stepped between his mother and Roosevelt and screamed, "Mother, shut up, shut up!" Then he turned to a relative and said, "For God's sake, get mother off to one side and tell her this is the president of the United States' daughter. If she makes too much of a fuss the newspaper reporters are going to make a big thing and it's going to ruin the whole visit."

Apparently, journalists didn't learn of this episode or decided not to embarrass the McIlhennys by writing about it. A few days later, the McIlhennys and the young women took a train to Avery Island for the party in the salt mine. Unfortunately, specific details about who said or did what to whom at the event have been lost. But descendants of salt miners who worked for the McIlhennys said that, according to their own family lore, the merrymaking went on well into the night.

The miners, of course, weren't invited to the party, but their children and grandchildren—many of whom were born and raised in the one- and two-room bungalows in Avery Island's Salt Village—

recalled hearing stories about the line of expensive horse-drawn carriages with leather seats and fringed roofs making an annoying racket as they pounded up the dirt roads to tour the island long beyond midnight. The clatter awakened the workers, who had to be at work early the next morning. In the following minutes, many of the miners stood on their front porches or at their windows watching the loudly chattering revelers go by. Some accounts said they got a glimpse of Alice Roosevelt and she waved to them.

Any ill will about the party at the time has long since been replaced by the glow that this still unforgettable event has left on the McIlhenny family's reputation in the region. While the McIlhennys— then or now—would never achieve the national prominence that John and his siblings had desired, a hundred years after the affair, it is brought up as the defining moment when people in Iberia Parish realized that the McIlhennys weren't quite like everyone else in the area.

"This put them in another category," said W.J. Trappey, chuckling about the incident. Trappey is the grandson of Bernard Trappey, who worked for the McIlhennys as a blacksmith in the late 1800s. W.J., now in his eighties, has forgotten a great deal of the past, but without any difficulty vividly recalls pivotal, ineradicable moments in his family's life, including the bruising legal battles between the McIlhennys and the Trappeys over whether the Trappeys would be allowed to produce a competing Tabasco sauce. "A lot of people down here a long, long time ago had been plantation owners and had slaves, for that matter, and had a lot of money at one time or another. But in the early 1900s, most families in southern Louisiana were still struggling to get back on their feet again. We didn't have the rich and fancy showing up at our parties the way the McIlhennys did. And a party in a salt mine? Who would have even thought of that. That was beyond everybody's comprehension and expectations. In the South at that period, you didn't even hope to be privileged in that way anymore."

Of course, if the McIlhennys were to retain their position in southern Louisiana, the Tabasco business would have to be attended to. John was clearly not cut out for running the company, a reality finally addressed in 1906. Sixteen years after John took over the family business, a friendly accommodation was worked out, allowing him to leave the company for a post in the Theodore Roosevelt administration as Civil Service commissioner, a job he held until 1919, when Woodrow Wilson appointed him financial adviser to Haiti during the U.S. occupation of the Caribbean nation. By the early 1930s, McIlhenny had retired to his estate in Charlottesville, Virginia, for a life of golf and preferential D.C. social clubs. He died in 1942 at the age of seventy-five and was interred in Arlington National Cemetery, shunning the family gravesite on Avery Island where his parents and most of his siblings are buried. Upon leaving Avery Island, John never returned to live there again.

Chapter 6

GREAT WHITE FATHER

If McIlhenny Co. was to enjoy a second act, it would have to be written by Edmund McIlhenny's second surviving son.

Born in 1872, Edward Avery McIlhenny was appointed to head the family business in 1906 upon the departure of this elder brother, John. Of the two siblings, Edward was better suited to run the company. For one thing, his personal life was more stable. At thirty-four years old, Edward had been married six years and had three daughters when he became president. John, a bachelor, had only just turned twenty-three at the time he was hurriedly handed the job. Moreover, Edward was instinctive, unconstrained and self-possessed, traits closely matching the innate, untaught talents that Edmund McIlhenny believed were prerequisites for a prosperous business leader. Unlike John, Edward didn't brood or fear making a wrong decision.

Edward hid few facets of his personality, but McIlhenny family members cited one incident from his youth that more than any other perfectly captured his spontaneity and self-confidence. It occurred on Easter Sunday in 1891 or 1892. Not yet twenty, E.A. or Ned, as family and friends called him, had returned home from Lehigh University in Pennsylvania for the holidays. He was wearing his church best, too formal for his liking. His white shirt was overly starched, and the string tie holding the collar shut on his beefy neck was tight, while his ivory seersucker suit felt like a sponge in the tropical heat. Sweat laced the young man's brow as he sat rigidly on the front porch of his family's Avery Island villa, awaiting guests.

Under orders to stay put, Edward could scarcely control himself. Since childhood, he had been uncontainable, constantly in fast or slow motion, kinetic and curious. Growing up on the island, E.A. had spent countless hours in the meandering bayous noiselessly inching a flatbed boat through the reeds to, for instance, watch the anhinga, a bird resembling a black snake with wings, dip its dagger-shaped bill into the water to stab a fish, flip it into the air and gulp it down headfirst. Or he could be found admiring the crystalline plume of the snowy egret as it waded in the still waters to stir up crabs and insects. Even as a boy, he took diligent notes of his observations in the field.

His athletic skills were legion as well. Among his brothers, cousins and other children on Avery Island, E.A. was the best swimmer, runner and hunter. "He wrestled with alligators for the sheer fun of it and he regarded it as unsportsmanlike to hunt the Louisiana brown bear with anything but a knife for a weapon and a heavy leather guard-sleeve for defense," wrote Hermann B. Deutsch, a Louisiana journalist who befriended the McIlhennys.

Edmund boasted, "Ned could hit carpenter bees on the wing with a shot from a single-barreled target pistol."

But on this Easter, likely the first following Edmund's death, E.A.'s mother had sternly told him to dress up properly and stay at the house until family members and friends came for dinner. She asked that he demonstrate his intelligence, breeding and schooling and not embarrass her with his country-boy, backwoods predisposition. Through the open windows in the estate—a dark Georgian manse built by Edmund, with cavernous, high-ceilinged rooms and a gallery surrounding three sides of the dwelling—E.A. could hear the kitchen help busily planning the dinner. He could see the maids setting the table as the butlers dusted the front room. There were few times on Avery Island that he had been this restless or bored.

E.A. hoped to comply with his mother's desires. But a calamity requiring his presence intervened, he would say years later in proudly (and often) telling this story. Suddenly, there was a commotion by the alligator pens, a set of cages a hundred feet from the house where E.A. kept the large reptiles that he was studying for a book he planned to write about them. The black help ran in all directions, yelling that Frank, an eleven-foot alligator, had broken out. The alligator was heading toward the birds' nests in the lake. Afraid of Frank's cranky temper and his iron-lock jaws, none of the workmen attempted to stop him.

Upon hearing the tumult, E.A. jumped down the porch stairs and raced across the lawn and down the bank of the bayou toward the fleeing alligator, overtaking Frank just seconds before he disappeared into the pea-green water. E.A. tackled the alligator and wrestled him into submission on the muddy shore. After tying Frank up with ropes, E.A. and the workmen dragged the alligator back to its cage.

His white clothes mucked up and a successful fight with an enraged deadly animal under his belt, McIlhenny felt more like himself once more. He walked slowly back to the house, with a lilt in his step, just as the guests arrived.

"He liked to say that there was never a question or doubt in his mind about what to do; the alligator was out, get him back," said a family member who was close to Edward. "There isn't an imagination big enough to come up with the life that E.A. led."

During John McIlhenny's troubled tenure, Edward was largely removed from the Tabasco company. In 1892, E.A. apparently (the family is mum about this) dropped out of college. Almost immediately, he booked passage as a naturalist on the relief expedition to the Greenland ice cap, bringing supplies and aid to explorer Robert Peary, who had taken a crew there a year earlier. In the midst of this journey, McIlhenny produced the first known charts tracing the routes taken by Arctic migratory birds, a few of which he had earlier seen wintering in Louisiana.

Five years later, McIlhenny financed his own expedition to Alaska, traveling deep into the region to northernmost Point Barrow, where he explored the glaciers and hunted wolves in Siberia. He returned home with nearly 1,600 artifacts of North Alaskan Eskimos and hundreds of pages of detailed notes describing the way the indigenous population lived, a treasure trove from a virtually unexplored region. McIlhenny deposited most of his findings in the University of Pennsylvania Museum of Archaeology and Anthropology, where they remain. Out of this venture grew an invaluable book exploring the rich tradition and structure of the many Eskimo languages.

In between these long-distance journeys, McIlhenny would invariably return to Avery Island, where he began his pursuit of banding birds to monitor their movement, social structure, behavior, life span and reproductive patterns. In his lifetime, McIlhenny tagged the legs of well over 300,000 birds—mostly waterfowl—an enormous collection for a single person, and he produced voluminous logs of data, more than any other individual, pertaining to the size, weight, condition and habitat of the birds living in the Gulf region.

Charting the patterns of life of people and creatures—their homes, their interactions and the family structures they formed—drew E.A. back again and again to reflect on his own family's existence on Avery Island. E.A. had always loved the island; although it was a mere six miles in circumference, he viewed it as an illimitable paradise, a fantasia of wildlife and flora. But he knew its magnetic effect on his family had as much to do with its physical beauty as its commercial potential. The McIlhennys had carved out an existence on Avery Island that E.A. believed forever tied the property to the family, the way birds are compelled to return to the same place season after season. It was a life that Edmund had cultivated out of vanquished southern soil.

E.A. was comforted by the notion that the Tabasco name his father created was potentially a priceless heirloom, one that could sustain the McIlhennys for generations to come. If only—a big "if" because the family business was in dire trouble. That was when, with some urgency, E.A. made his move. He approached his mother, brothers and sister and asked them to give him control of the family business, allowing John to move on.

Edward's first task was to correct the errors his older brother had made—primarily to simplify the company so it again reflected his father's vision. "John had tried to fix the company by altering it, which was contrary to the company's personality; he nearly demolished it," said a McIlhenny family member, currently one of the company's managers. "Ned was determined not to make the same mistake so he set out to undo what John had done."

The unprofitable oyster and shrimp lines were scrubbed, replaced by a renewed effort to increase sales and production of the flagship Tabasco product. Wholesale prices of Tabasco sauce had stabilized at about 50 cents a bottle by the time E.A. took over the company, half of what Edmund McIlhenny could command, but more than 40 percent higher than they had been in the late 1890s. By steadily boosting the number of retail outlets carrying Tabasco sauce, E.A. believed he could generate consistent revenue growth for the company from this single brand without any additional products. Until the market for Tabasco sauce peaked—which may have actually occurred only a few decades ago—it was foolhardy to distract the business with disparate offerings, McIlhenny asserted.

To reach a greater number of customers, E.A. canceled untargeted consumer advertising, and instead drew up a sales strategy that would concentrate on wholesalers. The idea was to better relations with distributors—even by paying them a little money on the side as needed—and through them negotiate for supplementary shelf space in stores. After firming up these agreements with distributors, McIlhenny felt he could seek their help in further promoting Tabasco sauce by making sure that important restaurants in their regions placed the product on their tables.

Convincing middlemen to more aggressively peddle his product would be relatively easy, McIlhenny assumed. Tabasco sauce was popular wherever it was sold, and it consistently outclassed the competition at major U.S. commercial fairs, winning gold medals at the 1901 Pan-American Exposition in Buffalo and the 1903 Louisiana Purchase Exposition in St. Louis. Considering the obvious appeal of Tabasco sauce and its market leadership, if more retail outlets and restaurants carried the product and storeowners already selling it were coaxed into larger displays, word of mouth among the growing legions of hot-foods addicts would inevitably increase the brand's sales exponentially, E.A. concluded. In other words, let the loyal customers promote the product, the precise way Tabasco sauce was marketed in the first place.

Edward McIlhenny possessed just the right touch for this type of mano a mano marketing strategy. He was a big, impressive man—not especially tall, but large-boned with ample arms and bearlike hands. His ruddy complexion lit up his face lunarlike when he smiled. He exuded warmth and had a large, outsized personality. Spinning jokes in a deep southern drawl, E,A, would laugh at them himself, loudly and contagiously, and then turn expectantly to those listening to see if everyone got the humor; if someone didn't, he'd look into that person's eyes, his own eyes twinkling, and repeat the punch line until he or she did. People were drawn to E.A.'s natural charm and his accomplishments as a naturalist, author and sportsman, which he would recount skillfully at every opportunity, usually to rapt audiences.

Like his father, E.A. frequently relied on a tall tale, often an adornment to a true story, to buoy his image, sell his product and lure people into his confidence. In a somewhat bizarre example, during his initial sales calls around the country, E.A. apparently took to embellishing his Arctic exploits—in a most inventive way. After reciting the actual details of his daring self-financed expedition in 1897 to Alaska's Point Barrow on the Arctic Ocean and describing in minutiae how he hunted Siberian wolves and returned with more Eskimo artifacts than anyone had ever seen before, E.A. would wait for the appropriate wide-eyed response and then offer an unexpected kicker.

Toward the end of his journey, McIlhenny found nearly 200 men shipwrecked in dangerous Sea Horse Shoal. He and his crew rescued them and brought them back safely. But here's the interesting part E.A. would add: "One of the rescued men was Jack London, the writer. He was using the name Jack Edwards then. But he spoke with such a Cockney accent, I called him London. He kept the name."

In the first few decades of the 1900s, when McIlhenny related this incident, it commanded attention. At the time, Jack London was a national celebrity, the best-selling, highest-paid and most feted American author. To come upon London in the streets was an appropriately noteworthy event. But to save London from certain death in the frozen North, that was stunning.

The story seemed plausible. For one thing, it was obvious from London's writings that he spent a lot of time in Alaska. Some of his greatest books, including *The Call of the Wild, White Fang* and *Burning Daylight,* were cliff-hanging adventure tales that took place in the Klondike. And McIlhenny, one of the few people in the world besides London who had traveled to that alien region, was surely courageous and charismatic. Amid a rescue attempt, London could have conceivably been so overcome with appreciation for McIlhenny's lifesaving gesture that he changed his name in homage.

Indeed, the tale was so believable that no one questioned it. In reality, though, Jack London was born John Griffith Chaney in Oakland, California—the East Bay, not the East End. It's generally agreed that he was the illegitimate son of journalist and astrologer William Chaney, who deserted Jack's mother when she was pregnant with Jack in 1876. Eight months after Jack was born, his mother married John London, a Civil War veteran and spiritualist, a newcomer to San Francisco. Jack was given the surname of his stepfather but didn't learn about any of this until he was in his twenties.

Not only did Jack London already have the name that he became famous for prior to being ostensibly saved by McIlhenny, it's unlikely that he—or any large group of people—was rescued by E.A. at all. According to the Web site of the U.S. Minerals Management Service, which tracks Alaskan boat accidents, there were two shipwrecks in the Sea Horse Islands in 1897 and none in 1898, the years that McIlhenny was there. And in both 1897 incidents, the crews weren't saved; instead, they walked through the tundra many miles to Point Barrow for shelter.

Although some or all of these details—particularly those concerning London's birth, the origin of his name and his nationality (American, not British)—were available in the dozens and dozens of biographies and articles written about the writer over the years, McIlhenny's story somehow stuck; it was never exposed as being false.

Such stories bolstered Edward McIlhenny's celebrity reputation in the food industry. Told over a few beers—and, sometimes, Tabasco-laced Bloody Marys—they could be the lubricant that convinced distributors to draw closer to this larger-than-life figure and take on additional inventory of Tabasco sauce.

If exaggerated tales of his exploits weren't enough, McIlhenny would tell other types of fibs to coax rack jobbers or retailers into promoting his products enthusiastically. For instance, he wasn't above sharing with Distributor A the apocryphal news that Distributor B had made overtures to McIlhenny Co. and was willing to carry much more Tabasco sauce than Distributor A, in exchange for an exclusive arrangement with the McIlhennys. E.A. would even produce trumped-up contracts to support these assertions. Or he might notify a storeowner that its nearest competitor three blocks away was planning to install a display case with Tabasco sauce in the front of his store, when no such possibility existed. Taking a cue from his father, E.A. believed fact and fiction were powerful tools that could be applied interchangeably to achieve his sole aim: sell greater amounts of Tabasco sauce.

Toward the end of his life, Edward's notion that the truth was negotiable without penalty rebounded against him, ultimately to blemish his memory. But much of the time he turned this dubious principle to his advantage.

"Mr. Ned was determined to make sure that nothing got in the way of what he wanted to accomplish," said Joseph Dubois, referring to Edward McIlhenny with the name used by employees living on Avery Island. Dubois began working for McIlhenny Co. in 1939 and eventually rose to head of production. "Everything he did—good or bad—he did to make money for the business. Sometimes that meant, I guess, that he'd have to lie a bit or cut corners. They say he got this from his father, but Mr. Ned was more calculating, and, I suppose you could call it, selfish. Mr. Ned was always the center of his very big world."

Edward McIlhenny's strategy to court middlemen, storeowners and restaurateurs with only a single product and his charm couldn't have been better devised. Almost immediately after E.A. took over the reins of the family business, sales rose—and continued to climb virtually every year that he ran the company. Early in E.A.'s tenure, McIlhenny Co.'s annual output exceeded 1 million bottles, a significant milepost. At Edmund McIlhenny's high-water mark, it would have taken fifty years to produce that much Tabasco sauce.

A welcome bounty, but escalating demand exposed another pressing concern that required immediate attention. Though McIlhenny Co. had many more customers to supply, its production facilities hadn't changed since its founding; the family was still making Tabasco sauce in Edmund's one-room "laboratory" with manual sifting and filtering devices and hand-poured bottles. This system was clearly outmoded, inadequate to keep up with new orders; grudgingly, E.A. conceded that a full-fledged factory would have to replace it. But while making this accommodation with modernity, E.A. was intent on not altering his father's basic business calculus: low overhead and inexpensive, streamlined manufacturing. To wit, automated mass production—an expensive option and the founder's least favorite wrinkle of the Industrial Revolution—was out of the question.

The plan E.A. devised was elegant. It successfully rivaled his father's in its simplicity and thrift, yet it was sufficiently complex that much of it continues to be used by McIlhenny Co. today. However, the system differed greatly from Edmund's in one notable respect: management style. Edmund was remote, diffident; he supervised his relatively small operation at arm's length. E.A. chose the opposite path. He was the visible heart of his company. The business circled around him and he was actively involved, ubiquitous, on the factory floor and in the pepper fields.

The starting point of Edward McIlhenny's manufacturing system was Avery Island's pepper fields, where acres and acres of perfectly formed burgundy red plants bloom in the humid Louisiana hothouse from July through September. During the growing season, E.A. drove to the tracts at approximately three in the afternoon, just as the pickers were wrapping up for the day. He'd playfully tease the workers and check the color of the chilies they had pulled from the vines. At times, he squeezed a few peppers to examine the consistency of the thick juice.

If McIlhenny approved, the chilies were loaded in boxes onto pickup trucks and carted to the factory. This brick, Cajun-design building, built by E.A. in the early 1900s, was distinguished by an unusual series of facades, whose sides rose nondescriptly and then three-quarters to the top unexpectedly tapered into a stepwise pattern to meet at a peak. With their sharply defined shoulders and narrow crest, the facades resembled—purposely, it's safe to assume, but not overtly—the shape of a bottle of Tabasco sauce. The current factory, constructed in 1978 and expanded a decade later, is a virtual replica of E.A.'s plant.

As the crates arrived at the factory, a McIlhenny employee standing on a platform tossed salt over the peppers, about 8 pounds of salt for 100 pounds of chilies. Next, a lift carried the crates toward the ceiling and emptied them into suspended vats that served as crushers, where at once club-like pestles ground the salt and pepper mixture into mash. With that completed, workers used hoses connected to twin spouts at the bottom of the crushers to drain the gummy liquid into fifty-gallon white oak casks on the factory floor.

These casks were another of E.A.'s favorite haunts. Here he could view the blend produced from the day's chili crop and make certain it bore the pungent odor and bloody pigment that would in time produce a flawless bottle of Tabasco sauce, imperceptible characteristics that most of the McIlhennys could seemingly recognize well after their other senses have deserted them. On E.A.'s approval, the workers secured the lids of the barrels with a mallet.

Five tiny holes were drilled into the lids. Filled with salt, these holes permitted the gases produced by fermentation to escape but prevented outside air from entering the casks. Finally closed and sealed, each barrel was lifted by a hoist and carried along a cramped hallway to a vast aging shed, where it remained untouched for three years alongside hundreds of barrels.

To satisfy McIlhenny Co.'s need for a steady supply of casks, E.A. signed a deal with Jack Daniels, the Lynchburg, Tennesseee–based whiskey distiller whose roots date back to 1866, a year before Tabasco sauce debuted. Under the agreement, still in existence today, McIlhenny Co. has bought tens of thousands of Jack Daniels's used barrels, which arrive at Avery Island smelling of hard liquor and charred from years of storing sour mash whiskey. After the casks are scoured and smoothed with wire brushes, they're put into service.

"Some of these barrels are eighty or ninety years old," said Hamilton Polk, McIlhenny Co.'s head cooper who worked for the family for more than three decades. "If you have a break in the barrel, we'll turn it around and wax it. It'll last another ten or fifteen years. The barrels that are bad, we'll cut them up and make wood chips and sell them to a smokehouse in Kentucky."

By the time the pepper mash was fully aged, following three years of fermentation, a labyrinth of spiderwebs had grown on the casks, a phenomenon viewed now as both utilitarian and sentimental. "The spiders and their webs quite effectively control the fly population," Took Osborne said recently. He's E.A.'s great-grandson and McIlhenny Co.'s current vice president of agricultural operations. "Besides, the webs are part of the tradition of the place."

Each morning, E.A. made his way to the aging shed to inspect the mash that had completed its thirty-six-month hibernation, the putative next generation of Tabasco sauce. The lids creaked like rusty hinges as they were pried off. When the fresh pepper mash was exposed to the air, the pungent odor burned the eyes and the throat down to the lungs. McIlhenny examined the liquid carefully, stirring it gingerly with a long wooden spoon. Color again was critical, as was consistency; every batch of Tabasco sauce must look the same and have the same texture. And the taste, of course, had to be equally unvarying. McIlhenny would dip a pinkie into the residue on the spoon and put it to his mouth. Sometimes, uncertain about a blend, E.A. would ask the workers to test it as well.

Some mash was rejected; over 90 percent typically made the grade. Given consent to proceed, the workers emptied some 400 gallons of mash from the casks into a 2,000-gallon wooden vat and added about 1,400 gallons of 100-grain vinegar, twice the strength of normal salad vinegar. This mixture was stirred for twenty-eight days. Historically, women were hired for this job, but recently they've been replaced by automated agitation machines. Each vat contained 1,600 gallons of Tabasco sauce, after seeds and skins were removed.

"The seeds and skins were bagged and sold to locals for crawfish boils," said Shane Bernard, McIlhenny Co. historian. Today, manufacturers use it in cinnamon red-hot candies and Dentyne chewing gum.

The strained mash, now Tabasco sauce, was then pumped the short distance to the bottling plant, where workers drained it into jars, primarily the familiar two-ounce versions, which were subsequently labeled and readied for shipment. Currently, McIlhenny Co.'s century-old, semi-manual manufacturing system, has the capacity to produce approximately 600,000 bottles of Tabasco sauce a day.

Edward McIlhenny undertook one idiosyncratic rite of fall alone. Each day or so in the late harvest season, E.A. would arrive at the pepper fields with swags of Spanish moss in his hands. He walked up and down the long rows of plants, gazing at the chilies without slowing his pace. Every now and again, he insouciantly draped a swag over a bush. These plants so marked were chosen because they were peerless among the crop. The color and size of their peppers, the shape and health of the plant, all played a hand in the split-second decisions that Edward made. The swags warned the pickers not to touch these chilies.

After the selected plants ripened, the seeds would be stripped and placed in a New Iberia bank's safe-deposit box. In the dead of winter, these seeds would be sown in greenhouses before being transplanted to the fields as the subsequent year's crop. If E.A. made the right choices, these Tabasco peppers would be identical to the ones picked the year before and the year before that.

Remarkably, it appears likely that all McIlhenny presidents have chosen unerringly: the Tabasco pepper used in the sauce today is so unaltered by time that it is believed to possibly be a near biological duplicate of the first chili planted by Edmund McIlhenny in the 1860s. This discovery was made recently when company agriculturalists were testing a pepper-picking machine, which they ultimately decided against adopting. As they drove the equipment through rows of plants, some peppers were disturbed by the movement of the machine in their midst and fell off the bushes on to the ground. Other peppers resisted the machine completely and clung to the bush. Neither of these strains was particularly productive. They were short on pepper juice, and the juice they had was inconsistent and of low quality. But the middle strain, the one the mechanized picker easily collected, excelled; it was brimming with dense, burgundy red juice. Moreover, these plants' seeds matched those that the McIlhennys, following Edward's tradition, had selected by eye for the current year's crop and also were a carbon copy of seeds tabbed in prior years, going back to the early days of the company's history.

"Before then, we didn't realize that there were at least three different strains of peppers in the fields," said Gene Jefferies, McIlhenny's agricultural chief from 1976 to 1999. "Over the years, the McIlhennys instinctually bypassed the hard-pick and easy-pick plants and others like them, and chose the best Tabasco peppers, those with the right genotype—without machines or equipment to help them. They have a sixth sense about which Tabasco pepper is the right one, about which one has always produced the best pepper sauce. I've never seen anything like it."

Edward McIlhenny's presence throughout the manufacturing process, his frequent appearances in the pepper fields and in the factory to rub shoulders with employees and inspect the product as it matures from raw material to Tabasco sauce, has become ritualized at McIlhenny Co. Every head of the family business since him has assiduously emulated this approach. Even as the company's output and global reach have multiplied the demands on its top executives, the hands-on, ubiquitous management style E.A. pioneered remains in place. It's the difference, family members say, between bottles indistinguishable from one to the next and a product that varies too widely to command a premium price.

Chapter 7
FIGHTING WORDS

As sales of Tabasco sauce surpassed 1 million bottles a year in the first decades of the twentieth century under E.A.'s leadership, the McIlhenny family's brand rose to the level of a qualified blockbuster, a name synonymous with its product category. To most people (as well as most dictionaries) then and now, Tabasco was simply another, more common term for pepper sauce.

However, a company realizes maximum benefit from such a recognizable brand only when it has the name to itself. And in the early 1900s, while McIlhenny made the best-known Tabasco sauce, the phrase was like ketchup, mustard, horseradish or pickled cucumbers—many companies sold products with the word *Tabasco* on their label, piggybacking on McIlhenny's success. Edward McIlhenny knew well the potential treasure awaiting his company if he could win sole use of the Tabasco name. And as he did most everything, E.A. pursued this aim aggressively. Even so, often he was far from certain that his efforts would prove out; this very same dilemma had bedeviled his brother and father before him without a successful conclusion.

Almost from the moment Tabasco sauce was launched, Edmund McIlhenny was wary of competitors appropriating the name of his product. Indeed, he was one of only a few pioneering American entrepreneurs who intuitively grasped what is now accepted wisdom in marketing circles: a dominant, exclusive brand can greatly influence consumer behavior. Its mere mention can expose positive associations regarding the product's taste, texture, quality, strength, innovation, trendiness and any number of other attributes. Ultimately, consumer loyalty and repeat purchases hinge on how well the brand consistently matches people's expectations for it.

There are a handful of old products—Coke, Pepsi, Jell-O, Band-Aid and Spackle, among them—whose trademarks alone are worth billions of dollars because of the substantial sales and goodwill they generate. Remarkably, these trademarks, long protected, are frequently of greater value than the company's hard assets. But in the chronicles of consumer goods, many more brand names—aspirin, cellophane, yo-yo, dry ice and granola, to name a few—have carelessly been allowed to lapse into generic use.

Edmund McIlhenny's concerns notwithstanding, he was unable to obtain control of the word *Tabasco* in his lifetime. Although McIlhenny hired attorneys to marshal legal strategies for gaining preferential rights to Tabasco, he lived in an era before federal trademark protection existed and, hence, was powerless. At the time, the states enacted their own trademark rules, creating a mishmash of edicts that ended at each state border with few regulators to oversee them.

Nonetheless, Edmund was determined to have his product perceived as one-of-a-kind, peerless—despite others on the market with similar names. McIlhenny's cheeky attempts to thwart rivals from mimicking his efforts—or, if they did, to produce an inferior product—included patenting a fabricated recipe for Tabasco sauce in 1870. And in 1888, McIlhenny quietly paid a Geneva, New York, botanist a tidy sum to declare that the pepper grown in Avery Island fields—and only that pepper—was a new variety of the *Capsicum frutescens* chili called Tabasco. He bragged about this self-bestowed honor in marketing materials.

Such unorthodox actions helped somewhat, but it wasn't until Congress passed the Trademark Act in 1905 that the McIlhennys finally got the chance to claim the word *Tabasco*, though they did so with an apparent bit of chicanery. Under this law, which extended trademark protection to commercial activity throughout the United States, for the first time the logo, name and packaging of a product manufactured in Atlanta could be safeguarded from imitators in Tallahassee, San Francisco or Augusta, Maine. To grandfather these new rules among existing brands, the legislation permitted products to receive national trademarks if no other business had used the same name for the prior ten years. Incomprehensibly, the McIlhennys seized on this part of the law to apply for a trademark on Tabasco.

To do this, of course, John Avery McIlhenny, then president of the family business, had to tell a not inconsequential lie. McIlhenny stipulated to the U.S. Patent and Trademark Office that his was the sole company making a pepper sauce called Tabasco, a fact contradicted by the presence in the marketplace of at least a dozen other Tabasco sauce manufacturers. They included B.F. Trappey and C.P. Moss in New Iberia; Hirsch Brothers in Louisville, Kentucky; Frances H. Leggett in New York; A.E. Mass in Atlanta; H.J. Heinz in Pittsburgh; and Campbell Soup in Philadelphia.

Yet, despite the obvious fabrication, McIlhenny Co. was awarded a trademark in 1906. Competitors were stunned. It was mystifying that McIlhenny would be given exclusive rights to a brand name that had been used by numerous pepper sauce manufacturers in full view for at least a decade. One explanation, although troubling, made the most sense: the McIlhennys had drawn on their political connections. John McIlhenny was a close friend of Theodore Roosevelt and would within months be appointed a Civil Service commissioner by the president. McIlhenny detractors assumed Roosevelt had a hand in the patent office's dubious decision.

Bernard F. Trappey, who was well acquainted with the McIlhennys, led the charge against this questionable trademark. Until the mid–1890s, Trappey had been a blacksmith on Avery Island. While working there, he grew close to both Edmund and Mary McIlhenny, but was envious of their business success. Trappey and McIlhenny routinely had conversations about Tabasco sauce, during which they discussed how it was made and the operational aspects of distribution networks. Trappey was confident that with little difficulty he could re-create Edmund's recipe, manufacturing process and regional sales channels.

One night in 1895, Trappey skulked out to the pepper fields on Avery Island and pocketed some Tabasco chilies to use for seed; he then abruptly quit his job. He planted the peppers in his backyard in nearby Jeanerette and set up a small factory in a shed on the property. A year later, Trappey introduced his own pepper sauce, called Tabasco Pepper Sauce Made by B.F. Trappey & Sons. Priced below McIlhenny's product, Trappey's sauce gained enough of a local following to dent McIlhenny's Louisiana sales. To the McIlhenny family, Trappey was a niggling but persistent irritant.

A decade later, when McIlhenny Co. obtained the federal trademark on Tabasco, the family joyfully believed they were rid of Trappey, as well as all of its other competitors, forever. Indeed, to be certain that the ruling was obeyed, newly named president Edward McIlhenny ventured into the trademark effort by sending an advisory notice to retailers and wholesalers, sternly warning them not to sell any other hot sauce but McIlhenny's with the word *Tabasco* on the label.

Larger companies, such as Heinz and Campbell's, generally decided that the cost of contesting the agency's decision was too high and not worth the effort. They stopped producing Tabasco sauce, turning their attention instead to their growing number of other products. E.A. presumed that smaller competitors would follow suit and that Trappey and its ilk might even fold up shop, unable to afford the exorbitant expense of altering their production, marketing and distribution arrangements and launching a new brand.

Trappey, though, and a scattering of other regional pepper sauce companies refused to cave in. They knew John McIlhenny had falsified the application to get the trademark and felt that this bit of impudence was worth questioning. As they saw it, it would be less expensive to challenge the patent office's ruling than to create a new brand of hot sauce, particularly because any pepper sauce not called Tabasco was unlikely to be well received. Hence, Trappey defied federal authorities by continuing to distribute his version of Tabasco sauce. Simultaneously, Trappey spent tens of thousands of dollars in lawyer's fees to petition the agency and the courts to overturn McIlhenny's Tabasco trademark.

"My grandfather was stubborn and he was fit to be tied at the McIlhennys; he took it very personally," said W.J. Trappey, who was president of B.F. Trappey & Sons from 1948 to 1980. "Maybe that's not a very smart way to run a company but I think it was him against the McIlhennys. My grandfather was at times it seems more interested in their business than he was in ours. He should have known he couldn't win."

Trappey's sales eroded, primarily because some distributors and retailers, mindful of the patent office's ruling, declined to carry the product anymore. Still, B.F. Trappey persevered and won—once— an enormous victory. In 1909, patent regulators rescinded the Tabasco trademark, three years after it was awarded. Responding to Trappey's unrelenting complaints, the federal agency finally recognized that John McIlhenny had, indeed, stated incorrectly on the trademark application that no rivals were using the name *Tabasco*.

With that basis for a trademark assertion eliminated, the agency also decided that the McIlhennys had no other right to claim the name *Tabasco*. Patent examiners noted correctly that New Orleans plantation owner Maunsel White had been growing chilies from the Mexican state of Tabasco on his property as early as the 1840s, and he sold a hot sauce called Maunsel White's Concentrated Essence of Tabasco Peppers locally. Consequently, they said, Tabasco is clearly both the name of a place and a generic pepper and thus couldn't be awarded to a company as an exclusive brand. It is perhaps coincidental, but worth mentioning, that when the patent office voided McIlhenny's copyright, Theodore Roosevelt had just departed the presidency.

When word surfaced that John McIlhenny had lied on the patent application, Democrats called for him to step down from the Civil Service Commission. To quell the furor and retain his job, McIlhenny grudgingly apologized—almost. He said he had committed a "grave error," but he signed the application "upon the advice of counsel and against my own convictions."

Edward McIlhenny was flabbergasted by the patent office's change of heart. The Tabasco trademark was a crucial component of the family's business strategy, and simply accepting the decision would have been suicidal for the company, he believed. So E.A. opted for an odd, even supercilious response: he refused to publicly acknowledge the agency's new stance. While quietly lobbying political leaders and judges in Louisiana, hoping to convince them to help overturn the agency's reversal of its earlier decision, E.A. publicly acted as if the ruling never occurred—curiously similar to the defiant posture taken by Trappey when McIlhenny first received the trademark.

E.A. sent "reminder" letters to retailers and distributors, which never mentioned the patent decision but pointedly noted that it was still illegal for them to sell any Tabasco pepper sauce other than McIlhenny's. Tabasco sauce competitors learned of this intimidation tactic when they began to receive nervous telegrams from their customers, such as the one sent by an East Coast distributor to a McIlhenny rival in 1915 that said, "Do not ship us any more Tabasco sauce. See letter." Attached was McIlhenny's unnerving correspondence.

McIlhenny also threatened restaurateurs with litigation if they carried any Tabasco sauce besides his, although the patent agency had stripped him of the legal right to do so. A typical incident occurred during a visit to New York City when E.A. stopped for lunch at Whyte's, a high-class businessman's eatery on Fulton Street. He asked for Tabasco with his meal; the waiter brought out a Tabasco pepper sauce made by another Louisiana manufacturer, Lowell Gaidry. Within days, Whyte's owner received a terse note from McIlhenny's lawyers. Whyte's would be sued for stocking an illegal product if all bottles of Gaidry's Tabasco sauce were not discarded immediately, the attorneys wrote.

Unwilling to engage in an expensive legal battle with McIlhenny—and not particularly interested in whether McIlhenny's or Gaidry's hot sauce was on the restaurant's tables—Whyte's owner signed an order promising to solely carry McIlhenny's products. This case, initially seen in New York as an amusing curiosity—a battle between a sophisticated New York restaurant and a southern bumpkin defending his family's pepper sauce—ultimately proved to be a valuable tactic. Upon learning the outcome, other restaurateurs in New York and other big cities in the United States followed Whyte's lead, fearful of a nuisance lawsuit.

Notwithstanding these victories, McIlhenny Co.'s hold on the hot sauce market was in doubt. Competitors gradually persuaded distributors that the McIlhennys had lost their claim to the phrase *Tabasco sauce*. That accomplished, rivals attempted to gain market share by undercutting McIlhenny's Tabasco sauce in price and in barbed ads attacking McIlhenny Co. for making inflated claims about the distinction of its brand.

These were relative boom times for B.F. Trappey. His Tabasco sauce continued to sell reasonably well in McIlhenny's home turf, and he could take great pleasure from imagining the discomfort felt by E.A. and his kin when they saw Trappey Tabasco sauce next to McIlhenny's on store shelves. For a time, Trappey naively believed that his Tabasco sauce would overtake his former employer's brand.

That possibility ended in 1918 with a stunning decision in southern Louisiana, when the U.S. Court of Appeals for the Fifth Circuit in New Orleans reversed the patent office's decision to remove McIlhenny's trademark on Tabasco sauce. In a ruling that took hot sauce makers completely by surprise, the court said McIlhenny's assertion of "a common-law trademark" for the word *Tabasco* "was in good faith."

To reach this conclusion, the court chose to ignore the evidence provided by Trappey and others to the patent office, which chronicled the growing of Tabasco peppers in the United States in the early part of the nineteenth century and Maunsel White's introduction of Tabasco sauce in the late 1840s, well before McIlhenny's product debuted. The court also overlooked John McIlhenny's lie in 1905, which stipulated falsely that his family was the sole company to use the term *Tabasco sauce* during the preceding ten years. Dismissing these facts without commenting on them, the court inexplicably awarded the Tabasco trademark to McIlhenny on the basis of the founder's original fairy tale depiction of how his company started—the Friend Gleason story.

The Fifth Circuit judges described the origins of Tabasco in this way:

"Several years prior to 1868 a man who at the time had recently come from Mexico gave to Edmund McIlhenny some peppers having a peculiar and agreeable flavor and aroma, all or a part of which were planted by Mr. McIlhenny on his place on Avery Island, near New Iberia, La., and thereafter he continued to grow them there; he being the first person to grow those peppers in the United States. In 1868 he began the manufacture and sale of a table sauce made from that pepper. . . . There was no name by which [this] pepper . . . was known when Mr. McIlhenny began to grow it, or when he started the manufacture and sale of the sauce made from it."

From this the court decided that "the word 'Tabasco,' as applied to pepper sauce, indicates origin of manufacture; that is to say, that the sauce to which the term is applied is the sauce made by E. McIlhenny of New Iberia, La., and his successors in title."

Had the McIlhennys written this ruling themselves, it would not have offered a better rendition of the family's less-than-honest portrayal of the development of Tabasco sauce. Indeed, it's commonly surmised in southern Louisiana, even among McIlhenny relatives, that E.A. probably did dictate the New Orleans court's findings.

"I have to admit it was favoritism," said a McIlhenny Co. heir who has meticulously maintained a record of the family's history. "E.A. was at the height of his power, John Avery was running the Civil Service Commission in Washington, the McIlhennys were a politically astute group with a lot of money to donate to politicians and a reputation for post–Civil War commercial success that no one could match in their part of Louisiana. The appeals court was hamstrung on this one. How could the judges rule against the McIlhennys and potentially destroy the family's national franchise and its substantial economic value to Iberia Parish? It would be similar to a Michigan court deciding that any carmaker that manufactured a car that looked like a Model-T could use the Ford nameplate."

With the appellate court ruling, McIlhenny's rivals ceased to call their products Tabasco sauce—all, that is, except Trappey. Though outmanned, financially depleted and with few options, Trappey did not capitulate. In contempt of court, he continued to peddle his version of Tabasco sauce while lodging complaints about McIlhenny's trademark claims to judges in Washington, Philadelphia, New York, Galveston and New Orleans and suffering tremendous losses in sales. An exorbitant obsession, this quixotic pursuit would occupy the attention of Trappey's company for three decades following the New Orleans decision in favor of McIlhenny.

In 1948, Trappey & Sons' legal options ran out. After the U.S. Supreme Court refused to hear the trademark case, a Louisiana judge ruled definitively that the McIlhennys owned the word *Tabasco*. In a ceremony that for the two families felt like the surrender at Appomattox, the Trappeys conceded defeat by signing an agreement to remove the name *Tabasco* from their product forever—and at once.

"The McIlhennys took no pity," W.J. Trappey recalled. "Every label we had, they forced us to destroy immediately. We tried to get their permission to let us use up the labels we had. We didn't have a whole lot of money. And, we didn't want to just throw away perfectly good labels. But they wouldn't let us. The whole affair, from start to finish, was a big loss, big loss."

And one that intellectual property experts are still dumbfounded by. Generally, geographical destinations like Tabasco are not given trademark protection; for instance, a company could not expect to own the exclusive right to name a product Idaho potatoes or Wisconsin cheese. Also, it's highly unusual for a business to receive a trademark on a generic ingredient that conceivably anyone can use in a product; all companies, not just one, can make soy sauce. McIlhenny Co. is arguably the only American business to successfully overcome both extremely high barriers to a trademark.

"Owning the name Tabasco is like owning the name jalapeno or chili; it's quite an accomplishment for the McIlhennys," said Jason Bernstein, an attorney at Powell Goldstein, who at one time worked for the white-shoe Atlanta law firm that handled McIlhenny's trademark cases. "But when they got the Tabasco trademark things were a bit different—the rules and the courts were not as strict as they are now. And the McIlhennys, from what I understand, were unrelenting."

Since obtaining its first trademark on Tabasco, McIlhenny Co. has been single-minded about challenging every individual or company—and there have been hundreds—that dared to adopt the name for any type of product. For years, the company retained Julius Lunsford, the high-powered Atlanta attorney credited with protecting Coca-Cola's trademarks, to handle Tabasco cases. Merciless in his approach, Lunsford relied on McIlhenny family members, who were on notice to be vigilant for trademark breaches as they traveled, and a team of researchers to uncover trespassers, each of whom received the same cold message: either discontinue using the name *Tabasco* and any of the other trademarks owned by McIlhenny—including one for the shape of the pepper sauce bottle and another for the look and feel of its distinctive diamond-shaped label—or face litigation. In Lunsford's approach, no room for negotiation existed no matter what the circumstances. Following Lunsford's death in 1999, his equally unforgiving son, J. Rodgers, took over principal trademark duties for the McIlhennys.

In the years following McIlhenny's decision in the early twentieth century to obtain and then enforce the Tabasco trademark at all costs, dozens of companies chose an entirely different route, relinquishing control of some of the most valuable brand names ever. They did this in part because they were unable to envision the long-term legal implications under trademark rules of their initial marketing strategies. A classic example is aspirin. Developed by Bayer Co., aspirin was originally sold to the public through pharmacies, which would package the pills and often market it to consumers as simply Aspirin or sometimes add the name of the drugstore on the label as well. The word *Bayer* never appeared. Accordingly, around 1915, when Bayer opted to sell its own version of aspirin and demanded that pharmacies and other drug companies stop using the term, the courts ruled against Bayer. By permitting drugstores to freely market their own aspirin products for so long, Bayer had conspired in making the name generic, the court said.

In a large number of cases, companies forfeited prized trademarks because they failed to anticipate the monopolistic effect their successful products would have on the free market. For instance, Otis lost the trademark for the term *escalator* because in the four decades or so that it took for the company's various patents on moving stairs to expire, *escalator* was the only term used for such equipment. As a result, the patent office ruled in the 1950s that it would be impossible for a new moving stairs manufacturer to compete with Otis if its product was called anything but escalator.

DuPont faced a similar issue with nylon, which rapidly became so synonymous with women's stockings that the chemical giant could not retain exclusive rights to the name when other companies sued to enter the market. Mindful of this outcome, some years later, when DuPont introduced Dacron, the chemical company took pains to call it a polyester fiber. This gave competitors the opportunity to sell their own brands of polyester to clothing manufacturers, while DuPont held the sole claim to Dacron.

By some estimates, McIlhenny Co. has initiated, either through attorney's letters or actual lawsuits, thousands of separate legal actions in the past century addressing possible trademark violations. The extent of McIlhenny's legal activities was evident in the in-house attorney's office at the company's headquarters on Avery Island. In the corner of the room there was an ample cabinet with shelf upon shelf of bottles that one way or another had reminded McIlhenny too much of its own brand, and thus were recipients of McIlhenny litigation threats. One was from Honduras. It was a hot sauce that looked exactly like Tabasco, except the name on the label was A–1. "They managed to infringe two trademarks with one product," said Edmund McIlhenny, the founder's great-great-grandson and a former lawyer at the company. Many of the cases have been small, even comical. Among the targets was Cajun Tan Systems in Baton Rouge, which hastily agreed to redesign its suntan lotion bottles after McIlhenny filed court papers claiming they resembled bottles of Tabasco. Another case involved four Mexican immigrants from Tabasco state who were intimidated by McIlhennys' legal tactics into changing the name of their Marion, Iowa, eatery, Tabasco's Mexican Restaurant and Patio, to Villa's Patio, at a cost of over $100,000 for new signs and materials.

But by far the most bizarre trademark infringement brouhaha stirred up by the McIlhennys involved Evangeline Tabasco, the pseudonym for a New York City artist, in 1979. Evangeline, whose real name was Sam Wiener, thought Tabasco would be a campy moniker for a satirical set of works he was planning, never once considering that the McIlhennys would be offended or even find out about it. Wiener wasn't especially well known; he didn't imagine his new name would attract much attention outside of experimental art circles.

However, the McIlhennys pay their legal team well to unearth any mention of their brand, no matter how obscure. And when they discovered Evangeline, they rapidly showered him with letters demanding he change his surname, unless he could prove it came from his family and not from the pepper sauce. One of the pieces of correspondence, written by current CEO Paul McIlhenny, said: "Can you shed some light on the origin and background of your name?

We do know that a state, a river and several towns go by the name Tabasco in Mexico, but we've never seen it used as a person's name."

Wiener playfully retorted: "If you only saw my art work, rather than focusing solely upon my name, I feel certain you would understand that it is the work that's important. For as Will Shakespeare put it: What's in a name? That which we call a rose by another name would smell as sweet."

But the McIlhennys could see no humor in the situation and responded with a final letter from their attorneys, threatening legal action if Wiener persisted in using the name. To no one's amazement, Evangeline Tabasco soon disappeared from the scene—although, perhaps to pique the McIlhennys, as late as the mid-1990s, Wiener would on rare occasions resurrect his Evangeline Tabasco works for a retrospective art exhibit.

When Edward McIlhenny was wrestling for exclusive rights to Tabasco, he could not have foreseen that hard-earned pepper sauce revenue would be spent on attorney fees to stop performance artists from using the name for their own impish purposes. But E.A. certainly wouldn't have been opposed to the idea. Little was of greater importance in the early twentieth century than consolidating the family business's image, particularly by transforming its product into a household name the McIlhennys alone controlled.

Indeed, handling the somewhat sordid details surrounding the Tabasco trademark—preparing legal arguments as well as pressuring judges, politicians and restaurateurs to see it his way—monopolized much of McIlhenny's efforts away from Avery Island during the first decade or so that he ran the family business. But on the island, where he much preferred to spend his time, E.A. was involved in a more pastoral and pleasing pursuit: designing the village of workers and managers that would be the true fulcrum of the company's growth throughout the twentieth century.

Chapter 8
TANGO

By any important measure, Edward McIlhenny's tenure as head of the family business was an instant success. From his first year on the job in 1906, sales consistently rose, Tabasco sauce's reputation grew and the distribution channel for the product widened significantly. But almost immediately an old dilemma surfaced: how to satisfy rising demand for Tabasco while minimizing costs sufficiently to maintain high profit margins.

Decades earlier, when the family business was relatively small, Edmund McIlhenny had relied on inexpensive transient labor; a relatively limited manufacturing schedule in a streamlined factory setting: and a few, fairly straightforward distributor relationships to produce an uninterrupted stream of profits. E.A. didn't have it so easy. To build a substantial inventory of Tabasco sauce and fill the rising tide of orders generated by his assertive sales tactics, McIlhenny would need more workers to perform at much higher levels in a roomier plant that, while still not overly automated, had to meet strict distribution deadlines. Moreover, these new employees would have to be full-time, permanent, more skilled and responsible; McIlhenny couldn't afford any glitches in output. This meant that their wages would escalate along with their productivity.

For a medium-sized family business like McIlhenny Co., increasing salaries was not an acceptable option, as it was for bigger manufacturers, which could grow faster than their expenses by, for instance, revitalizing old products, introducing new brands or acquiring other business lines. Mostly by design, McIlhenny Co. had a far different personality. It was a one-product company with its manufacturing operations confined to a tiny island. The McIlhennys viewed anything more complicated than that as anathema to the prosperity of their family business. If McIlhenny Co. were a wide-ranging operation with dozens of products and factories around the world, the need for additional capital and greater international presence would almost certainly result in the family losing control of the company through public stock sales, joint ventures, armies of creditors or even a hostile acquisition by another consumer goods outfit, the McIlhennys believed. So without the benefit of a large organization that could potentially dilute the impact of expenses on the bottom line, E.A. was left with no other choice but to limit labor costs, just as they were about to skyrocket.

To solve this problem, E.A. returned to his father's design. By mirroring on a much grander scale Edmund's modest Salt Village community, E.A. could offer hundreds of Tabasco workers lower salaries in exchange for virtually free housing. Once the homes were constructed, McIlhenny Co.'s costs to maintain the village would be minimal. After all, the McIlhenny family lived and ran its business on Avery Island, so the roads, utilities and other infrastructure had to be kept up anyway. As they settled in and raised families on the island, the workers would be increasingly bound to the business.

But beyond its size, E.A. had a more aggressive goal for the Tabasco company town than his father. He perceived it as less a basic worker village—in which employees and management lived as neighbors, socialized at times and crossed paths, but otherwise remained relatively independent of each other—and more a feudal settlement. The McIlhennys—or simply, E.A. himself—would be the spiritual masters, the true landlords, of the community, to whom workers could come for advice, shelter, money, protection, quality of life, medical care and, of course, jobs.

By any measure, it was an audacious plan, one that in its strange, antiquated social arrangement—it dated back to centuries before American plantations—outdid the craziest egotistical antics of any company leader in memory. But it also had a practicable symmetry. It deftly fit E.A.'s magnified image of himself—the global adventurer cum raconteur cum intrepid naturalist—while providing the permanent brake on labor costs McIlhenny Co. required to thrive. And it offered workers no-cost housing on a piece of land as valuable as it was idyllic, an island well beyond the budget of nearly everyone living in Iberia Parish, rich or poor.

Some say the idea for this grandiose experiment came in 1900 (six years before E.A. was named company president) at a party on Avery Island celebrating Edward's marriage to Mary Matthews. Surprising everyone, the company's employees put on a moving but oddly provincial display of affection for the couple.

St. Louis socialite Lucy Matthews Chambers described the event in her unpublished autobiography: "After we had eaten heartily the whole house party gathered around the bride and groom who were seated in the middle of the front porch near a large table on which was a handsome bowl filled with claret punch, a silver ladle, and glasses. A few minutes after we sat down we heard music out on the lawn and along the drives and walks approaching the house. There were violins, harmonicas, banjos, and combs covered with paper for the children. We heard the deep plaintive voices of Negroes singing spirituals. This large crowd of whites and Negroes consisted of those employed in the salt mine, Tabasco sauce factory, gardens, and offices on the island. People of all ages from little children to grisly-haired old retainers came up the West steps to the front gallery and bowed to the bride and her radiant husband who stood up to shake hands with them. Children placed on the table a flower or some small gift they had made for the bride. All then walked to the other steps and left."

McIlhenny's colleagues and relatives recalled that E.A. spoke about this incident often. This was evidence, he said, that the family had taken on an iconic status in Iberia Parish, a plateau achieved because the McIlhennys were a rarity in the region—a success in a place that success hardly ever visited anymore.

"It was an astounding outpouring; it was then I knew that our standing in the Parish had produced a unique relationship with the workers that no other company I had seen could claim," McIlhenny told people close to him. "It was clear that we had the chance to create on the island a very different type of community that didn't exist anyplace else."

E.A. McIlhenny broke ground for the new Tabasco company village soon after being named head of the company in 1906, and construction continued for a decade or more. By some accounts, it is to this day one of the most ambitious housing developments ever undertaken in south-central Louisiana.

Upon clearing the centuries-old underbrush and expanses of ancient trees on the north side of the island near the Tabasco factory, McIlhenny built as many as seven rows of homes, six to a row, on this relatively diminutive parcel. With houses shoehorned into a cramped area, the new community instantly assumed the unfortunate look of a shantytown. E.A. also sprinkled additional housing on the far eastern side of the island near the pepper fields and in Salt Village. (By this time, the McIlhennys had seized full control of the island's salt mine and expanded its output, greatly increasing the family's potential revenue stream from it, under a new McIlhenny entity called Avery Rock Salt Mining Company.)

In general, the newly built homes were similar to the one- to three-bedroom bungalows Edmund McIlhenny had initially constructed near the salt mine, but there was also a handful of more commodious five-bedroom dormitory-style dwellings. Architecturally, these homes followed the same blueprint as the smaller ones, except two of the bedrooms hung awkwardly off of the sides of the houses like misplaced pieces of a cube, and they were topped with a distinctively irregular, oddly space-age, pyramid-shaped roof. As many as a dozen unmarried workers could be wedged into these dorms.

By the time the building spree was completed, E.A. had constructed well over sixty houses. Including those who resided in the homes built earlier by his father, more than 500 people would eventually live in Avery Island's worker villages.

To support the commercial needs of the population, E.A. erected two company stores. The one in Salt Village was a two-story, 5,000-square-feet, barnlike structure with a steep-sloped Cajun roof, a predominant design feature on almost all Avery Island buildings. Its U-shaped sales counter in the center of the ground floor gave it the contours of a vast convenience store. The store on the Tabasco side of the island was a more squat, 1,400-square-foot building that resembled a rural grocery with a narrow sales counter off to one corner and a separate delicatessen section. In both stores, scrip given to many of the factory, salt mine and pepper field workers in lieu of salary was the preferred form of currency.

Another new building, the Bradford Club—named after Sidney Bradford, an engineer and McIlhenny in-law who ran the salt mine for the family from 1902 through 1931—served as a worker's gathering area. Located in Salt Village, it was an open twenty-six-foot-by-forty-foot room, primarily used for McIlhenny company functions, weekly medical and dental clinics, dances, beer parties, worker safety discussions and Boy Scout meetings.

As the number of people on Avery Island swelled, McIlhenny used his clout as one of the largest private commercial taxpayers in Iberia Parish to convince local politicians to invest in the island and, in so doing, confer legitimacy on it as a community. Bowing to McIlhenny's persistent requests, parish officials agreed to build a tiny post office in the middle of the island; more suburban-style than classical, it is now unattractively covered with overgrown crawling ivy. And just yards down the road from the post office, the education board constructed two public elementary schools—one for white and the other for black children.

The company town was called Tango Village, though no one is quite sure why anymore. Some people who worked with the McIlhennys believe the name originated from the tango parties that Avery Island black residents held on Saturday nights in a makeshift nightclub set up near the Tabasco carpenter's shop. But there's an additional, more provocative possibility. It could be a wry, nearly cruel antebellum reference to the constrained living conditions of the workers in Tango Village. In various dialects of the Congo, the ancestral home of many Louisiana slaves, tango meant closed or shut off. Consequently, slave traders often used the word *tango* to describe the gathering places of slaves. It's entirely conceivable that either the McIlhennys or the workers themselves lifted the name *Tango* from their plantation-era memories, perhaps as an edgy joke or an arch commentary on the dark side of the congested and captive company town on Avery Island.

It would indeed be ironic if the name *Tango Village* originated from either a black practice or an African tongue, because virtually no black people ever lived there. By designing Tango Village in the style of a feudal duchy, McIlhenny fashioned a distinct caste system on Avery Island based primarily on ethnic background and color. The Anglo-Saxon McIlhennys were, of course, the bosses. The few non-McIlhenny supervisors, such as longtime plant manager Joseph Dubois, were generally of mixed origin, part Cajun and part French, Spanish or Anglo. Most of these trusted employees were given homes on the island a little roomier than those of the common worker and ordinarily set apart from Tango Village. A family of four might have a three-bedroom house. One step below the non-McIlhenny managers were the factory hands, who were nearly all Cajun and consigned to the less luxurious quarters of Tango Village. The pepper pickers, who were black, belonged to the bottom caste. None of them was allowed to reside on Avery Island. In fact, the only people of African or Caribbean descent with homes on the island were McIlhenny servants. They lived in dwellings built near the family's mansion.

This caste system and the lowly place reserved for black people in it tell only part of the complex racial story played out on Avery Island, as in the rest of the South; in truth, Edward McIlhenny had an ambivalent relationship with black people, somewhat unusual for its time and place in either of its extremes.

On the one hand, E.A. was known to use primitive and denigrating language when speaking of black people. For example, in 1933, E.A. published a book of African slave songs called *Befo' De' War Spirituals*. In it, he described with some tenderness the music of the antebellum period. "Negro spirituals sung by uneducated Negroes in the South can never be adequately written down because it would require unconventional notation," E.A. wrote. "They should be recorded in their environment in some way so that the beauty and the manner of their singing would not be left out." But in 1934, after folklorist Alan Lomax sent a letter to McIlhenny asking if he could tape the pair of Avery Island black women mentioned in the book, E.A. responded with a curt note spiced with a derogatory term for blacks that had fallen into disfavor decades earlier even in the deepest South and was only heard anymore at meetings of racist organizations. E.A. wrote to Lomax that one woman had moved away and the other was sick and couldn't sing, before adding, "I sincerely regret that at this time it is impossible to record the spirituals as sung by these two old darkies."

A more public expression of McIlhenny's disregard for blacks in the community was his involvement in a conspiracy of silence surrounding the worst racial episode in New Iberia's history.

What's now known as the New Iberia incident occurred during the week of May 15, 1944. A year earlier, local black residents had formed a chapter of the NAACP, then considered a radical group in the South. The New Iberia branch was especially active, with well over 100 members, many of them respected professionals—physicians, pharmacists and hospital administrators. Headed by J. Leo Hardy, a former insurance salesman and a Louisiana NAACP member since 1927, the group's focus was on voting rights.

World War II had brought a surfeit of industrial jobs to Iberia Parish. But black people were considered unskilled for these positions. To overcome this bias, in 1944 the NAACP convinced the federal government to mandate that local authorities establish a welding school for them in New Iberia. Even prior to the opening of the school on May 7, the white leadership of the parish, led by education superintendent Lloyd Porter, conspired to derail it. The school was placed next to a white neighborhood, where black residents were intimidated and afraid to walk, and its hours were limited, ensuring that they could not receive sufficient training to convince employers they were qualified for skilled positions.

Hardy protested these conditions in letters to Porter and the federal government. That infuriated Porter, who was particularly incensed at Hardy's temerity in bringing the federal government into Iberia Parish racial affairs again. On May 15, Hardy was picked up by deputies at the welding school and taken to Sheriff Gilbert Ozenne's office, where Porter was waiting. According to Hardy's account, the sheriff bullied him with questions asked in a harassing tone: Did he realize his letters to Porter were insulting? Did he know his place in the community?

Afraid of being beaten, Hardy turned timid; he apologized and repeatedly uttered the word "Yassuh" in response to every question. Porter screamed: "You yellow son of a bitch. You are saying 'yes, sir,' but deep down in your heart you would cut my throat."

Told to leave Iberia Parish by ten o'clock the following morning, Hardy didn't obey. At eight in the evening, sheriff's deputies apprehended him outside of a bar and drove him to Ozenne's office again. There, Ozenne kicked and beat him while his arms were held by the deputies. Bloody and barely able to move, Hardy was dragged to the sheriff's car, taken to the parish limits and dumped on the side of the road with the warning not to return.

The following night, other NAACP members met the same fate. Two black doctors, Ima Pierson and Luins Williams, and a teacher, Herman Faulk, were pistol-whipped, lashed and thrown out of police vehicles on the outskirts of town. According to Faulk, his assailant spat at him and said: "You are one of those niggers going around telling other niggers they will be voting soon. We are going to beat the hell out of you for the first ballot you cast."

In subsequent days, other black people left the parish on their own, including the welding instructor and Dr. E.L. Dorsey, who ran a sizeable clinic and a funeral parlor. Dorsey was smuggled out of Iberia Parish in his hearse. Most of the people who fled or were cast out never came back to New Iberia.

Although shocking, the expulsions were generally met with silence from white residents. Local newspapers played it down or ignored it completely; church leaders refused to discuss what they knew; and the business establishment never questioned or condemned it. Meanwhile, Ozenne and Porter incomprehensibly claimed no expulsions had occurred.

Even now, books about the region fail to mention the New Iberia incident, a name apparently given to it by the NAACP. Indeed, the book *New Iberia,* a complete account of the city's past, written by the highly respected Southern Louisiana University professor Glenn Conrad, lists some of the black community's most prominent citizens, such as Pierson, Williams and Dorsey, but neglects to say that these men—all of them physicians—were forcibly expelled.

The McIlhennys chose to publicly keep mum regarding this assault on black neighborhoods in New Iberia, where many of their workers lived. E.A. McIlhenny bemoaned the incident in private, but he usually begged off any discussion of taking a stand against it by telling relatives his hands were tied. "I hate what happened," McIlhenny said. "But what I can do I try to do on the island; they don't listen to me in the Parish."

An untruth, obviously, considering his elevated political sway in the community. But E.A. was correct in implying that on Avery Island, where he was the final arbiter, the McIlhennys promoted black rights in a manner greatly exceeding what could be typically expected from southern white males—and certainly southern white bosses. That, in fact, was the other, more endearing extreme of E.A.'s equivocal relationship with black people.

E.A., more often than not, displayed a great deal of natural affection and genuine affinity for the black workers in his midst. He and the many black employees E.A. hired not only for what they could do around his house but for their skills in the woods would regularly spend full days together on boats in the bayou watching alligators, banding birds or hunting in the Avery Island underbrush. During these expeditions, E.A. treated his help like companions—freely sharing food, drink, stories and songs with them. Impressed by their seemingly effortless instincts in nature, McIlhenny frequently deferred to their judgment when they came upon dangerous or unexpected situations.

Little is preserved of these unusual friendships, except in the sketchy recollections of McIlhenny family members and, at least until recently, in a curious vestige at the McIlhenny cemetery on Avery Island. Amid the magnolia-scented grassy circle that serves as the family's burial ground, there was an opening in a hedge, which separated McIlhenny graves from those of the black workers dating back to plantation days. Peering at Edward McIlhenny's tombstone through this fissure was a granite slab over a small, barely discernible mound. It stood out for two reasons: it was the only marked grave in the "colored" section of the cemetery; and its less than generous tombstone was blank, uninscribed. Doc Russell, E.A.'s black childhood playmate, was buried there.

Although they met as youths, Russell and E.A. were lifelong friends. The pair spent countless hours together on the back porch of McIlhenny's mansion, sometimes in serious political discussion but also sharing, perhaps for the hundredth time, their favorite slice of ribald humor. E.A. so enjoyed Russell's company that he gave him lifetime employment to do odd jobs at the house or in the Tabasco factory. After his death in 1949, E.A. stipulated that Doc Russell must have a gravestone and not suffer the anonymity of the other black people buried on the island, or so the legend goes. Though the McIlhennys followed E.A.'s wishes, they apparently couldn't bring themselves to put Doc's name on his tomb.

"It's strange when you think of it, but in those days if you were white you had to pay blacks to be your friend," said Michael Bell, an organizer in New Iberia's black community, "because you certainly would never reveal publicly in Louisiana that we were around because you liked us."

Bell and other black residents of New Iberia point to a much more concrete symbol of McIlhenny's desire to have black workers participate in community activities on Avery Island, even if he wouldn't let most of them live there. In the height of his construction efforts, McIlhenny turned his attention to building a Baptist church on a patch of land near Salt Village. A rustic, sturdy rectangular building, seventy feet by sixteen feet, it sat on concrete joists, with an unassuming ten-foot cupola on the roof near the entrance. Inside, the building felt cavernous. It had a fifteen-foot wooden ceiling that echoed and filled the room with the deep humming vibrato of gospel prayer, sounding like the susurrus of thousands of leafy branches, as the voices coming from the eleven rows of pews rose skyward. At the front was an unadorned pulpit; behind it, a baptismal pool.

The church was E.A.'s gift to the black workers on Avery Island, many of whom were Baptists. The McIlhennys were Episcopalians and the Cajun Tabasco and salt mine workers were generally Catholic. They all had to leave the island to pray. Only the black employees had a sanctuary on Avery Island, a building so popular that New Iberia residents journeyed to the island en masse every Sunday, often staying to have picnics on the property afterward. They celebrated weddings, funerals and baptisms there. Because of the church, to the religious among the black workers—which meant most of them—the island became home as much as their own dwellings in New Iberia.

McIlhenny was guided more by practical impulses than altruism when he decided to construct the Baptist church. E.A.'s vision of the company town was shaped by one overriding goal: procuring cheap, disciplined and loyal labor for the family business. By tying workers to the land and, thus, making it socially and economically unfeasible for them to either perform poorly at their jobs or move away, the McIlhennys could secure their services for generations. But the black employees, living off island, had no reason to be loyal; they could come and go as they pleased, be as irresponsible as they chose and take a new job someplace else without any notice. And this raised the threat that at a critical point in McIlhenny Co.'s agricultural cycle—for instance, in the peak of pepper season, toward the end of the summer or early fall—the crop would go unpicked.

So if racism prevented McIlhenny from integrating Avery Island and offering homes to the black workers, he could alternately attempt to win their commitment to the family and its business with a house of worship. As it turned out, for most in the black community, the Baptist church throughout the South was such a palpable spiritual symbol and the communal locus of their struggle for freedom both prior to and after the Civil War that McIlhenny's instincts were unerring. Today still, black Tabasco workers' memories are sweetened by the presence of the simple barnlike church, which overshadows their position at the bottom of the caste on Avery Island.

Dorothy Spencer, a seventy-year-old New Iberia resident who picked peppers on Avery Island as her mother and father had before her, expressed this best when she said, "My parents would say that their God lived on Avery Island, even if Mr. Ned didn't let them live there. And to them that was more than good enough."

But sentiments like these raise a puzzling discrepancy. While the presence of the Baptist church on Avery Island clearly loomed large in the recollections of black people in New Iberia, they seem to have utterly forgotten another, historically more momentous step concerning race relations taken by Edward McIlhenny. White residents of the region spoke of it routinely, however: Although Avery Island was segregated in the literal sense, the most prevalent aspects of racial segregation—that is, exclusive facilities for blacks and whites—were banned there. In a remarkable gesture repeated in virtually no other southern workplace, E.A. outlawed separate bathrooms, water fountains, shelters, dining areas, stores, commissaries and common rooms. There was no back and front of the bus in vehicles that drove onto the island. Signs that read COLORED and WHITE, so starkly idiomatic to the language of the grainy photos of the rural South in the first half of the twentieth century, did not exist on Avery Island, one of the southernmost locations in the nation.

To defend this unconventional racial stance, McIlhenny somewhat quixotically relied on the same private property justification used by many bigoted southerners to accomplish the opposite end—specifically, keep blacks from entering their stores or restaurants. It was his island, McIlhenny argued, "and I'll do what I damn well please with it. I'll make the rules on my property."

That local authorities chose to ignore E.A.'s obvious disdain for the region's racial rules was a tribute to McIlhenny's clout in the parish—influence he ironically claimed he didn't have during the New Iberia incident. Indeed, by the end of E.A.'s life in 1949, the McIlhennys had become so politically autonomous in south-central Louisiana that soon after his death the family implemented one of E.A.'s more audacious goals: to integrate the elementary school on Avery Island. Coming five years prior to the 1954 Supreme Court decision that called for the elimination of separate schools for blacks and whites over time, and decades before this ruling was actually enforced in the South, it was a little-noticed but nonetheless uncommon achievement.

The Avery Island schools opened in the 1920s. In their initial years, each had two classrooms and thirty to fifty children attending grades one through five. Of the pair, the white school was better equipped with new textbooks, a complete selection of art and vocational supplies, a lending library and a challenging curriculum that aimed to prepare students for middle school off of the island. The black school, by contrast, best resembled an ill-stocked day-care center.

Moreover, the white students were Avery Island's next generation, the prized children; they enjoyed a Huck Finn existence tied to the rhythms of the island community. Their reminiscences were colored with arcadian nostalgia. It wasn't unusual, a former student said, to stumble upon an alligator wandering the paths of the island that the children took to get to school. "That would happen three or four days a week and it was fortuitous, because it meant that we would get a lift," said Eleanor Dore, who attended Avery Island School about thirty years ago and now teaches there. "We'd call the McIlhenny men to report the alligator, and after they came out and tied it up, they'd load us up in the back of their truck and take us to school. We felt so privileged to arrive at school on McIlhenny's truck. It was like a limousine."

Many times a year, E.A. would speak at assemblies in the white school to discuss possible careers on the island and a future in the Tabasco business. The McIlhennys were keenly interested in the progress of the white children, customarily asking school officials for performance measures and demanding they do better if the school fell behind others in the region. And the children made sure to bring their report cards to E.A. as soon as they received them, many times before showing them to their parents. E.A. felt that the grades of the white students were a direct reflection on his role as steward of the island.

No such importance was placed on the black children, many of whom didn't live on the island (that is, were not the children of E.A.'s in-house help) and who mostly kept to themselves on the way to and from school. The McIlhennys and their employees barely noted the existence of the school and hardly ever showed up for activities there.

By the late 1940s, like the majority of black schools in the South, Avery Island's had so declined from a lack of resources and an abundance of neglect that it had become an embarrassment. An empty shell without aspirations, it was nothing more than a pen for a handful of black children during the day. In time, it became so desolate that most of the black Tabasco workers took their kids out of the school and instead sent them to parochial schools in New Iberia, if they could afford to, or to larger public schools, hoping to find more educational opportunities for their children at a bigger institution.

When the black school's enrollment had dwindled to a mere ten, E.A. decided it had to be shut. He had two concerns about it: it obviously failed the children and, as important to McIlhenny, it did little to build loyalty among black workers toward the island and the family. If anything, it bred resentment.

Still, closing the black school and moving its few students into the white school was a brazen request, which parish educational authorities were not prepared to grant without a fight. McIlhenny may have gotten away with setting his own racial rules for the island's facilities because Avery Island was his property, but the schools were not his. Initially, the school board was unwilling to consider Edward McIlhenny's request, which was tantamount to rewriting the discriminatory regulations that had guided Louisiana and the rest of the South since Reconstruction. In no other Louisiana city or town was school integration even a remote possibility.

E.A. McIlhenny died without resolution of this issue. But two years later, the education board relented and allowed the McIlhennys to shutter the black school. There are no accessible records that indicate why the school board suddenly changed its mind, nor contemporaries of the period who remember. But the consensus in Iberia Parish was that, yet again, the McIlhennys had flexed their considerable muscle in a region where their tax payments were desperately needed.

There was little reaction on the island to the integration of the schools. "Maybe we weren't very street smart, but when the ten black kids moved into the white school there was no ruckus or complaints, unlike what happened in the rest of the South in the years that followed," said Joseph Terrell, teacher Eleanor Dore's father and McIlhenny Co.'s former chief accountant. "I guess we were used to mingling with the blacks because that was the way of life on Avery Island. It was a good thing that the black school was closed; the teachers they had at the black school, they weren't very good."

But if E.A.'s progressive policy of shared facilities among the races on Avery Island was such a singular achievement in a region where integration was yet decades off, it is odd McIlhenny's black employees don't speak about it or appear to recall it, while to the white community it is as vivid as today's newspaper. There is one intriguing explanation, though. For the white people, the more lenient racial attitude on Avery Island was noteworthy more so because it was unique to McIlhenny's property—it could be viewed as another twist in the story of the eccentric McIlhenny family, like turning a fallow plantation into a pepper sauce factory or founding a feudal worker village more than that it represented a more significant shift in the South. Away from the island, there were still unquestioned rules ensuring black suppression; in other words, in almost every place in the area besides Avery Island, the typical, manifest forms of southern racism predominated.

Meanwhile, for the black people of Iberia Parish, a more enlightened attitude on Avery Island was barely noted for precisely the same reasons that the white residents recollect it so well: for those who lived under the sword of segregation every day, one small village where it was less practiced—but where they weren't allowed to reside—was simply not remarkable enough to be memorable.

Chapter 9

NIRVANA

On Avery Island, Edward McIlhenny determined the tone, style, landscape, pace and tasks of the closed world his employees inhabited. He was at his desk in McIlhenny Co.'s executive office, up the stairs from the Tabasco factory he built, by four o'clock every morning. He left work at six in the evening and was in bed at ten. McIlhenny expected the same punctuality, though not the same hours, from every worker.

E.A. had lunch each day promptly at noon. So did everyone on Avery Island. When McIlhenny walked out of his office to go home and eat, triangles sounded and the entire business shut down for an hour. Even the switchboard closed. The factory workers ate at their houses in Tango Village. The black pepper pickers and maintenance staff, and anyone else who didn't live on the island, bought food at one of the island's general stores and ate in the dining hall or outside. By one o'clock, everybody, including E.A., was back at work.

McIlhenny's handiwork was visible everywhere on the island. His magnetism, bonhomie and vitality fashioned an uncommon rapport with the residents of Tango Village, who enjoyed the intoxicating privilege of being in E.A.'s indefatigable orbit; his passion for nature produced a backdrop of wild landscapes, lavish wildlife and an odd but treasured religious icon, most of which had not been seen before in Louisiana or anywhere in North America.

Yet, evident from time to time was a somewhat less attractive side of Edward McIlhenny. Eager to repeat the commercial success of the Tabasco company with unrelated projects that, like the pepper sauce business, would take advantage of Avery Island's plentiful resources, E.A., perhaps naively, ventured into ill-chosen efforts that led to disturbing or at best embarrassing results.

If the family business was Edmund's likeness, a picture that Edward McIlhenny could inspirit here or there with color and design but never truly alter, then Tango Village was E.A.'s personal palette. Just as E.A. had envisioned, within months of its opening Tango Village had become a thriving, self-contained worker's community. Residents participated in their favorite hobbies and recreation, formed their closest friendships, received basic medical care, got an education and bought most of their food and clothing on Avery Island. Few reasons could be found to cross Bayou Petit Anse to the mainland, McIlhenny delightedly told friends.

And if a family absolutely had to leave—for example, to go to church, shop for special items, visit relatives or see a physician about a problem that the island clinic's doctors couldn't solve—E.A. usually arranged to take them. In the early days of Tango Village, a mere handful of the workers had an automobile. Relying on the McIlhennys for mobility was frequently the sole option.

Confined as they were, Tango Villagers grew dependent on each other as well, an impulse E.A. encouraged because it served to bind the community even more. Acts of kindness and charity were customary. If a child became seriously ill and required constant attention for a long period of time, making it difficult for his mother to care for her other children and maintain her home, Tango women divided the mother's chores among themselves. Similarly, the men organized home repair teams that traveled from house to house on nights and weekends to attend to deteriorating plumbing, electrical fixtures in disrepair, walls and ceilings or much-needed paint jobs.

That the community crystallized so perfectly is a testament to Edward McIlhenny's instinctual understanding of the era's management-labor dynamics—particularly his conviction that workers primarily desired protection from the worst dangers of the free market: i.e., the threat of without warning losing their livelihoods and, hence, their ability to take care of their families. Indeed, much to the McIlhennys' pleasure, E.A. was as aptly suited to oversee Tango Village as he was to run the Tabasco company.

"The people of Tango worshipped Edward," said a descendant of the Averys, whose mother was raised on Avery Island. "He was the thread that wove the company into a community, albeit one that was spun to benefit the Tabasco business."

In recollection upon recollection, E.A.'s generosity toward Tango Village was mentioned. People spoke of the day camps he organized during the summer, the baseball teams he coached, the trips to the movies in New Iberia on rainy days, the gifts at Christmas time, the support—financial and emotional—when an employee was having marital difficulties and the paychecks in periods when Tabasco sales were weak and there was little work to be done.

In fact, the job security and the stability of the community—the knowledge that Edward McIlhenny was boss *and* guardian—were the primary reasons so many Iberia Parish locals freely accepted lower wages and relinquished much of their autonomy to work for the McIlhennys and live on the island.

As a child, Edward Terrell witnessed the irresistibility of Tango Village for economically vulnerable families. Soft-spoken, approaching seventy years old, with sad, deep-set, dark eyes, leathery Cajun skin and a nasal, Louisiana drawl, Terrell was born on Avery Island. His grandfather and father worked in the salt mines, and he, his parents and sister initially lived in a two-bedroom house in Salt Village. They moved to a three-bedroom home in Tango Village when Terrell was a teenager, soon after his father had transferred to the Tabasco business, eventually to rise to general manager.

"Those were small houses on a small island," Terrell recalled. "You couldn't take a piss without the neighbor flushing his toilet."

Terrell and his wife, Pal, left Avery Island in the late 1950s as newlyweds. Terrell had taken a job in the front office of McIlhenny Co.—he would become vice president of accounting before retiring—but Pal wanted to raise children off of the island, hoping to rear them in a less-provincial environment. Until recently, the couple—their children grown and out of the home—lived in a fabulously ornate, two-story, eight-bedroom, mid-1800s Greek Revival estate in the heart of New Iberia, a far cry from his upbringing in the squat, nondescript worker shacks in Salt Village.

Although Terrell has been away from Avery Island for well over forty years, in many of his dreams he lives there yet.

"Avery Island was a safety net," Terrell said, explaining its hold on his imagination. "I remember my daddy telling me that during the Depression the Tabasco business was slow. Demand was down. Tabasco was a luxury that many people couldn't afford. But Mr. Ned didn't cut salaries or lay anyone off who lived on the island, even though there wasn't enough work. He told my daddy, 'You'll make it up to us sometime when things get better.' That's a hell of a safety net, when people off of the island were standing on relief lines. Whatever personal price you pay to live on the island—you lose some privacy and life there is slow and a bit unsophisticated—for a lot of workers that seems like no cost at all if you don't have to worry about the basics of life.

"I have something to confess," Terrell continued. His eyes lit up, the hint of a mischievous smile creased his lips. "When I was a boy, I ran with another boy named T-Foot Delcambre, whose father was Foot Delcambre and mother was Miss Punk. When we were eleven years old, me and T-Foot hauled the mail by bike every day from the Avery Island post office to Miss Sadie [Edward McIlhenny's sister] and Miss Mary [Edward McIlhenny's wife] in huge mailbags. That was hard work and they paid us just five cents a week. Sometimes they told us to take the money from the cookie jar or someplace like that. If they weren't looking, we would grab more money than we were supposed to. Hell, we were underpaid. I never told my parents.

"But here's the funny part: T-Foot and I felt so guilty about this that we would spend hours talking about it, fearful that if Mr. Ned found out we were stealing a few pennies—that's all it was—our families would get thrown off the island. Just like that, with no questions asked. At that time, we could do nothing worse to our parents, there was really no worse penalty in the world that we could think of."

Particularly, Terrell added, when many residents of Tango Village were still recounting with amazement the details of a summer day in the 1930s during which Edward McIlhenny revealed shaman-like qualities. After that unforgettable moment, few people on the island wished to stray far from E.A. and his voodoo talents.

It occurred in a baseball game pitting Tango and Salt Village on Avery Island. E.A. was the designated pitcher. A Tango Village teenager, about sixteen years old, hit a ball into the gap in left-center field. Retrieving it, the center fielder threw it to the shortstop, who relayed it to the catcher. It arrived just as the teenager slid into home plate. In the collision between the runner and the catcher, the teenager's leg was wrenched backward, so forcefully that the crack of his bone, followed by a screeching cry, was all that could be heard on the field.

Everyone gathered around the boy. There were murmurs about getting him to the hospital quickly, but McIlhenny's voice cut through the chatter. "Carry him to my home, fast," McIlhenny said.

Only a small number of the workers had ever been in McIlhenny's Georgian manse, but at that moment they didn't notice the house. All eyes were on the teenager, now on the long, rectangular kitchen table, looking skinny and frail, his expression twisted with pain and his bare leg bent like a clover. McIlhenny—his 200-pound frame making him the most imposing figure in the room—stood over the boy. He had washed his hands and collected a pair of scissors, plaster of paris, water, tape and bandages.

As E.A. began to work on the leg, the boy shrieked and everyone cringed.

"But Mr. Ned didn't skip a beat; he kept his attention on the leg and kept fixing it," said Antoine Broussard, whose parents lived in Tango Village. "And then Mr. Ned did something that took everyone's breath away. He started talking in this soft, purring voice about anything and everything, nonstop. He spoke about his trips to Alaska and the flowers in his garden and the Tabasco factory and what the Eskimos were like and whatnot. The thing is, he never stopped talking for a second and he never changed his tone of voice and he never stopped fixing the bone. Just the sound of his voice quieted the boy, whose face seemed to soften. It was as if Mr. Ned put everybody in a hypnotic trance. There wasn't a sound in the room but him. And then suddenly, when everyone awoke, that's how I explain it, the boy's leg was in a perfect cast. Very eerie."

While some slight variations of this tale are offered, generally this telling is faithful to how people in the area recall the incident. It's entirely possible, though, it didn't happen the way it is remembered. There are no firsthand accounts, no one alive now who was present at the event. Initially, some old-timers said they were there. Then, inevitably, they would realize that their desire to believe the story—and that E.A. possessed supernatural skills—addled their memories and led them to mistakenly conclude they were in the room.

Apocryphal or not, it was easy for Tango Village residents to believe that the boss was a bone healer. For one thing, southern Louisianians were no strangers to the presence of the metaphysical through Caribbean sorcery, if they were black, or Catholic mysticism, if they were Cajun. For another, who else but a man possessing magic could have molded the elysian setting on Avery Island that E.A. had willed into being on his own. Visually and viscerally moving, entirely out of the ordinary and inspired, the environment McIlhenny designed was a stunning tableau abutting the workers' drab village of shanties and huts. "It was like watching the Garden of Eden materialize," said Joseph Dubois, a McIlhenny manager and company town resident.

McIlhenny's most provocative brushstroke was the 900-year-old Buddha sitting cross-legged on a lotus leaf in a glass house overlooking a blue-green lagoon. Young and thin, the Buddha had an oddly distorted expression, one of wide-eyed puzzlement, the innocent face of somebody who believes he knows too little rather than too much. His robe was worn toga-like, the right side of his torso from his chest to his shoulder unclad. Even seated, he was six feet tall and four and a half feet wide.

E.A. placed the Buddha in an ideal spot for meditation, where it still remains today, a location so quiet only the hollow cackle of unseen birds and the burp of lapping water could be heard. Planted directly in front of the statue were seven sacred hillocks of Chinese flowers—irises, creeping juniper, all manner of camellia and honeysuckle—an arrangement also repeated at the other side of the lagoon. In bloom, this dense flora provided a clattery counterpoint to the silence of the Buddha's gaze.

Arches of wisteria and titan sixty-foot-tall bamboo combined to produce a set of playfully baroque entrances to the site from almost any path. Cut and bundled, some of the bamboo framed the fluted columns of the Buddha's ten-foot-by-ten-foot shrine, itself raised on a pedestal of metallic-hewed contoured rocks and embellished with a cluster of delicate colors: a pink-red door, yellow curtains and a ceiling of pastel.

In this ethereal scene, workers recalled enjoying the simple passages of life—Sunday picnics, first kisses and family walks at dusk when the tropical air turned balmy. "My parents proposed to each other in front of the Buddha," said Emile Breaux, who was born on Avery Island and works for the Louisiana Department of Wildlife and Fisheries. "They were good Christians, but to them that seemed to be an appropriate place to take their first vows."

Sculpted in about 1100, the Buddha's original home was the Shonfa temple, now destroyed but once a prominent Buddhist shrine in northeast Beijing. During the fall of the Chinese empire in the early 1900s, a general looted the Buddha and shipped it to New York with orders to have it sold to a museum. Before the deal was consummated, however, the general was captured and beheaded. Orphaned, the Buddha gathered dust in a downtown warehouse.

A few decades later, in the mid-1930s, the owner of the warehouse rediscovered the Buddha buried in the back of the depot. He placed it on the auction block. A pair of Edward McIlhenny's East Coast friends saw it and knew immediately that this was the perfect gift for their eccentric buddy who made pepper sauce in Louisiana.

To McIlhenny, the arrival of the Buddha symbolized the coming of his spiritual alter ego. Uncomfortable with organized religions, McIlhenny believed in a Rousseauian state of grace, marked by a unity with nature that allows individuals to experience spiritual revelation at their death. In Edward McIlhenny's worldview, people's fates weren't decided by a higher being, but by the depth of their relationships with the natural world.

E.A. so identified with the Buddha's search for Nirvana that he wrote an intimate poem in the mystic's voice and etched it on a granite plaque at the hushed entrance to the shrine. Among the elegantly framed stanzas:

Long days of travel have brought me from my home,
Yet I have known no hour of calmer rest.
My thoughts are like the swaying bamboos' crest
Waved to and fro above the rippling stream,
Clear and blue
As from a glorious dream.

Surrounding the Buddha on 250 acres was McIlhenny's Jungle Gardens, a panoply of nonindigenous plants and trees E.A. acquired through painstaking negotiation with botanists in distant places, trading in some of the most exotic items on Earth: papyrus from the Nile Valley; Tonkin cane from Southeast Asia; and a rare Tibetan podocarp, an overgrown evergreen with needles like sharp swords that is one of the few vestiges of the coal age, a period more than 200 million years ago when there were no flowers, birds, butterflies or bees on the planet, only cockroaches, dragonflies and tiny reptiles. He imported Japanese bamboo that could grow as much as eighteen inches in three hours, finger bananas from China, Indian soap trees, and about 1,000 varieties of cherished camellias.

The Wasi orange tree, whose fruit was hallowed and reserved solely for the enjoyment of the Japanese emperor, was obtained in a fashion somewhat more heroic than a meager purchase, McIlhenny claimed. According to his telling, during a rescue mission in the Arctic, E.A. saved the lives of three high-caste Japanese. The mikado offered to reward McIlhenny for his valor with a decoration and a gift of money. But McIlhenny turned him down. Instead, he asked for a Wasi tree, an audacious request because it existed in no other garden in the world but the emperor's. Charmed by McIlhenny's brazenness, the emperor assented.

Given these prodigious achievements in recomposing the landscape of Avery Island and McIlhenny's many responsibilities at his day job as head of the Tabasco company, it would seem E.A. would have been hard-pressed to find time to protect a dying species. But there they are, observable from a wooden bridge spanning a thirty-five-acre pond beyond the iris gardens: tens of thousands of snowy egrets—two-foot-long ivory birds with silky white beards, stark black bills and legs and bright yellow feet—in full plumage. Perched on a platform the size of a football field rising ten feet above the pond, they were ubiquitous—on each other's backs, entwined as they jockeyed one leg then another for position on the bamboo, flying in and out of the trees and bushes, and diving into the water for food. Their raspy, clipped call, the sound of choking, echoed against the woods encompassing the preserve. By most accounts, this is the largest egret community in the world.

What's startling is not that there are so many egrets on Avery

Island now, but that there are any. In the early 1890s, the snowy egret was virtually extinct. There were fewer in the United States than buffalo—and there were only about 800 of those. At the end of the nineteenth century, egrets were stalked for their pure, white, flocculent feathers, which were in bloom during the spring nuptial season and prized for upscale women's hats. Hunters would search the swamps in the bayous for nesting colonies of the birds and kill the adults while they watched the babies. Then the hunters waited, sometimes for hours, for the mates to return with food for the nest—and those birds would be shot as well. The babies were left to starve to death. Twenty feathers on each shoulder of the egret—forty plumes in all—were worth $40, paid in cash, to the Louisiana woodsmen.

E.A. McIlhenny grew up enchanted by the egrets, which lived on Avery Island in the spring and summer and migrated to Central and South America for fall and winter. As a youth, he shadowed their graceful movements from a skiff in the dank waters of the island, painting elegant portraits of them or writing poems about their balletic dives. But in 1892, when E.A. was nineteen and home from Lehigh University, he was dismayed to find that the egret population on the island had thinned measurably; the birds had been decimated by poaching, impossible to police on an island thick with trees and accessible by shallow waterways overgrown with vegetation.

Besides petitioning politicians to outlaw the hunting of egrets, which he did to no avail, McIlhenny at first believed there was nothing else he could do. The snowy egrets, it appeared, were on a certain path to extinction. Then McIlhenny recalled a conversation at the dinner table some years earlier when his father and mother were entertaining an Indian viceroy. The guest had told a story that in hindsight provided a possible solution for the egret's woes.

According to the viceroy's account, an ancient raja tried to please a capricious wife by building a giant cage of bamboo and putting brightly colored birds from every region of India in it. It was not known whether the raja's wife was happy with the gift or not, because his tenure was insignificant and little else was remembered about him. Subsequent monarchs, however, neglected the bamboo cage, and in time it decayed and splintered, enough so that one winter the exotic birds were freed and many flew away. But most surprising, the viceroy said, was what happened the following season, after the frost had passed: the birds came back to the bamboo cage, rather than to their original home, the natural environment for their species.

Although migratory habits of birds are reasonably well understood now, a century ago they were still a mystery. In fact, it wasn't until 1902 that Dr. Paul Bartsch of the Smithsonian Institution developed the first scientific bird-banding program in North America to chart their paths, a program Edward McIlhenny would enthusiastically join. By his death, he placed more identity tags on birds' legs and necks than almost any other individual in the country, a status he holds to this day. But with limited information available about bird activities in 1892, the viceroy's story was eye-opening: it indicated that some, perhaps many, migrating birds not only returned to the region they had left during the prior season, but also to the very same spot.

From this possible clue, McIlhenny hatched a plan. Over many days in early spring, he and two black employees, John Goffney and Pierre, waded "waist deep in palmetto and cypress swamps, . . . crawling through cane brakes and thickets until they located eight young egrets," wrote Harris Dickson, the Louisiana journalist, in the *Saturday Evening Post*. The men placed the birds in a twenty-foot-tall wire and bamboo cage they had constructed in an artificial pond created by damming a bayou near the Tabasco factory.

Each morning, McIlhenny dispatched his employees to catch fresh shad, shrimp, shiners, minnows and tadpoles, which E.A. fed to the fledgling egrets by hand. By October, the birds had matured and grew noticeably restless as shorter, cooler days brought the urge to fly south. E.A. opened the door to their cage to let them go. But the birds didn't leave. They chattered a lot and circled the pond, but that was all.

So E.A. destroyed the cage. Nonetheless, they stayed. For three days, the egrets flew frantically to different parts of the pond; they were literally aflutter, looking puzzled but determined not to go just yet. That night, frost appeared on the lily pods. The next morning, when McIlhenny arrived at the pond, the birds were gone.

It would be an anxious winter for McIlhenny—"the longest I ever endured," he told friends—as he nervously waited to learn if the viceroy's dinnertime tale would prove to be prescient. The answer arrived on March 18, 1893, three days before spring, when four of the egrets returned. McIlhenny found them sitting in the bushes within feet of where their cage had been. Two days later, another pair returned. The birds lived at the pond through the summer, and in the fall a total of thirteen egrets—five adults and eight born that year—flew south.

As the years passed, the population of Bird City, as McIlhenny called it, ballooned exponentially. By 1908, McIlhenny estimated that at least 10,000 egrets lived there. Within seven more years, the size of the community had doubled. In 1920, Avery Island was home to well over 90 percent of the egrets in North America because it was practically the only place on Earth where the birds were safe from hunters. To accommodate the crowd, McIlhenny expanded the pond considerably and built the huge deck that serves as part of the nesting ground for the 100,000 egrets on Avery Island now.

Delighted by his success, McIlhenny imported a motion-picture camera from France, one of the first ever in the United States, and made a documentary chronicling the revival of the near-dead species. He planned to use this film to convince federal lawmakers to pass legislation protecting the bird from hunters.

But there's a strange twist to this story: While E.A. was lobbying Congress, he toyed with a plan to make money off of the very egrets he had assiduously labored to save—this being one of many inexplicable schemes McIlhenny hatched to augment Tabasco revenue in the family's coffers. With thousands of birds in the pond every spring, each of them displaying a superb array of white feathers, McIlhenny saw another lucrative, recurring revenue stream for the family. He realized that with no difficulty he could catch a few birds each year, cut their valuable plumage off without killing them and offer a dependable supply of feathers to international hatmakers, who were desperate for feathers now that the egret was extinct everywhere but Avery Island.

"It would be like giving the birds a haircut," McIlhenny confided to a reporter. "It wouldn't harm them and their plumage would grow back next year. And what a sound commercial proposition for the family it would be."

It's not clear exactly what year McIlhenny devised this plan, but it was likely around 1910. He plucked ten adult egrets and sold their feathers to a wholesale milliner for $550—at $55 a bird, a full $10 more than poachers were getting just a few years earlier before Bird City was built.

McIlhenny's dubious venture came to an abrupt halt after just one year, however. Pro-preservation Louisiana politicians warned him that his egret feather enterprise was derailing their efforts to persuade Congress to outlaw the killing of the birds. It made E.A.'s campaign to save the birds look like a poorly disguised attempt to put competitors out of business and gain a monopoly on the egret plumage for himself. Moreover, McIlhenny was reminded that by selling egret feathers, he would reignite the market for their plumage. That would, no doubt, inspire additional poacher activity, because as prices for the egret's plumage rose, poachers would be willing to go deeper and deeper into the Gulf's swamplands to hunt the bird.

This embarrassing episode notwithstanding, McIlhenny worked unceasingly for a law to protect egrets. He wrote letters to dozens of congressmen, goaded state legislators and politicians to keep up the heat on Louisiana's delegation in Washington and invited anyone whose attention he could command to come to Avery Island and watch his rudimentary but effective documentary on Bird City.

Finally, in 1918, with the help of his brother John Avery McIlhenny, then Civil Service commissioner, E.A. had amassed sufficient political capital to win the lengthy battle. That year, the Senate ratified a 1916 agreement between the United States and Canada prohibiting the killing or capturing of migratory birds. In subsequent years, Mexico, Japan and Russia would agree to the same rules. It took three decades, but due in large part to McIlhenny's efforts, the snowy egret was saved from extinction.

For most naturalists, the sheer awkwardness of being caught trying to make money from a cause they espoused would have prevented similar questionable ventures in the future. But Edward McIlhenny's commercial instincts couldn't be restrained by common sense. Consequently, in 1938, McIlhenny puzzlingly decided to create a market in the United States for the soft fur that lay under the ratty coat of the queer-looking nutria—a semiaquatic, beaver-sized rodent indigenous to South America, with sickly orange teeth, prickly hair and inch-long claws. Launching this business, E.A. paid a trader $112 for fourteen adults and six babies.

Two years later, after his original colony of 20 animals had grown to more than 500, McIlhenny sold many of the adult nutria to breeders throughout North America for $1,000 each. At the same time, he released the rest of the animals into the Avery Island marshes, opening a concession that let hunters to trap these animals in exchange for a share of the profits they generated.

With these measures, the nutria fur frenzy in the United States took flight. At one-tenth the price of expensive furs, nutria rapidly became a popular alternative to mink and fox. Cajun trappers on Avery Island grew rich on the pelts of "le rat Ned," and McIlhenny had a lucrative new venture that allowed him to take credit for single-handedly creating the nutria industry in Louisiana.

"I originally brought 15 pairs of the animals from the Argentine . . . and have liberated probably 150 pairs of these animals in Iberia Parish since 1940," McIlhenny boasted in a letter to a member of the Terrebonne Parish Chamber of Commerce. (True to course, E.A.'s description of his activities contains a lie or two; he claimed to have purchased ten more nutria than he actually did, according to receipts. And he bought the animals from an American seller, not an Argentine.)

The nutria craze was short-lived, lasting but three decades, ultimately a victim of the collapse in the fur industry worldwide. In 1976, nutria harvests in Louisiana peaked at 1.8 million animals. By 2002, hunters trapped fewer than 30,000 nutria. As nutria hunting declined, the animal became a public nuisance—and not just in Louisiana. There are tens of millions of nutria roaming the reedy grasses of at least thirteen states, from Oregon to Maryland, virtually all of them descendants of McIlhenny's initial brood. They're multiplying alarmingly fast. Reaching sexual maturity at six months, nutria have two to three litters a year of up to thirteen offspring and are in heat again forty-eight hours after giving birth.

"They're in our ditches. They're in the suburbs. They're everywhere. They're like cockroaches," said Gloria McKinnon, of the New Orleans chapter of the Audubon Society.

The nutria has inflicted its greatest damage on the nation's threatened wetlands, where the rodents devour marshes and leave behind mudflats and dead swamps. It's estimated that as many as 50,000 nutria in Chesapeake Bay, Maryland, have chewed up 8,000 prime acres. In Louisiana, where the nutria population is higher, the devastation is far worse. Approximately 100,000 acres of wetlands have been destroyed by nutria alone.

The McIlhenny family is so embarrassed by Edward's role in the nutria fiasco that it has asked its paid, full-time historian, Shane Bernard, to unearth facts to counter E.A.'s involvement. But the incident has been impossible to debunk.

"E.A. was an outstanding naturalist," said Greg Linscombe, director of the Louisiana Department of Wildlife and Fisheries. "So you have to wonder, 'What was he thinking?'"

The answer to that provides a telling glimpse into Edward McIlhenny's personality, as well as his family's. While a dedicated environmentalist, E.A. was a McIlhenny first, and the McIlhennys have always viewed Avery Island as, simply put, raw material for the growth of the family's fortune. Every precious resource on the property has either been turned into a revenue stream—the salt mines, the pepper fields, the oil and gas buried deep in the rocky isoclinal folds, and even E.A.'s beloved Jungle Gardens (which costs $6 to visit)—or has been refashioned to minimize overhead for a McIlhenny enterprise (i.e., Salt Village and Tango Village). E.A. believed he had two primary responsibilities: to preserve the family business and the island. His artisanship on Avery Island was dazzling, but it so drew his workers closer to him, the Tabasco company and his ever-expanding legend that it could be aptly viewed as a profit center. In truth, E.A., like every McIlhenny, was a better steward of the company than the land.

A short time before he died, Edward McIlhenny's image—for much of his life remarkably immune to criticism—was stained by a nickel-and-dime incident involving unsavory elements of Louisiana politics.

The events allegedly took place between 1937 and 1940. Huey Long, the southern populist paradigm, had been assassinated in 1935. During his frenzied seven-year run as Louisiana's governor and senator, Long molded the disenfranchised poor into a prevailing political force and held his coalition of blacks, Cajuns, white farmers and urban working class together by building schools, universities, hospitals, clinics and bridges, handing out free textbooks and paving roads. Less than shy about admitting that he frequently took a piece of these deals for his personal treasury, Long famously remarked in a speech at Louisiana State University: "People say I steal. Well, all politicians steal. I steal. But a lot of what I stole has spilled over in no-toll bridges, hospitals . . . and to build this university."

One of Long's closest associates, state judge Richard Leche, was elected governor in 1936. He, too, made no attempt to be anything but candid about what attracted him to public service. "When I took the oath as governor," Leche said, "I didn't take any vows of poverty." Leche was in office a mere three years, but in that short time he caused enough havoc to "go down in history as perhaps the most corrupt man to ever serve as Governor of Louisiana," said Charles

Cook Jr., the editor and publisher of the *Cook Political Report* and a native of the state.

In 1939, Leche was indicted and convicted of mail fraud for collecting $31,000 in kickbacks on the purchase of 233 state trucks. And at various other times, he faced charges for taking bribes from lobbyists and contractors; double-dipping, in which the state paid twice for constructing buildings, with the second payment pocketed by Leche and his cronies; and selling oil on the black market in violation of federal law. When Assistant Attorney General Oetje John Rogge was sent to Louisiana to untangle the messy affairs of the state, he found that Leche had earned $282,000 in 1938 on a governor's salary of $7,500.

E.A. met Leche through his brother Rufus McIlhenny, who was head of the Iberia Parish policy jury and active in Louisiana Democratic Party politics. While it's not clear that E.A. and Leche were close friends, they had reason to be acquaintances. As a major landowner and head of one of the state's predominant businesses, McIlhenny carried considerable weight in Iberia Parish among the judges and corporate executives, people Leche sought for support; and a relationship with the governor was essential for E.A. to gain backing for his various commercial activities and naturalist causes.

On September 28, 1940, this little-known relationship between the two men made news across the country. That day, McIlhenny and Leche were indicted by a federal grand jury on charges of mail fraud in connection with landscaping work for Louisiana State University. According to government prosecutors and state and civil lawsuits, Leche forced LSU to hire McIlhenny to manage a beautification program at the university by threatening to cut off funds if E.A. wasn't chosen for the job. As the sole bidder, McIlhenny estimated that the landscaping project, which chiefly involved plants he raised on Avery Island, would cost about $46,000. However, LSU was billed upwards of $122,000 for the work, a massive overrun that McIlhenny, Leche and school officials concealed from the school's board of supervisors, authorities alleged. This occurred just five months after McIlhenny's landscaping contract with Southwestern

Louisiana Institute was canceled by the state board of education because of $9,000 in overcharges.

A few days after the indictments came down, McIlhenny turned himself in at the federal courthouse in New Orleans. He posted $5,000 bond and returned to Avery Island. McIlhenny declined to ever publicly discuss the case in detail; instead, he vowed to clear his name and attacked federal authorities for being "runny-nosed carpetbaggers." But privately, McIlhenny was deeply ashamed and brokenhearted at the episode's potential impact on his legacy.

"He was devastated," said a relative on the Avery side. "He let the lawyers take care of it, and I think he knew that he'd never serve time. But he was humiliated to be seen around the state and around the country as just another Louisiana crook following in Huey Long's footsteps."

The tight-knit, circle-the-wagons nature of Louisiana justice appears to have interceded in the case of Leche and McIlhenny. Though many of the government's claims about the promised estimates and excessive overruns were true, conspiracy was hard to prove. Witnesses vanished, memories failed and paper trails stopped short of anything damning. The federal indictment simply faded away. Meanwhile, the state's Supreme Court took care of the local litigation, tossing it as invalid. McIlhenny wasn't required to pay the overcharges he collected.

After the indictment, though, Edward McIlhenny's usual immodest buoyancy—his self-assured egotism—was in scant supply. In mid-conversation, the memory of what the prosecutors said he did—of what people believed he did—would cross his face like a cloud's shadow, visibly dispiriting him.

In late 1946, E.A. suffered a stroke while pushing a boat through a duck blind on Avery Island toward the end of a hunting trip. The small group of black employees who had gone with him carried his inert body back to the family's mansion. E.A. never recovered full use of his hands and legs and was confined to his room, miserable in his inactivity. He died on August 8, 1949, at the age of seventy-seven.

The funeral on Avery Island was an enormous event, with hundreds and hundreds of people attending from all classes of life. Tango and Salt Village residents were there en masse, as were black pepper pickers, maids, butlers and hunting companions. And there were naturalists, artists and ethnoarchaeologists—and, of course, the extended McIlhenny and Avery families. As the sun set on the restless egrets and the Buddha stared dispassionately at the beautiful gloaming on the bayou, McIlhenny was buried in the family cemetery, where his headstone was the most unembellished of all. It read: EDWARD AVERY MCILHENNY. BORN MARCH 29, 1872. DIED AUGUST 8, 1949.

During E.A.'s long run managing the family business, annual Tabasco sales rose above $3 million from $100,000, an enviable growth rate of above 8 percent a year achieved despite the Great Depression and numerous other global economic bubbles and panics. Output topped 20,000 bottles a day, more than Edmund McIlhenny produced in a full year. In the process, through his trademark and one-on-one sales strategies, E.A. eliminated any direct competition for his brand.

But to read Edward McIlhenny's obituaries is to see two completely different perspectives on a life. The local obit from the *New Orleans Times-Picayune* had a tone that was part *Citizen Kane* and part *Heart of Darkness;* it reflected well the profound personal and emotional impact E.A. had on the lives of his company's workers and failed to mention, in some 1,500 words, the Leche affair: "Death came Monday to Edward Avery McIlhenny, nationally-famed naturalist, artist and author. . . . Salt and pepper were the tools E.A. McIlhenny used on an island to fashion a jungle kingdom where he ruled like a baron—a benevolent baron—over man, beast and plant. Seven hundred men, women and children looked upon him as the 'Great White Father,' bone healer, nurse, physician who gave them a living, translating Avery Island, off the Louisiana coast, into an American showplace. . . . In his kingdom, burglary was almost unknown."

McIlhenny's national obituary, prepared by United Press, ran in major American newspapers. Short—about 100 words—it would have confirmed E.A.'s worst fears: half of it, the first and last paragraphs, was given over to the Leche indictments and the Louisiana scandals.

In fact, both articles did Edward McIlhenny an injustice by overlooking what he excelled at most: he was an exceptional—in some ways, unparalleled—chief executive of a family business. In a forty-five-year-run—four decades at the top, in itself, is hard to match—McIlhenny guided his company successfully from the first to the third generation (an achievement only a very few family businesses can lay claim to), transforming an entrepreneurial venture involving a fledgling premium brand into an established, multimillion-dollar household name, while furthering the traditions implanted by its founder.

In other words, he lived up to a simple vow he had silently made upon being handed the Tabasco company: "It was my duty, I told myself, to pass it on to the next generation better than I got it."

Chapter 10
SIC SEMPER FIDELIS

At Edward McIlhenny's death in 1949, the natural choice to head the family business was Walter Stauffer McIlhenny. Natural, that is, to everyone but him.

The son of John Avery McIlhenny, E.A.'s predecessor, Walter was raised in Washington, D.C., where John moved his family after being named Civil Service commissioner. Walter was a stranger to Avery Island throughout much of his youth. He graduated with a degree in civil engineering from the University of Virginia and then took a job with Continental Oil. There Walter earned a reputation for simplifying complex machine processes and squeezing efficiency out of intricate mechanical systems. In 1940, when Walter was thirty, E.A. asked his nephew to bring his skills to the family business, hoping to further streamline manufacturing operations.

Walter agreed, primarily because he assumed it would be only a brief posting. By this time, Walter had already qualified as a sharpshooter in the Marine Corps Reserve, and he looked forward to being called to active duty imminently, once the United States entered World War II. Beyond that, who knows what? Walter thought. But more than likely, upon returning home, he would pursue something away from Avery Island. Perhaps he would become a Marine educator or simply travel the globe courtesy of his father's Tabasco wealth.

His plans were disrupted, however, within months of the war's end when E.A. took sick. As E.A. lingered, the Tabasco business stood still. Some in the family feared that would-be competitors—small national brands like Baumer Foods' Crystal Hot Sauce or Bruce Foods' Louisiana Hot Sauce—would use this opportunity to make inroads with distributors in regions where McIlhenny was weakest, like the Midwest and the Northeast. Consequently, Walter was hurriedly called back to Avery Island to fill the leadership vacuum and run the family business, at least temporarily

Walter shared his father's ambivalence about Avery Island. They both appreciated its atavistic charm but found it confining. And certainly the Tabasco company was a grand idea that put a lot of money in the family's hands, but Walter, like John, was more disposed to an occupation that afforded personal independence than managing a company isolated on an island.

Nonetheless, in Walter's worldview—crystallized by the Marine code to extol honor, courage and commitment—family obligation prevailed over his own desires. He returned to Avery Island willingly, privately harboring hopes that someone else would be found to permanently take over the reins of the business. But when E.A. died, Walter was still the only option to manage the Tabasco company, a distinction he would carry and regret until he died more than thirty-five years later.

"I could have been a typical rich man's brat and ridden fast women and walked with slow horses," Walter said in January 1975. "If I had my druthers, I'd be a Marine. If I couldn't be a Marine, I'd be a farmer. I'd much rather be driving a tractor or following a mule than sitting at a desk."

Walter—whose "term of office," as he called it, lasted until mid-1985—brought a thoroughly different management tone to the job than his uncle. E.A. is best remembered for his charisma and wizardly accomplishments, served up while running the company with a regal hand. Walter, by contrast, was all business; he was serious, formal, aloof and disciplined—traits he mastered during five grueling years at war.

E.A. was a freethinker and something of a hedonist in his eating and drinking habits. He had very little vanity about the way he dressed; his sartorial style, what there was of it, was mostly relaxed. Walter, a clean-cut bachelor with perfectly erect posture, deep-set dark eyes and, later in his life, a distinguished handlebar mustache, was old-fashioned; he disdained modernity in ideas and in the clothes he wore. He was more comfortable in a suit and tie than casual wear.

Clearly, Walter had huge shoes to fill. E.A. was beloved, the only boss the employees who lived or worked on the island had known. Most of them had never met Walter or said more than a few words to him. It helped, though, that Walter came back to Avery Island a military legend. Celebrated as the romantic Tabasco Mac in dozens of stateside articles cataloging activities at the front, Walter was a certifiable American hero, having won widespread renown for commanding Marine troops through a series of daredevil maneuvers in the assault on Guadalcanal.

One of his most publicized sorties took place in August 1942. Amidst a frontal attack on the island, McIlhenny organized a volunteer party to evacuate the wounded well forward of the battle line. According to Marine files, "First Lieutenant McIlhenny, armed only with a rifle, and while under heavy enemy mortar and machine gun fire, covered the advance and withdrawal of the rescue party, gallantly drawing enemy fire and silencing a Japanese machine gun nest. Although ill at the time and suffering shock from concussion of an enemy mortar shell, he returned to a vantage point close to enemy lines and, in the face of fierce sniper fire, acted as an observer, relaying accurate information until ordered by his superior officer to leave his post."

Three months later, McIlhenny attempted another death-defying maneuver when he led a patrol of twenty men to penetrate a dense jungle full of Japanese snipers and clear a path to the enemy's right flank. En route to their battalion upon completing the assignment,

McIlhenny's team was spotted by Japanese troops, who opened fire and pinned them down. "When almost all of his men were wounded, Captain McIlhenny, despite his own injury, was determined to carry the message [about enemy coordinates] himself and finally succeeded in reaching our lines," Marine files noted. "His great courage and unswerving devotion to duty enabled his company to attack the enemy's flank and capture their position."

At the conclusion of the Guadalcanal battles, McIlhenny volunteered for combat in two other Pacific forays—Cape Gloucester, New Britain, and Peleliu, Palau Islands. He resigned from active duty at the end of 1945 as a decorated major with a Navy Cross, a Silver Star, two Purple Hearts and a number of Presidential Unit Citations. Eventually, he received a promotion to brigadier general. One of Walter's favorite war stories involved the time his platoon partners were carrying him to safety after he had been shot. Before they could find a secure spot, they were set upon by a new round of snipers. So they dropped McIlhenny over the edge of a cliff to hide him. He emerged with severe acrophobia. "I cured myself of it," McIlhenny said, "Back home I stalked mountain goats all the way to their shelters in the highest peaks in the country until I wasn't afraid anymore of heights."

McIlhenny didn't stray far from the Marines. He cofounded the Marine Military Academy in Harlingen, Texas (on Iwo Jima Boulevard), a prep school for boys ages eight to twelve, and the sole institution in the world basing its curriculum entirely on the traditions and values of the Marine Corps. The school's strict mandate, still practiced, was to teach "self-discipline, teamwork, motivation, how to follow and how to lead," according to McIlhenny. A Marine insignia was religiously pinned to Walter's lapel. It's no surprise, then, that he ran the Tabasco company with military precision.

Workers could set their watches by Walter's comings and goings. At precisely 11:00 every morning, Walter arrived at the Tabasco factory to inspect the pepper mash. Julius Derouen, his factory foreman, was invariably by Walter's side. The Derouens were a familiar presence on Avery Island: Julius' father, Dutille, was a

McIlhenny blacksmith for forty years, and Julius had been born and raised there. Walter watched with a handheld spotlight as Derouen scooped the three-year-old mash out of each of the casks. Examining the aged pepper's color, smell and texture, Walter determined whether it met the standards set for the company's sauce. A nod, Derouen knew, meant to move on to an adjoining barrel.

Lunch was next, always at noon for an hour, in keeping with the custom established by E.A. McIlhenny. But under Walter, it was a more starchy, anachronistic affair, held virtually by appointment every day in the spacious dining room of Walter's house. An early 1950s *New Yorker* magazine article elegantly captured the peculiar design of Walter's home, particularly its homage to the past. Journalist John McNulty wrote: "In plantation days rows and rows of buildings (on Avery Island) constituted the slave quarters. Two of the buildings, constructed of brick handmade on the island, have survived in fine condition. They are low buildings, and in the century or more they have stood there, sun and rain have given the brick a texture and tint to be acquired by no hastier means. These two houses, overlooking a pond, Mr. McIlhenny has made into the bedrooms of the home. The two are connected at one end by a newer building . . . which contains a high-ceilinged open beamed living room, a kitchen, and quarters for the staff."

The dining room was located in the recently constructed portion of the house. Adjacent to it was the drawing room, decorated with tiger, lion and zebra skins Walter bagged in African safaris accompanied by the guide who traveled with Ernest Hemingway. Frequently, McIlhenny and his relatives who joined him for lunch would convene here in the moments prior to the meal. In due course, a black butler in a white jacket and white gloves would announce that the food was served.

Walter sat at the head of the long table. A portrait of the company founder, Walter's grandfather Edmund McIlhenny, hung behind his chair; on the opposite wall was a portrait of Edmund's wife, Mary Avery McIlhenny. On the wall to Walter's left was a painting of Zachary Taylor, the twelfth president and Walter's great-

great-grandfather on his mother's side. A typical menu chosen by Walter included braised pork, sweet potatoes, homemade rolls, and Tabasco sauce. Walter led the conversation but ate quickly. A half dozen black servants, all of them dressed in ivory outfits cleaned and pressed daily, ushered the food in and out obsequiously, bowing as they served and bused, so the McIlhenny men could be back at their desks by one o'clock.

At first unnoticed, the plantation-era facets of this daily event ultimately became a source of discomfort for black people in Walter's employ as well as for some McIlhenny family members. "As the years went by, it was hard to approve of the obsequiousness that these lunches demanded of the black help," said a McIlhenny relative, slightly younger than Walter, who lived on the East Coast. "It got so that when I visited Avery Island I found myself avoiding these lunches. But Walter was resistant to change. He continued to practice this lunchtime ritual until he died."

Although by the last quarter of the twentieth century hardly any companies would dare host functions like these for fear that they would be viewed as tacitly endorsing obvious racial stereotypes, Walter's response to those who found the lunches unnerving was predictably brusque and undiscerning. "These are routines, not political or social statements," Walter told relatives on more than one occasion. "Nobody is hurt by order."

Punctilious, Walter stopped short of being intimidating. While difficult to get close to—he warmed up to few people and revealed personal reflections to almost no one—Walter at times displayed a comical side to his squareness that his coworkers swore he must have seen the humor in. If he did, Walter's pride prevented him from admitting it.

One such incident took place toward the end of Walter's tenure at McIlhenny Co., when a diesel locomotive, instead of the usual steam engine, noisily clacked onto Avery Island to pick up crates of Tabasco sauce for distribution. To put this story into context, it's useful to recall that by this point the first personal computers had already been invented and VCRs were just a couple of years away.

Disturbed by the clamor of the diesel and used to the rhythmic chug of the steam engine, McIlhenny pulled Joseph Terrell, the company's chief accountant, into his office. Enraged, Walter yelled, "What is that thing out there? What's it doing here?"

"I think it's a diesel engine, Mr. Walter," Terrell answered.

"Well, I'm going to call the railroad superintendent and tell him that we don't want that kind of train on our island. It's disturbing."

Later, Terrell saw Walter in the hallway and asked him if he had spoken to the superintendent.

"I did," McIlhenny said, appearing confused, while his tone of voice was still prickly and defiant. "But he didn't understand what I was talking about. He said he couldn't do anything about it. And then he asked me if I'm still filling my Tabasco bottles by hand with an eyedropper. What the heck did that mean?"

If McIlhenny could be insensitive toward his black workers, he treated the white, mostly Cajun residents of Tango Village with the utmost care. Walter viewed residents of the island he governed as his responsibility, just as E.A. had. As such, he felt compelled to ensure their well-being on and off the job. This was evident by, among other things, his demand that employees notify him when their children took ill. "If a child was sick, by 5:00 at night Walter's big old Buick would be parked in the worker's driveway with the keys inside, just in case the car was needed after hours to get the child to the hospital or doctor off of the island," said Simon Freyou, a civil engineer and a longtime contractor for the McIlhennys.

Walter succeeded in gaining the respect of his workers, but he never won their loyalty. Most of the workers found him friendly on the surface, but he was too detached to seem genuinely compassionate. "I can't remember any of us ever sitting around and having a shoot-the-bull conversation with Mr. Walter; he just wasn't that type—he seemed uneasy in social settings," said Alex Guidry, who lived on Avery Island in the early 1980s before leaving McIlhenny Co. to become a mechanic in an Iberia Parish auto dealership. "And while offering us his car was a nice gesture, I doubt anybody ever actually took him up on it and drove it anywhere. What if you had an accident? How would you explain to Mr. Walter that you totaled his car? He was too much of a perfectionist to forgive a mistake that big."

The incipient distance between the workers and the McIlhennys weighed heavily on the Tabasco business—chiefly toward the end of Walter's tenure when about a quarter of Tango's 500 or so residents moved off of Avery Island. The benefits of living in the company town—virtually free shelter, a lifetime job, and the paternalism of the family business—were lost on some of the younger workers, who preferred instead a less-parochial existence. They hoped to raise their children in larger communities that would offer more individual privacy, potentially better schools, a greater number of cultural activities and the chance to purchase their own homes. Untethered from the McIlhennys, eventually they could seek job opportunities elsewhere with higher pay.

Such desires notwithstanding, most of the employees who left Avery Island held onto their jobs at McIlhenny Co. for at least a short period of time. Small comfort, however, for Walter, who could only watch impotently as the company town that his family had depended upon for decades as a cheap, reliable and permanent source of labor eroded.

Walter hardly deserved all the blame for the disillusionment in Tango Village. Post–World War II mobility influenced all sectors of society, and with the nation's industrial economy expanding rapidly during that period, U.S. workers were unexpectedly awash in palatable options. Against that backdrop, Tango Village, once a model worker community for the people of southern Louisiana, felt restricting and, worse yet, demeaning. Walter's dispassionate military bearing left him ill equipped to bridge the widening gap separating him from his employees. In retrospect, the McIlhennys failed to appreciate that a company town like theirs—or any isolated venture—relies on the personality of its manager to motivate the group so it pursues as one a goal assumed to be equally beneficial to the organization and the employees.

The many leadership lessons Walter learned from the Marines

didn't prepare him for that assignment. He was incapable of exerting the complexity of character to inspire people who had more free will than soldiers. Indeed, if Edward McIlhenny was the thread that wove the company into a community, Walter symbolized the shredding of the fabric as the connection began to unravel.

McIlhenny Co. ultimately paid a painful price for Walter's inability to address the revolt in Tango Village. But in some measure he made up for this shortcoming by adroitly tackling the most immediate and tangible problem threatening the Tabasco business's future: the urgent need for sales growth. With the third generation in charge of the family business, Walter had to generate sufficient revenue to support over fifty McIlhenny heirs with a claim to a portion of the company's treasury.

Edmund McIlhenny created a pool of shares when the family business was formed, which, under company bylaws, may be passed down from one direct descendant of his and Mary McIlhenny to the next. No one outside this group can own stock in the Tabasco business, and insiders may only sell shares to each other or back to the company.

That approach, practiced by many family businesses in the past, is increasingly out of favor because it is a silent time bomb, as the McIlhennys have learned. Supporting a growing number of family members with a stake in the Tabasco company has required increasing sales exponentially. Nonetheless, the McIlhennys believed (and still do so today) that shares in their company and the power to decide its course were a birthright of every McIlhenny heir. Consequently, the primary job of the family members directly managing the company's day-to-day operations was to produce enough profits so this group could live comfortably.

The company's $3-plus million in annual revenue at Edward McIlhenny's death provided ample earnings to finance the families of the six second-generation McIlhennys in reasonably high style. However, that was far too meager for the much larger third generation. To satisfy the cash needs of this group, Walter had to confront a concomitant challenge: by 1949, the company's sales had leveled off, and the McIlhennys had become complacent about it.

"The older generation was graciously pleased to (merely) fill orders that floated in over the transom," Walter said.

The U.S. market was practically tapped out. McIlhenny Co. had already negotiated aggressive distribution contracts throughout the country. And short of hiring dozens of new salespeople to extend Tabasco into regional pockets where historically the product hadn't fared well, Walter could do little to substantially improve revenue in the United States. Even a prolonged and expensive sales blitz could not guarantee that enough customers would be found to pay for the effort.

The possibility of expanding international sales, though, was an attractive alternative. The end of World War II marked the beginning of the internationalization of consumer goods to an extent never seen before. The reconstruction of national economies combined with the emancipation of colonies, the creation of trade blocks, like the European Common Market and the Latin Free Trade Association, and advances in communications and transportation produced a bonanza of global marketing. With only 2 percent of its sales in non-U.S. markets and the popularity of chili peppers in every region of the world, McIlhenny Co. was ideally suited to take advantage of this opportunity.

To explore this possibility, Walter essentially mimicked the strategy adopted by Edward McIlhenny decades earlier to extend sales in the United States. He met with distributors in key European, Latin American and Asian countries. By cajoling, browbeating, pleading, and offering gifts, Walter convinced most of the major grocery representatives to take a case or two of Tabasco and place the product on store shelves. His World War II exploits, well known in most of the world, were a big plus. Some distributors only came to these meetings to rub shoulders with a genuine Marine hero and ask for his autograph, but McIlhenny refused to let them leave the room without at least two dozen bottles of Tabasco sauce.

Although not an instant international success, Tabasco sauce finally won over global customers. And by the mid-1970s, 40 percent of McIlhenny Co. sales were from non-U.S. markets. Tabasco's popularity was greatest in Japan, followed by Germany, Canada, Britain, Spain and Venezuela. To produce Tabasco sauce for these markets at the lowest possible cost, McIlhenny broke with the family's traditions and embraced a modern technique being implemented by many companies: he opened bottling plants in Venezuela, Spain and Mexico, among a few other places, to serve as central hubs to pack and distribute the product. While Avery Island would remain the home of Tabasco sauce's single manufacturing plant, the product would be bottled in numerous locations around the world.

It might seem out of character for Walter, usually so orthodox, to seize upon a concept this fresh. But the idea emerged from his Marine experiences. During the war, he led enormous movements of troops and equipment, which had to meet stringent budgetary and scheduling guidelines. From those exercises, McIlhenny observed that logistic networks were most fluid when critical materials were available locally and needn't be transferred over long distances. The new McIlhenny bottling plants ensured that the final product—frequently, the most expensive item to ship in a supply chain—was prepared solely in its sales region. By adjusting operations in this way, McIlhenny saved more than 50 percent on transportation and labor costs for overseas activities.

McIlhenny could have saved even more by also building facilities to manufacture Tabasco sauce away from Avery Island. But that would have radically altered the company's business model, and Walter was unwilling to consider such a step. Oddly enough, however, he would soon be induced to employ a tactic a great deal more disruptive than that.

Tabasco sauce revenue ballooned to aproximately $40 million in 1985, a thirteen-fold spike since Walter was named president in 1949. With that performance, he successfully stilled the demands for higher dividends by McIlhenny family members. But the upsurge in sales had an unanticipated consequence. For the first time since very early in the company's history, McIlhenny Co. was unable to manufacture enough Tabasco sauce to fulfill demand.

Harvesting Tabasco peppers is a labor-intensive process, requiring about five pickers per acre. As McIlhenny Co.'s production requirements spiraled upward to as many as 60 million bottles per year, thousands of new acres of chilies had to be planted on Avery Island. In turn, tens of thousands of additional pepper pickers were needed to gather the crops. At a salary of 10 cents per pound of pepper, these jobs proved impossible to fill. McIlhenny tried hiking wages a bit to lure pickers, but to maintain 25 percent plus profit margins—especially on overseas sales, which were more costly to ship and distribute—he couldn't raise compensation to a desirable level.

The result, first felt around 1975, was an acute shortage of aged pepper mash. Confronted with the unacceptable prospect of leaving orders unfilled, Walter made what he later termed "a terrible decision," one that he dearly regretted, but was forced into by circumstances, he believed: he compensated for the inventory deficit by using mash that had not fermented in casks for the full three years. Some of it, in fact, was only two or two and a half years old. To justify this step, a radical departure from the way Tabasco sauce had been made for more than a century, Walter promised to always age the mash for at least "three warm seasons." That could include a temperate spring and summer in the same year. To further amplify the supply, Walter secretly added to the pulp non-Tabasco peppers purchased from U.S. growers. Thus produced, the sauce was patchy and thick, its taste was pungent but not smoothly so, and even Walter McIlhenny was heartbroken by his own actions.

"It tore him up," said a former McIlhenny manufacturing supervisor who worked closely with Walter. "His grandfather's recipe had been protected for over a hundred years and he, probably the most traditional of all the McIlhennys, had dishonored it. He couldn't explain it to himself in a way that made it acceptable."

What a Gordian knot Walter faced: the family business had to continually expand to meet its present sales obligations, but by doing so it could not produce enough mash to satisfy its promise to its past. Walter's solution, of course, was only a short-term fix anyway. With the dearth of pepper pickers in Louisiana, in a short time he would exhaust the surplus mash created by his program. One way or another, McIlhenny had to find a means to pick many more Tabasco peppers quickly.

The answer came from an unlikely source. A few years before the pepper mash shortfall, Nelson Rockefeller, then governor of New York, had approached Walter with an intriguing offer. Rockefeller had a coffee farm in Venezuela, which operated six months out of the year. He suggested that Walter try growing Tabasco chilies there when the land was fallow, putting his idle agricultural managers and farmhands to work.

The connection between the Rockefellers and the McIlhennys dated back to the early twentieth century, when Edward McIlhenny and his friend Charles Willis Ward, a wealthy East Coast birdwatcher and flower enthusiast, hatched a plan to convert a series of islands in the Gulf of Mexico into Louisiana's first wildlife refuges. Seeking funding, the pair approached philanthropist Olivia Sage, the widow of industrialist Russell Sage. It took some coaxing, but she eventually purchased a 75,000-acre island in Vermilion Bay and deeded it to the state as a sanctuary.

Sage introduced McIlhenny to John D. Rockefeller Jr. In 1914, after a series of letters, John D., through the Rockefeller Foundation, agreed to take over a portion of McIlhenny's $212,000 mortgage on 86,000 acres in the Gulf. Five years later, that property was transferred to Louisiana and renamed the Rockefeller Wildlife Refuge, a seaside research center with 200 miles of canals and bayous and one of the most biologically diverse animal populations in the nation. To finalize this deal, McIlhenny had to overcome an early faux pas when he mistakenly called John D. by the surname "Rockfellow" in a note. But Rockefeller apparently never noticed, and the two families, while not close, have remained collegial. When Walter first heard Nelson Rockefeller's idea, he demurred.

According to McIlhenny lore, the Tabasco pepper's only home had been Avery Island soil—a narrative questioned, of course, by 1840s plantation owner Maunsel White, early pepper sauce rival Bernard Trappey and others. Walter didn't want to pollute the purity of the Tabasco line by planting the pepper anyplace else.

But the scarcity of pepper mash changed his mind. McIlhenny realized that acceding to Rockefeller's offer and, more broadly, growing Tabasco in perhaps many low-cost agricultural nations was his only hope of extricating the business from an untenable predicament. On balance, cultivating the pepper away from Avery Island was a far more acceptable break with McIlhenny tradition than continuing to compromise the Tabasco sauce recipe and putting out an inferior product. So in 1977, Walter hired Gene Jefferies to manage Latin American growing operations for the family business.

Jefferies was an inspired choice. A graduate of Arizona State University with a master's degree in agricultural economics, Jefferies had managed a highly productive team of farm development volunteers for the Peace Corps in Campo Grande, Brazil. Subsequently, he became an agricultural specialist for the IRI Research Institute in northeastern Brazil and then Venezuela, teaching local communities modern farming methods. When the IRI project lost its funding and Jefferies' position was terminated, he was told about the McIlhenny job by a friend who had learned of it through a contact at Louisiana State University.

Jefferies, to meet now, is a soft-spoken, tall, angular man with leathery skin, weathered by many hours in the sun. He exudes confidence, but humbly so—a style he borrowed from his days as a cowpoke and ranch hand, jobs he held prior to college at age twenty-five. Jefferies' years of experience with small farms south of the border, his prepossessing personality and his reputation as a responsible, fair-minded and organized overseer equipped him well for the job of exporting McIlhenny's culture to Latin American growers.

Walter placed two conditions on the Latin American plan: only real Tabasco peppers could be bred, and these peppers must be offspring, or close to it, of the original Tabasco seeds planted by Edmund, as it was believed were virtually all the peppers used in the sauce since the company was founded. These rules were relatively easy to satisfy. Rather than permit the Latin American farmers to propagate the seeds from one year to the next, Jefferies would send seeds from the Avery Island harvest to the growers, choosing from the clutch of prime Tabasco plants picked and set aside in a safe-deposit box each year by McIlhenny chief executives for their likeness to the original pepper.

The Rockefeller tract in Venezuela was the first Tabasco field in Latin America. But Jefferies rapidly added sites in Honduras, Panama, Haiti, the Dominican Republic, Colombia and Brazil. In each location, he hired local agricultural managers, who contracted with dozens and dozens of individual farmers—in Honduras, as many as 700—to grow the pepper. Every region had a receiving station, where the farmers brought the chilies after harvest. There the peppers were ground immediately—"Tabascos don't hold up for very long after being picked," Jefferies said—and placed into a hammer mill, in which they were mixed with about 8 percent salt. Finally, the blend was poured into plastic barrels.

"We kept it like that for two to six weeks," Jefferies said. "The mash was bubbling as the CO_2 gas was escaping. And once that settled down, we either put the mash into large shipping containers or stainless steel tankers, which hold about one hundred barrels, to be shipped to Avery Island and placed into the manufacturing process there."

Including fees to farmers, McIlhenny paid about 25 cents a pound for Tabascos grown in Honduras and a bit more in other Latin American locales, a tad higher than the company was offering to pay pickers in the United States at the time.

Before fully committing to this venture, McIlhenny and Jefferies considered using a mechanical harvester to pick peppers. But although useful for certain hardy peppers like jalapeños, automated equipment was disappointing in the Tabasco fields. The machine tended to rip apart the fragile Tabasco plant, and it couldn't tell a ripe pepper from one needing time to mature. More disturbing, because the mechanical harvester seemed to ruin as many peppers as it picked, it squeezed only two harvests out of a growing season before the field was played out; with manual labor, it's possible to get as many as six.

"The mechanical harvester would have cost us about sixty cents to pick a pound of peppers, so it didn't make sense," Jefferies said.

Jefferies knew that his loose-knit group of Latin American Tabasco farmers was anything but a permanent confederation, a thought that worried him quite a bit. Like most growers in poor nations, the agreements they made were only as good as the financial deal behind them. Jefferies was well aware that these farmers would drop the McIlhennys without any notice if they received a better offer, leaving the Tabasco business gasping again for raw materials.

To guard against this, Jefferies devised a novel payment arrangement. Considering that the Tabasco pepper had an unusually lengthy growing season—six months between planting and harvesting (two months in the hothouse and four months in the field)—Jefferies offered to pay the farmers an advance as soon as the crop was planted. And during harvest, he agreed to dole out additional payments based solely on monthly production reports. To make sure none of the growers were abusing his generosity, Jefferies and his agricultural managers often made spot visits to check the truthfulness of the farmers' planting and harvesting claims. Only McIlhenny proposed such flexible terms to Latin American farmers, who by and large couldn't easily afford to finance the crop themselves, especially with banks charging anywhere from 30 percent to 60 percent interest on loans. Jefferies' compassion for the farmers' conditions and his understanding of their financial requirements secured a dependable supply of cheap Tabasco peppers at a time when McIlhenny Co. was desperate for a stockpile. In turn, it could be said that Jefferies' actions rescued the brand, which was in danger of becoming so adulterated that the McIlhennys would have had to abandon their assertion of a unique, slow-fermenting process in the preparation of Tabasco sauce. Stripped of that distinction, the brand would inevitably lose its premium position and be indistinguishable from commodity pepper sauces on the market.

"When I came to work in 1977, McIlhenny still advertised the traditional three-year aging for peppers, but that wasn't true; in fact, we were down to about fourteen months inventory," Jefferies recalled. "We were buying cayenne peppers from New Mexico and mixing it with what Tabasco we had. We were buying a little Bahamian hot pepper from R.J. Reynolds Company in North Carolina, which was being harvested mechanically and brought down here to be blended. Those were dark days. When I left in 1998, thanks to the Latin American farmers, we had a four-year inventory of Tabasco mash."

Inside the McIlhenny family, the view of Jefferies' contribution is a bit less generous. As the McIlhennys frame it, Walter was responsible for bringing the family business back from the brink; at best, Jefferies played a supporting role. "Jefferies isn't a McIlhenny, so that automatically eliminates any hope of top billing for anything he did," said a McIlhenny relative who worked at the company when Jefferies was there. "In the family's version, Walter pulled all the strings; Jefferies just followed orders. But most of us realize that's not the case. Look, the way we were making Tabasco sauce in the 1970s was so dishonest that it could have destroyed a 100-year-old, consistently high-quality product, period. I don't want to be overly dramatic about this, but Jefferies may have saved the company."

Chapter 11

NEW IBERIA CONNECTION

The McIlhennys were delighted by the success of the Tabasco crop south of the border. Abundant inexpensive labor toiling in well-managed pepper fields was an irresistible combination to the family. Gradually, as it became apparent that the Latin American operations were reliable—more so than Avery Island's, because the Hispanic workers were unlikely to balk at the low pay—Walter McIlhenny transferred additional inventory to growers in Honduras, Costa Rica, Venezuela and Brazil. And by the mid-1980s, all of the peppers used directly in the preparation of Tabasco sauce were cultivated outside of Louisiana. Avery Island's fields were limited solely to the premium Tabasco plants that produced the high-quality, primordial seeds shipped each year to Latin America to grow the crop.

Although the decision to sharply curtail output on Avery Island was made after the pool of nearby applicants for jobs paying 10 cents a pound dried up, losing these positions nonetheless weighed heavily on a segment of the black community in New Iberia, where most of McIlhenny's Louisiana pepper pickers lived. In previous decades, generations of black New Iberians—hundreds at a time— found permanent employment on Avery Island. And while the work was difficult and the pay minimal, these pickers grew dependent on the financial stability that the McIlhennys offered and, in turn, contributed significantly to the success of the company town—even if they were not permitted to live there.

But with these jobs outsourced to less expensive regions, only a few dozen or so New Iberian pickers were still needed. Moreover, most of these local positions were temporary, staffed by day labor that had little contact with the McIlhennys. Consequently, the relationship between the McIlhennys and the pepper pickers—once so vital that Edward McIlhenny erected a Baptist church principally for them in hopes of wedding their identity more closely with the family and its business—was irretrievably severed.

In the streets of New Iberia, the memories of working with the McIlhennys are vivid, though. There is no shortage of stories—no scarcity of recollections, good and bad—about the bond that connected the community and the McIlhennys and what its passing has meant to the town and its residents. Many of McIlhenny's pepper pickers began life in the fields as teenagers, as Gladys V. did. Now forty-six, a divorced mother of two teenagers, Gladys didn't have to say that she had picked peppers for years; the appearance of her hands gave it away. Large, gray, soot-tinged blisters pocked her coffee-colored fingers. The blisters were firm and ingrained. "Peppers sting when you touch them, and if they burst they burn so bad that you want to lie down and cry," she said.

One morning in mid-August 1980, Gladys took the fifteen-minute ride from New Iberia to Avery Island in the ramshackle McIlhenny Co. school bus for the first time. She shared the bus with thirty of her neighbors—all, like Gladys, black. The others chattered about this and that, but Gladys barely spoke. Only twenty years old, she had never left her hometown and had no idea what to expect.

When the bus arrived at the Tabasco fields, Gladys stood on the bluff overlooking the chili plants, momentarily taken aback by the brilliant meadow of deep crimson, radiant enough to darken the hue of the sky and horizon. Her initial impulse was to run freely among the nearly perfect rows of incarnadine crops.

But minutes later, standing in the pepper fields she had admired from afar, the foolishness of her first impression became evident. Perilous, hot stalks, waist to shoulder level, the plants were menacing; she was overwhelmed by the heat and humidity. "Believe me," Gladys said. "The beauty was gone."

The day was interminable and taxing, worse than anything imaginable. Twelve hours spent hunched over searching for ever more hidden pieces of tiny fruit. Each minute seemed to last longer than the one before. Her back hurt; her fingers stung; from the hue of the plant, her eyes felt bloodshot.

Prior to being dispatched to the fields, the pickers were handed a "baton rouge," a red stick painted the color of a perfect Tabasco pepper—one whose complexion had completed its journey from yellow to green to bright red. The workers were instructed to pick only peppers matching the color of the stick. Stern warnings were issued to leave untouched any peppers not yet ripe. McIlhenny management hovered in the fields, primarily monitoring the productive pickers, who were given the best rows. Amateurs like Gladys were directed to skimpy bushes, guaranteeing that their wages would be low because workers were paid by how many pounds of peppers they picked.

At the end of each row, there were casks of water for drinking. "It tasted of stale, lukewarm pepper, because they gave us water out of old barrels that they had made the sauce in," recalled Michael Bell, who picked Tabasco chilies as a youth with his mother approximately the same time as Gladys did.

Bell's most indelible memory was of the McIlhenny foreman—"a guy named Ralph; big, with rolled-up sleeves, muscles like the tough guys I saw in comic books. Ralph carried this big stick and he walked around the fields and stuck it in our baskets. He wanted to make sure that we didn't have anything in there besides peppers, to make it look like we were working harder than we actually were."

At three in the afternoon, an old pickup truck trundled out to the Tabasco patch and slowly came to a halt in front of the workers. A McIlhenny—in recent times, one of the many cousins who work at the company as summer interns—stepped out of the cab and climbed on to the truck's bed, where the pickers had already lined up, their baskets of peppers in their hands.

One after another, the pickers handed their baskets of fruit to the field supervisor, who was stationed adjacent to the McIlhenny scion on the back of the truck. Wearing gloves, the foreman searched each basket, casually tossing out peppers that didn't make the grade. He put what remained on a scale and barked out the weight as if handling bagatelle and not the output of hard labor. McIlhenny counted the cash and handed the day's wages down to each picker. As the last picker was being paid, the school bus pulled up next to the truck. The workers, their denim clothes now dusty, their dew rags drenched with sweat, gingerly got on the bus for their return trip to New Iberia.

By 2000, the McIlhennys, struggling to find laborers for the fields, upped the salary to 60 cents a pound. An industrious worker, putting in a full day with few breaks, can pick eighty pounds or so—and take home about $50.

Remembering her first day, Gladys said, "Half of my peppers got thrown out of the basket, because they weren't ripe. I didn't know what I was doing; I just wanted to get the day over with. And standing there, watching the foreman cast aside a good portion of my work, was so disheartening and embarrassing. I hated that feeling and could only think, 'How could I let my life come to this.' I walked away with ten dollars and I swore I'd never come back to Avery Island. Obviously, I broke that promise. There aren't a lot of other places for me to work around here."

The black pepper pickers, now and in the past, predominantly live in New Iberia's Hopkins Street neighborhood, a scrum of slummy single- and two-family homes amid cheaply constructed, town-house-like public housing on narrow streets pocked with broken macadam. It's a harrowing place: upwards of 25 percent of families and 30 percent of individuals are below the poverty line, three times the national averages. About one-third of adults over thirty-five have not graduated from high school. Drug use and firearms are in plain view. And New Iberia recently passed an ordinance to outlaw carrying open containers of alcohol on the streets, mainly to stanch deadly nighttime brawls, a spectator sport in the Hopkins area.

Joe Lopez, unemployed with no prospects for work, exemplifies the lives led by former pepper pickers. A more trusted employee than most, Lopez didn't only pick peppers for the McIlhennys; he also planted and prepared the fields. For a long time, his father drove the school bus that transported the pepper workers to and from Avery Island. In his early fifties, Lopez lived in a featureless gray one-story house on Hopkins Street, which huddled directly behind a similarly nondescript home bordering a pebbled lot with heavy machinery. Through inheritance, Lopez owned both of these houses.

Dark-skinned and overweight, his breathing labored and stertorous, Lopez's expression was thoughtful, his coal-black eyes warm. A widower, he survived on disability checks because of his bad back, he said. Lopez had three children with his first wife. His second wife, also not working, had six with her previous husband; some of the children—the number changed weekly, Lopez joked—still lived at home.

Lopez had fond memories of his job with the McIlhennys; he was young and strong then. Working outdoors, even in the pepper fields, made him feel virile. Returning home with money in his pocket, no matter how meager, buoyed his self-respect. Picking peppers for the McIlhennys was an opportunity, he said ruefully, that doesn't exist anymore. "When I worked there, I felt like I was part of the family, so I worked hard and they treated me well in return," Lopez said. "It kept me off the streets and out of trouble. It gave me cash and something that seemed worthwhile to do every day. If I needed help—advances on my salary or sometimes personal advice—I could go into McIlhenny's offices and get it.

"It's not the same now. The pepper pickers come and go. Except for a few hard cores, it's a new group from day to day or week to week; they're nameless now to the McIlhennys."

The sound of children on bikes and an argument over a game of sandlot ball seeped through the shaded windows in the dark living room. Hopkins Street had changed considerably as well, Lopez said. "It gets worse with each new generation," he explained. "When I was a kid, there were stores of all kinds in this neighborhood and dance halls, a lot of business activity. They're mostly shut down because it's so unsafe. Dangerous things happen here, and it doesn't surprise anybody."

The McIlhennys have had ample social, political and commercial ties to New Iberia and Iberia Parish since the founding of the family business. They are by most accounts the largest private landowner in the parish and, hence, pay the highest property taxes. That distinction alone has afforded the McIlhennys valuable leverage in the region. Because of it, founder Edmund McIlhenny effortlessly convinced local authorities in 1886 to extend the Southern Pacific railway line from New Iberia to Avery Island, a bit of favoritism that slashed the fledgling Tabasco company's shipping expenses by half and arguably ensured the company's survival. Since then, McIlhenny Co. executives have had similar success in gaining Iberia Parish backing for beneficial dredging and widening projects linking the Port of Iberia and other Gulf channels with Avery Island's surrounding waterways.

The McIlhennys are longtime members of the Episcopal Church of the Epiphany in New Iberia, and many of their friends resided in the city. In addition, some of the McIlhenny children—chiefly the girls, who have generally been excluded from working in the family business—obtained their first jobs in New Iberia. And nearly all of McIlhenny's workers—not merely the pepper pickers but also the factory laborers who lived on Avery Island—came from New Iberia and had extended families there.

New Iberia—a town of 32,000 cast between New Orleans and Houston—would seem to be a conservative, buttoned-down community, a religious town with unusually high attendance at the

Edmund McIlhenny (1815–1890), founder of McIlhenny Co., sold the first bottle of Tabasco sauce in 1868 and ran the family business until his death. *Johannesburg Sunday Times*

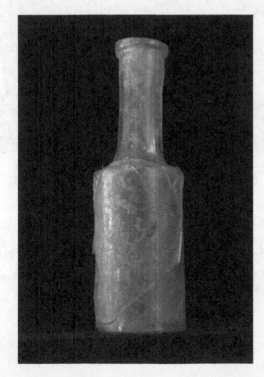

An 1870s vintage Tabasco bottle, the oldest ever found, was unearthed during an archaeological dig in 2002 at the Boston Saloon in Virginia City, Nevada. *Ronald M. James, Nevada State Historic Preservation Office*

Tabasco ads from the early 1900s.

Edward Avery McIlhenny (1872–1949), also known as "The Great White Father" by his workers, became president of McIlhenny Co. in 1906 and led the family business for 43 years.

BELOW: Edward Avery McIlhenny (right), posing with fellow legendary birder James Pond, built a bucolic worker's village on Avery Island. *Southwestern Louisiana Institute Photograph Albums in University Archives and Acadiana Manuscripts Collection, University of Louisiana at Lafayette*

A worker's home on Avery Island in the first half of the 20th century. A McIlhenny employee who likely was a domestic in the family's mansion is seated on the porch with a child. *Collection of the Louisiana State Museum*

An architect's rendering of a 1920 worker's home in Tango Village on Avery Island. *Library of Congress, Prints and Photographs Division, Historic American Buildings Survey/Historic American Engineering Record, Reproduction Number HABS LA,23-AVIS,2-B*

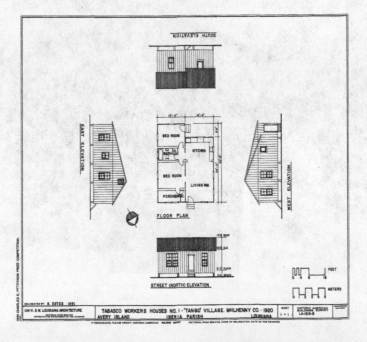

Live Oaks reflected in a
pond on Avery Island,
a photo taken by Edward
Avery McIlhenny.
State Library of Louisiana

LEFT: Pepper pickers in the
Tabasco fields on Avery Island.
State Library of Louisiana

BELOW: The Baptist church on
Avery Island, built by Edward
Avery McIlhenny primarily for
the company's black workers.
*Wetmaap (Wetland Education
Through Map and Aerial Photogra-
phy) a cooperative program
of the U.S. Geological Survey
National Wetlands Research
Center, Lafayette, LA and Chadron
State College, Chadron, NE*

The grave of Felicite, a Haitian servant honored as the foremost citizen of New Iberia, where most of McIlhenny's pepper pickers live, after singlehandedly nursing the town's sick and dying during a Yellow Fever epidemic in 1839. *Jeffrey Rothfeder*

The 900-year-old Buddha placed by Edward Avery McIlhenny on Avery Island in the mid-1930s in a setting of Live Oaks with Spanish moss and arches of wisteria. *Jeffrey Rothfeder*

Walter Stauffer McIlhenny (1910–1985), seen here circa 1945, was a World War II Marine hero known as Tabasco Mac before he became head of McIlhenny Co. in 1949, a job he held for 26 years. *Official Marine Corps Photo*

The Tabasco production line on Avery Island in 1961. *State Library of Louisiana*

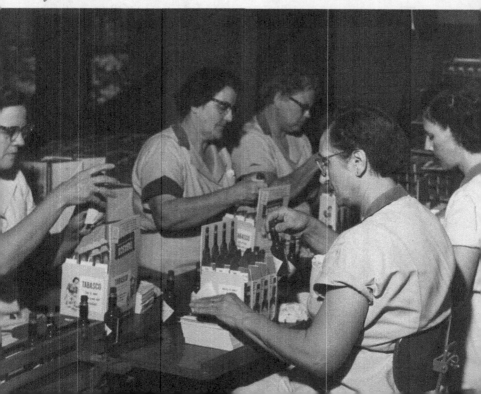

Tabasco peppers growing on Avery Island. *USDA Photo Research*

Paul McIlhenny (left), current CEO of McIlhenny Co., wrested the company back from its only non–McIlhenny family CEO in 1998. In this 2006 picture, he's talking to Cajun musician Joe Douglas. *Johannesburg Sunday Times*

three dozen or so churches of all denominations that dot the local landscape seemingly on every block. Hunting is popular, especially among the sizeable Cajun clans. And with scores of Iberia Parish's youth in the military, there is the distinct scent of patriotism in the flags hanging on doorways and the "Support Our Troops" decals on pickup trucks.

But examined more closely, the core of New Iberia's character is colored by an unexpected Bohemian streak. A number of the town's residents—even librarians and waitresses—claimed to be a painter, poet, photographer, folk artist, chronicler of southern weltanschauung or had ambitions of becoming one. Gay unions and vegetarianism, ideas that are taboo in much of Louisiana—a state described by one historian as south of the South—are openly practiced in New Iberia. While a majority of people in Iberia Parish—and, for that matter, Louisiana—votes Republican these days, New Iberia itself tilts Democrat.

In New Iberia, practically everybody speaks at least two languages, the influence of the multiple cultures that settled the city, a greater variety of immigrants than in any other section of the country, save perhaps New York. Before Anglo-Europeans and newly minted Americans arrived en masse in the early 1800s, Spanish, French, Cajuns, Caribbean blacks (many of them freed during the Haitian slave revolts) and Africans had already immigrated to New Iberia.

Each of these groups left a distinct imprint. In New Iberia's "historic" downtown, a two-mile stretch of quiet, lazy streets that sidesaddle the snakelike Bayou Teche and appear as if they would have been at home in the nineteenth century, many of the classical office buildings are built in double-balcony Spanish Colonial style. The village square, Bouligny Plaza, is dedicated to New Iberia's founder, Spanish lieutenant colonel Francisco Bouligny, who incorporated the city in 1779. The stores are owned by Cajun families like the Guidrys and the Babineaux.

Street and building names continue to honor the Duperiers, the French family that came to New Iberia via Haiti, whose plantation eventually encompassed much of the town. One of the best restaurants is run by Miss Brenda Placide, a Caribbean black. Little more than a shack across from the railroad, it features Louisiana soul-food-cum-Cajun-cuisine: gumbo, fried chicken, fish and crawfish étouffée. And a half dozen drive-through daiquiri bars—yes, people order drinks from the driver's seat of their automobiles—slake the region's thirst for the chosen drink of the West Indies.

This multiculturalism, along with New Iberia's relative seclusion—the town is a good two hours by car from any big city—bred a rare eccentricity, an acceptance of different ideas, customs and off-center behavior rarely found in the South. And considering the McIlhennys' steady interaction with New Iberia and its people since setting down roots on Avery Island, it's hardly a surprise that the family reflected the region's defining traits by combining the unconventional with the old-fashioned in the Tabasco business. Indeed, it could be said that the McIlhennys would not have been able to practice their oddly anachronistic brand of commerce anyplace else but in the iconoclast's isolation of the Iberia Parish bayous.

Curiously enough, a close friend of E.A. McIlhenny, the artist Weeks Hall, stands out to this day as perhaps the very best illustration of New Iberia's unorthodoxy. The final heir of the Weeks family, one of the preeminent antebellum sugarcane planters in the region, Hall antipodally dubbed himself the "last of the nigger lovers." Belying this description, however, Hall spent the final thirty-plus years of his life in the bedraggled family mansion on three acres in the center of New Iberia, painstakingly restoring it to the grand Classical Revival estate it was before the Civil War, when it housed hundreds of slaves. At Hall's death in 1958, Shadows-on-the-Teche, as the house is known, was converted into a museum and remains the foremost tourist destination in town.

Hall had been a painter of some promise early in his life, but by the 1940s he was an alcoholic and had lost his enthusiasm for art. Instead, Hall's passion was plying literary guests like Henry Miller, Gertrude Stein and Sherwood Anderson with plenty of brandy and then entertaining them by bouncing light off of still lifes and landscapes in the Shadow's angular, cavernous rooms to create shapes and patterns on the walls. And when alone, Hall could be found standing guard in his front yard, behind his bamboo cane fence and live oaks, wearing nothing but undershorts with a bottle of liquor in his hand, yelling obscenities at the garden-club ladies who had traveled by bus to look at his oversized estate.

In 1949, Hall's unpredictable behavior took another twist: he convinced a town priest to bury jazz cornetist Bunk Johnson, a black, impoverished New Iberia resident and one of Louis Armstrong's earliest teachers, in the otherwise lily-white Weeks family plot.

By placing Bunk Johnson for eternity next to a family of slave owners, Weeks may have been taking a page from the unusual final accommodations of New Iberia's most celebrated resident, a black Haitian servant named Félicité. In 1839, a yellow fever epidemic swept across New Iberia claiming the lives of half of the community. One of the earliest victims was Dr. Benoni Neal, the town's leading physician. Other doctors succumbed soon after. With no one to administer to New Iberia's citizens, Félicité took it upon herself to nurse the sick and dying. Miraculously, she never contracted the disease.

A plaque praising Félicité's stands prominently in front of New Iberia's civic center, the only person so honored. It says, in part: "[She] closed the eyes of the dead and wept over their graves. . . . She was an angel of mercy in a time of pestilence. Her name shall not be allowed to drop into oblivion."

Defying the rules of caste, at Félicité's death in February 1852, "this old colored maid," as local accounts called her, lay in state at her former master's home. On the day of her burial at St. Peter's Cemetery in the heart of the city, all businesses in New Iberia closed for the funeral and the entire town attended. When they passed on, Félicité's owners were entombed in the same crypt as her. Such mixing of the races, especially involving death and the hereafter, was—and still is—unheard of in Louisiana.

Michael Bell, a civil rights activist who has recently devoted himself to promoting the memory of Félicité, said that a clear connection can be made between the black maid's place in New Iberia history and E.A. McIlhennys' unlikely response to the racial divide in the 1940s. "Félicité's life is so uniquely a story of New Iberia—it's full of black pride and a rare degree of tolerance for it in a southern town—that no one doubts Edward McIlhenny's decision to desegregate Avery Island would have brought opprobrium down on him, no matter how powerful he was, had Félicité not already been adopted as New Iberia's most important citizen," said Bell.

Yet despite the many aspects of New Iberia's character that can be found in the McIlhenny family—and notwithstanding the strong social and economic bonds linking the McIlhennys to Iberia Parish—the McIlhennys have generally neglected the area's poverty; throughout its history, the family business has contributed little to diminishing the privation. For a long time, this disinterest could be dismissed as routine. Until at least the 1980s, most companies had generally ignored the underprivileged in their backyards—even those on the payroll. But in the past two decades or so, these attitudes have conspicuously changed in corporate America and around the world as well. Instead of indifference, CEOs—particularly family business owners, who are not only employers but lifelong residents of the communities housing their headquarters—have generally assumed a broader social obligation to the towns that support them, their families and their companies with natural resources, a labor pool, education, infrastructure and quality of life.

Unlike other companies with annual sales below $1 billion who undertake social responsibility efforts, McIlhenny Co.'s idea of giving back to the community, as cataloged on the company's Web site, has been curiously self-serving. In one case, the company asked marketing departments at five black universities in Louisiana—Grambling State, Xavier and Dillard among them—to have their brightest students put together a campaign with "innovative ways to present information to African-American families about Tabasco sauce . . . [and to] create acceptance, build loyalty, and generate

(Tabasco) usage in eating and cooking activities," McIlhenny said on its Web site. The students received a minimal stipend for their hard work and, according to McIlhenny, "much of the research, strategies and ideas they generated have now been incorporated into [Tabasco] marketing."

Other McIlhenny "charitable" programs included a cookbook award, with a first-place prize of $2,500 earmarked for the author's favorite charity, and an annual contest to choose the U.S. fireman who invented the best-tasting dish with Tabasco sauce in it. In these and the few other McIlhenny philanthropic efforts, the company never passed up the opportunity to promote its flagship product; virtually all of the family's charitable programs are branded with the Tabasco logo.

McIlhenny Co.'s clumsy attempts at charity were in large part a reflection of what made the family's business so successful. When corporate generosity can be combined with product marketing, as the McIlhennys have chiefly done, the McIlhennys deem it worth considering. Otherwise, corporate giving seems to be a diversion in search of a reward.

Chapter 12

HOT ENOUGH FOR YOU?

Walter McIlhenny died on June 22, 1985, just days after suffering a stroke. A bachelor, only the family business survived him. He left it healthier than it had been some thirty-six years earlier when he became president. At his death, sales of Tabasco sauce, racing toward $50 million a year, were at record highs in both the United States and overseas. And thanks to the opening of Latin American Tabasco fields, the pepper shortage was only a memory. Perhaps most importantly for the McIlhennys, Walter had held the family together, providing ample annual dividends to the cluster of McIlhenny heirs so that the company could be passed intact to the fourth generation.

But to whom in that group? Like his predecessors (except his father, John Avery), Walter passed away on the job. And as was the case before when McIlhenny presidents died, a clear-cut succession plan did not exist. No McIlhenny had been designated to be next in line and trained in the marketing, management or manufacturing skills required to run the family business. Generally, it was assumed that the McIlhenny family member who had the greatest familiarity with the company would be handed the top job.

That's a dangerous way to pick a company president, and more and more family businesses—fearful of management becoming overly inbred and not sufficiently knowledgeable about business trends and ideas—have developed strict policies against such an approach. And yet, rejecting this notion, the McIlhennys roll the dice with each chief executive and constantly confront this question: What if the McIlhenny heir picked to run the company doesn't possess the keen commercial instincts of Edmund, Edward or Walter? The lack of a McIlhenny succession plan belies the fact that with every new president the family business—its external environment as well as its internal obligations—becomes increasingly complex and difficult to manage, making it acutely necessary that there be a positive outcome each time this question is faced. Indeed, at Walter's death, McIlhenny Co. was about to enter the most turbulent period of its history—which continues to this day—during which the survival of the family business would again be put to the test.

More a result of boardroom politics than anything else, Edward "Ned" Simmons, Edward McIlhenny's grandson, succeeded Walter as head of the Tabasco company. Pauline "Polly" McIlhenny, the first child of Edward and Mary, was Ned's mother; his father was Fisher Simmons, a Colorado businessman who died in 1941 when Ned was twelve. With a degree in zoology from Tulane, Ned Simmons was another in the line of McIlhenny executives with no marketing or consumer goods expertise.

Although fifty-six years old upon taking over the reins at McIlhenny Co. in 1985, Simmons's maturity couldn't make up for his limited management background. Walter had kept his own counsel when he ran the family business, and Simmons wasn't prepared for how multilayered the job of chief executive was. He never quite mastered the combination of intuition and analysis that guides successful top managers, and he had little patience for the rigors of decision making—particularly the process of having to carefully weigh choices based on the impact of all possible outcomes.

As the Tabasco company grew unyielding to easy solutions, Simmons seemed to disengage from the company. "His style was benign to almost hands off," said a McIlhenny vice president who worked with Simmons. "It was like he wasn't enthusiastic about running the business."

This was precisely the wrong moment for management indifference. For the first time since McIlhenny took full ownership of the word Tabasco in 1918, there were dozens, if not hundreds, of companies competing against the Tabasco brand. Hot sauce and chili salsa—prior to the mid-1980s, unknown fare save for McIlhenny's product—had suddenly seized the fancy of the mainstream public. And Tabasco, the originator of the flavor, was under attack from multiple parapets.

Food historians attribute the unexpected popularity of so-called Tex-Mex pepper condiments in the United States to the increasing interest in natural, vegetarian and low-fat foods. Traditionally, in most cultures, "the heavier the dependence on plant or vegetable foods, the more pronounced the seasonings; the heavier the consumption of animal foods, the less pronounced the seasonings," wrote Elisabeth Rozin in *The Primal Cheeseburger*. "Those cuisines that clearly demonstrate a highly spiced or complex seasoning profile—Southeast Asia, India, Africa, Mexico—all have long relied on high-plant, low-meat diets."

In other words, as the American diet became health conscious, the foods we chose to eat needed spicing up—a lot of spicing up—to enjoy in large doses. "The unique stimulation [that pungent chilies] provide is an important compensation for foods that are somehow less satisfying, less perfect when eaten unseasoned," Rozin explained.

The hot condiments flooding the market found a perfect outlet in a separate food-related trend sweeping the nation: gourmet stores carrying exotic but wholesome products from smaller manufacturers, usually not available in major supermarkets. Chili sauce was an ideal fit.

By 1989, thirty-five manufacturers in Louisiana alone produced roughly a hundred different brands of hot sauce. And there were any number of companies with similar ambitions sprouting up in Texas, New Mexico, California and Arizona—even Vermont and Massachusetts. These pepper sauce entrepreneurs knew that they couldn't compete with McIlhenny Co. on quality. None had the inclination or the financial backing to ferment their pepper mash for one year, much less three years. In addition, McIlhenny controlled the distribution channels into traditional groceries so the start-up brands would not be able to make significant headway there; their physical shelf space for the foreseeable future would predominantly lie in gourmet or natural foods retailers. (Some years later, the Internet would play a big role in their marketing efforts.) Consequently, with few other sales options, the new products were mostly targeted at the extreme, niche customers in McIlhenny's universe.

If McIlhenny Co. viewed the typical Tabasco sauce consumer as daring but tempered by good taste, McIlhenny's competitors tried to attract a freewheeling, undisciplined caricature of these customers—people they called chiliheads. "That's the kind of person who likes roller coasters, fast cars, and stays up late looking for excitement in his life," said Chris Schlesinger, the Cambridge, Massachusetts-based manufacturer of Inner Beauty hot sauce, a wild concoction that consists of very hot chopped habaneros, mangoes, cheap yellow mustard, brown sugar, and vinegar. "It's benign masochism; they experience danger through our hot sauce without actually being in it."

Chiliheads are drawn primarily to the red pepper's perilous heat, manufacturers like Schlesinger maintain; metaphorically, and perhaps literally, they are addicted to the pain and pleasure of capsaicin, the alkaloid responsible for the pungent taste of Tabasco and similar peppers. It's believed to be an irresistible combination: the severe burning sensation of chilies lassoing the brain until it releases endorphins that counteract the discomfort—a high-octane yin and yang that some researchers contend results in a feeling of euphoria. To tap this market, manufacturers leapfrogged each other with spicy claims, offering unabashedly diabolical and sinister condiments to whet the piquant palate. And to back their assertions, they exhumed the sole measurement that could vouch for the potency of capsaicin in their products: the oddly contrived Scoville unit.

Wilbur Lincoln Scoville is not the sort of person you would normally link with adventurous gastronomical tastes like hot sauce and chili peppers. A skinny-necked, ungainly, reclusive chemist who lived in the early twentieth century, he looks positively dyspeptic in his photos. Yet due to a relatively minor experiment, Scoville's name, which would have been long forgotten by now, comes up practically any time the pungency of chilies is argued.

In 1912, Scoville, forty-seven at the time, worked for the pharmaceutical company Parke-Davis in Detroit. During this period, drugmakers were keenly interested in the potential medicinal properties of capsaicin. For centuries, South American tribes had successfully used capsaicin as a pain reliever, a fumigant and curiously a digestive aid (presumably, it is now believed, because capsaicin numbs the nerve endings in gastric sores). The hope was to transform these homeopathic cures into modern medicines.

But pharmacologists inevitably encountered the same roadblock upon attempting to design capsaicin-based treatments: the level of capsaicin in individual peppers varied so greatly—this was true even among chilies of the same species—that consistently predicting the potency from one unit to the next of products manufactured from these plants was impossible. Scoville encountered this obstacle while working on Heet, the muscle-ache salve. "The pharmacist cannot, by specifying a certain species of Capsicum (the genus of most chilies), be sure thereby of securing the most active medicinally," Scoville wrote in a report to the *Journal of the American Pharmaceutical Association*. A method for accurately measuring the pungency of capsaicin in a chili was desperately needed for the development of capsaicin-based treatments to progress, Scoville asserted.

Initially, Scoville thought this problem could be solved easily with recently discovered methods for extracting and comparing the chemical content of elements. But he was quickly disappointed. Unlike many alkaloids, capsaicin doesn't readily react with other chemicals. Using a chemical catalyst to gauge capsaicin levels, as Scoville had hoped to do, wasn't practical.

Scoville grew obsessed with finding an answer. At Parke-Davis, he wrote and rewrote variations on an array of formulas; at home, he daydreamed about the problem perpetually. Finally, after months of wrestling with the dilemma, Scoville jiggered a method to measure capsaicin so rudimentary as to be laughable. Indeed, he rejected this idea numerous times, but kept coming back to it, and ultimately concluded that there simply wasn't a more sophisticated way to determine the heat level of peppers.

The crudest—and most dubious—aspect of Scoville's system was the tasting apparatus he chose: the human tongue. Instantly, this got him into trouble with some colleagues, who complained that the tongue was too subjective to be useful for scientific calculations. Something more mechanical was needed, they said. Scoville responded that no device could identify the presence of capsaicin so well. "Physiological tests are tabooed in some quarters, yet when the tongue is sensitive to less than a millionth of a [capsaicin] grain, it certainly has an advantage," Scoville said.

Pressing ahead despite his critics, Scoville soaked three varieties of hot peppers—Japan, Zanzibar and Mombasa—in alcohol overnight to separate the capsaicin from the chili. He then added sweetened water to each of these extracts and repeatedly sampled them until the pungency of the capsaicin had been diluted to the point that his tongue couldn't detect its presence any longer. It took a 30,000 to 1 ratio of sweetened water to capsaicin before the pungency of the Japanese chili was imperceptible. Consequently, Scoville awarded the Japanese pepper a rating of 30,000 Scoville heat units. The Zanzibar required nearly twice as much sweetened water before it was sufficiently weakened; it received 50,000 Scoville units. And the Mombasa was the spiciest of the three peppers, breaking the 100,000 Scoville unit barrier.

Though the test lacked scientific rigor, Scoville units were a god-send for pharmacologists experimenting with capsaicin-based treatments and for manufacturers producing these products. With these readings capsaicin of a specific strength could be called for in a formula with reasonable confidence of reliably producing the desired heat range. To make Scoville results more precise, researchers often asked five people, instead of one, to test for capsaicin levels in a pepper and then averaged their responses.

The Scoville system had one expensive flaw, however. After a few rounds of pepper tasting, most people lost the ability to determine whether a drop of water was more or less pungent than the prior one before. So new groups of tasters—fresh tongues, as the pharmacologists called them—had to be constantly convened.

Scoville units, rudimentary but accurate, silenced the naysayers. Feted as a savant in the pharmaceutical and chemical communities, Wilbur Scoville was honored with citations and awards. Pharmacologists anticipated that Scoville's invention would unleash a glut of pepper-derived treatments. But his celebrity was short-lived. Within a decade or so, Scoville's system merited nary a mention. Though the technique was still plausible, the promise of capsaicin as a medicinal chemical had faded.

Fast-forward to the 1980s. The chili craze is in full swing, and Scoville ratings have been rediscovered. Anxious to prove their spicy bona fides, manufacturers of hot and hotter products began to conduct hundreds and hundreds of Scoville tests around the country on all manner of piquant sauces and peppers. Jobs for tasters were at a premium, with pay scales at double and triple minimum wage.

Rescued from obscurity, Wilbur Scoville became the darling of the chiliheads. They avidly relished each fresh high-water mark in ever-escalating Scoville readings; these mounting numbers were testament to their fearless eating habits and their daredevil disregard for pain. Newsletters devoted to Scoville tests and increasingly outlandish pepper sauce piquancy claims were published; within a decade or so, Web sites would appear in which chili lovers would argue over the validity of the latest Scoville ratings, while in other places on the Internet pictures of Scoville and even his grandchildren were lovingly displayed; and at fiery-foods.com, chili expert Dave DeWitt created a coveted annual Scovie award for the best hot sauces, salsas and pepper-based recipes. In an unlikely turn of events, Scoville was once again, decades after his death, the king of capsaicin.

"The name of Dr. Wilbur remains on the tongue of every chili-head, as we boast about our latest foray into the Scoville zone," said Canadian pepper fanatic Ian Chadwick, without a hint of forced solemnity.

By the 1990s, virtually all peppers had been tested and a Scoville hierarchy was established. (In most chili labs, the traditional primitive Scoville test had generally been replaced by high-performance liquid chromatography, a computerized tool that "visualizes" the amount of heat in capsaicin extract by exposing the alkaloid to a light beam and measuring its fluorescence. The outcome, nonetheless, was translated into Scoville units.)

The cherry pepper braced the bottom rung of the scale with a rating of 100 Scoville units; the jalapeño and the chipotle earned 2,500 to 5,000 units; the Tabasco came in at 30,000 to 50,000 units; and the chiltepin, the tiny, berrylike pepper that grows wild throughout Central and South America and is believed to be the primogenitor of all chilies, reached as high as 100,000 units.

Until recently, the Red Savina habanero, an evil-looking bloodred pepper with a daggerlike point, was considered to be the hottest chili in the world, at upwards of 500,000 Scoville units. But in 2000, a team at an agricultural laboratory in India claimed that the local Naga Jolokia had topped the Red Savina with an unheard of Scoville rating of 855,000. Although initially few believed that any chili, particularly this orange, wrinkled, febrile pepper from Asia, could compete with the mighty habanero, extensive testing over many years finally convinced the skeptics. Indeed, in a current round of laboratory results, the Naga Jolokia—this one grown in New Mexico—exceeded the original assertions made for it. Its Scoville rating was, remarkably, over 1 million.

The ratings of the peppers themselves are merely a sideshow to the real Scoville frenzy, which pits the sauces made from these peppers against each other. Routinely the newer hot sauce companies combine multiple types of peppers or add capsaicin extracts to their brands, hoping to achieve the very highest Scoville ratings possible, readings that skyrocket well beyond those of individual chilies. Outrageous examples of this heated competition are on display annually at the Fiery Foods convention, usually held in the Southwest. The McIlhennys never participate in the event—they fear that their presence would by association legitimize their upstart rivals—but virtually all of McIlhenny's chilihead competitors can be found there. Once a sparsely attended affair with two dozen or so sleepy exhibitors, lately it has housed upwards of 300 companies offering hundreds of products to thousands of visitors from across the country, some of whom have traded in their prized vacation time to attend. It would hardly be a stretch to suggest that the Winnebago company could take pictures of the convention's parking lot for a product brochure.

At a Fiery Foods show in Albuquerque, New Mexico, Blair Lazar, wearing a T-shirt that said, "Blair's Death Sauce. . . . since 1989," stood at a prominent booth near the front of the exhibition hall hawking a product called 5A.M. Special Edition. An unfathomable 5 million Scoville units, it was pure capsaicin extract in a bottle. The seal on the lid was a baleful melted blend of white and platinum Italian wax with a human skull peeking through, its face contorted into the demented look of a man consigned forever to burn in Hades. A bottle of 5A.M. cost $100. Its warning label left no room for confusion: "Use Extreme Caution! This is NOT a sauce! This product must be used as an ingredient only!" Said Lazar, "If you survive, you'll feel alive."

Dave DeWitt, the organizer of the show, said he had to take out a $2 million liability insurance policy because the hottest of the sauces were so toxic. He also insisted that exhibitors let people sample the sauces on the end of a toothpick only. "One company didn't listen and a man put a whole potato chip slobbered with hot sauce in his mouth; he fainted right away on the floor," DeWitt said. "There's been spontaneous vomiting and dizziness. I'd like to ban the superhot sauces, but it's a big part of the business."

Clearly, in the past couple of decades, the once relatively stable market, dominated by the sharp elbows and understated marketing of the McIlhennys, has become a free-for-all with rambunctious participants like J. P. Davis, whose booming, circus-barker voice was louder than anyone else's at DeWitt's convention. "You want to see a grown man weep and a demure lady sweat?" he bellowed, pointing to a bottle of his sauce, Tejas Tears. On the label was a woman's face that looked like a fright mask; she was screaming, and tears in the form of chili peppers were running down her cheek. Above her was the slogan: "It's hot enough to make you cry."

"I invented it, because I couldn't find a sauce strong enough for my taste buds," Davis said.

He was dressed in a Hawaiian shirt and casual khakis. How Davis got here was typical of the recent-vintage hot sauce manufacturers, who were frequently at aimless points in their lives when they read or heard something to persuade them that their future was in chilies. In the late 1980s, Davis was a bartender in Austin, Texas—"I was mostly unemployed and broke," he said. A friend told him about a local chili convention where cash prizes were awarded for the best hot sauce.

Davis needed the money and was hooked on spicy foods—nothing was too pungent for his palate. Confident in his knowledge of chili-head preferences, Davis entered the contest. Over a weekend, he experimented with numerous recipes and ended up with Tejas Tears—an incendiary mixture of habaneros, carrots, onions, water, vinegar, lime juice, garlic and canola oil. Davis poured five gallons of the sauce into sixty-four ten-ounce soda bottles.

Davis lost the challenge, but sold his entire inventory at the convention, netting nearly $500—more than he had in the bank. Flush for the first time in quite a while, Davis continued to manufacture the item and peddle it at farmer's markets. Now, two decades later,

Tejas Tears is the flagship product in a line including chipotle sauce and pestos, sold nationwide via the Internet.

"Everybody here has a similar story," Davis said. "We're a bunch of little lonely accidental family businesses. Many of us are still making the recipes in kitchens at home."

One of the more crowded booths at the show was called Hot Shots, run by Charlotte, North Carolina, pepper sauce middleman Dave Lutes, who distributed 10,000 cases a year of the most ultrahot sauces he could get his hands on. Some of his products—such as Ground Zero, Cyanide D.O.A. and Sudden Death—were so lethal that Lutes asked customers to sign a waiver, releasing him from liability in case of injury or death after ingesting the sauce. And Lutes also carried what he called a fire extinguisher—an item called Burn Away—that could be sprayed on skin scalded by hot condiments.

"Do you want to see the spiciest sauce of them all?" Lutes asked, holding up a bottle of Da Bomb—The Final Answer. With its black label containing a drawing of an amateurish cartoonlike missile that had nosedived into a field of conventional-looking skulls and crude writing that said, "Quest for the hottest ends here," Da Bomb didn't look overly menacing. But the ingredients were nothing short of playing with fire: habaneros, capsaicin extract, apricot nectar, mustard flour, garlic, allspice and spices. "That's 1.5 million Scovilles," Lutes said, smiling broadly.

With so many new manufacturers joining the extreme wing of the hot sauce business, it has been difficult for any one of these start-ups to profit from their products. The manufacturer of Bayou Butt Burner boasted of selling 10,000 bottles a year. McIlhenny, by contrast, makes 600,000 bottles of Tabasco sauce a day.

"If Butt Burner is two or three dollars a bottle wholesale, well, just add it up—10,000 bottles a year doesn't net you a lot of money," Lutes said. "Of course, many of the small manufacturers now have multiple lines, so they're making more than that. And if they develop the recipes in their homes, farm out the manufacturing and sell their products over the Web, they can keep their overhead pretty low. But look at it this way: If we weren't here, we'd be at a Star Trek convention or buying comic books or driving a truck. Selling chili sauce beats that."

Heat may be the Holy Grail of chiliheads, but not so for the McIlhennys. The long fermentation process used in the preparation of Tabasco sauce and its carefully chosen ingredients are designed to moderate the spiciness of the product, articulating the pepper's flavor without enflaming it.

"The first thing that you taste is the salt and vinegar, then the pepper creates a kind of emotion that starts juices flowing," said Paul Prudhomme, the emblematic Cajun chef, who rode the recent wave of chili mania to fame. Prudhomme makes a brand of pepper sauce under his own name but still prefers Tabasco for many of his recipes. "Chilies elongate the taste. You swallow them and get the heat as well as the residual flavors. But too much spice destroys the palate that the pepper is meant to indulge."

That Edmund McIlhenny instinctually navigated a nearly flawless balance between heat and flavor when he invented Tabasco sauce is either dumb luck or yet another indication of his commercial genius. McIlhenny relied on intuition, not analysis, and a small group of ex-slaves and close friends to fashion the flavor they hoped people would find pleasing in a pepper sauce. Many years later, the Scoville test offered a statistical explanation for what McIlhenny achieved with no more than a hunch: his recipe in fact dampened the Scoville level in the Tabasco pepper, which would have been excruciating to eat raw. Or, in Scoville terms, Tabasco sauce rates aproximately 5,000 units—quite spicy, but one-tenth as hot as the Tabasco pepper itself.

This distinction, though, between Tabasco sauce and products like Blair's Death Sauce and Da Bomb—seemingly an advantage for the McIlhennys—proved somewhat less than beneficial. Though few start-up brands in the late 1980s and early 1990s were able to break McIlhenny's commanding grip on national supermarket chains, their strength in gourmet- and natural-foods shops hindered McIlhenny's attempts to expand its market share, even as interest in chili peppers escalated. In a period that should have been ideal for Tabasco sales, the racy tone set by manufacturers of chilihead products made McIlhenny's brand appear old-fashioned by comparison, missing the prerequisite pizzazz demanded by the hip hot sauce new breed.

Tabasco sauce faced an additional threat. A handful of national brands—some of which had been in existence for decades, though with very little consumer attention—tried to enliven their products by claiming they were a milder, tastier and inexpensive alternative to McIlhenny's pepper sauce; in essence, these companies wooed discount-conscious consumers who had unadventurous palates— those non-chiliheads who possibly had avoided Tabasco in the past, but did not want to be left out of the hot pepper craze. "McIlhenny is not much flavor, more heat," argued Terry Hanes, chief operations officer of Baumer Foods, in 1993. Baumer manufactures Crystal Hot Sauce. "Our product has one-fourth the heat level, and a lot more flavor."

Thus, portrayed as too mild for the chiliheads and excessively hot for the cautious, Tabasco sauce was sandwiched between two distinctly powerful marketing ideas, resulting in a troubling trend: from 1989 to 1992, Tabasco's sales growth flattened and its market share dropped five percentage points to 27.5 percent. Meanwhile, McIlhenny's rivals were moving in the opposite direction. During that time, Crystal Pepper Sauce and Bruce Foods' Louisiana brand each gained 2 percentage points in market share to 10.3 percent and 7.3 percent, respectively.

Walter McIlhenny's successor, Ned Simmons, was eager to reverse this course. With the fourth generation in charge of the family business, the number of McIlhenny heirs had swelled to roughly 100, twice the number of people that had relied on Walter for steady dividends. To satiate the financial needs of this large group, Simmons believed he must choose from two unpalatable options, both of which in all likelihood would cannibalize the Tabasco brand: produce a pungent, expensive pepper sauce that could take aim at the chilihead brands in gourmet markets or, alternately, manufacture a product able to compete against the discounters.

Simmons opted for the latter. He reasoned that efforts to build sales of a premium brand in specialty shops across the globe would absorb enormous amounts of resources while at best generating only incremental revenue, which would barely register on McIlhenny's top line for many years. By contrast, to sell a discounted and perhaps milder version of Tabasco would involve a campaign in supermarkets, where McIlhenny had experience and relationships and where, because of scale, instantly substantial revenue gains were possible.

If Simmons's choice could not be easily faulted, his execution was remarkable only in its foolishness. To expand McIlhenny's product line beyond Tabasco—and into the discount arena—for the first time in its history, Simmons incomprehensibly acquired Trappey & Sons, the New Iberia company that Edward Avery McIlhenny had left virtually for dead after seemingly endless litigation over the use of the word *Tabasco* on pepper sauce labels.

In 1948, with the nearly fifty-year Tabasco trademark war over, Trappey & Sons (the pepper sauce outfit launched by a former McIlhenny blacksmith) was vanquished, broke and in disarray. In the ensuing years, W.J. Trappey, the grandson of the company's founder, strove to revitalize the business by expanding the few product lines besides pepper sauce that his grandfather and uncles had developed, such as pickled peppers and canned sweet potatoes. But the distribution channels for a small company lacking a national customer base were limited, especially with giant food ventures like Heinz, Kraft, General Mills and Borden's using their muscle to offer discounts and promotions that monopolized supermarket shelf space. W.J. also had to contend with an undisciplined group of shareholders—uncles and cousins who were united only in their frustration with the company's inability to generate profits.

Considering the odds, it's stunning that Trappey & Sons remained independent as long as it did. But in 1980, Trappey family members demanded that W.J. find a buyer for the company. "The older ones saw an opportunity to make a little money by forcing the sale," Trappey said. "I would have kept it; things weren't going great, but I thought there was potential, if I made some changes. But what was I going to do? When you have relatives that are anxious to do something else and no rules in place to prevent them from getting their way, you have no choice."

Trappey & Sons was purchased by the Seguras, a prominent New Iberia agricultural family who invested the bare minimum in the company and had no real interest in reinvigorating the brand. And in 1991, Ned Simmons bailed the Seguras out, taking Trappey off of the family's hands for a couple of million dollars. The plan was "to get into the cheap hot sauce market without infringing on the McIlhenny Tabasco name," said a former McIlhenny executive, who opposed the deal because the asking price was far too steep "for basically a defunct company."

Moreover, the idea of selling a cut-rate sauce didn't sit well with some McIlhenny family members, who believed the company should not deviate from its traditional high-end perch, no matter the bleakness of revenue forecasts. "One director who opposed the deal said, 'It's like you take in a homeless guy from the street and bring him into the rich man's palace; he'll never fit in,'" said the McIlhenny executive.

Ned Simmons was unmoved. He was certain Trappey's inert pepper sauce brand had enough life to be a vehicle for a price war against companies like Baumer or Bruce Foods. With McIlhenny's credibility in supermarkets, the relaunched Trappey could quickly become the dominant player in the low end of this fast-growing market, Simmons presumed.

But Simmons failed to consider a wide range of possible questions that would ultimately determine the success of the plan. Among them: How do you implement a low-end/high-end product strategy without cannibalizing sales of the flagship Tabasco sauce? What types of promotions, distribution agreements and advertising campaigns are required to revive a moribund product? How do you minimize marketing and manufacturing costs for the discount brand sufficiently so it returns an acceptable profit margin? Which facets of Tabasco's and Trappey's operations can be shared to cut overhead for both sides of the business?

These issues would stymie skilled product marketers. To address them appropriately, Simmons would need knowledge, instincts and management skills well above those required to shepherd the relatively simple, one-dimensional Tabasco business model passed down through the generations by the McIlhenny family.

His first appointment, though, confirmed that Simmons had none of these. Soon after the acquisition was finalized, Simmons named his son, Ned, to manage Trappey operations and serve as liaison between the Trappey and Tabasco sides of the family business. Ned junior had no background in food manufacturing at the time he was hired by his father, having held lower-level management jobs at oil companies.

"He lacked any notion about how to manage dollars and cents," said a longtime McIlhenny executive. "And the Trappey purchase was all about controlling tight budgets and being efficient to squeeze the most profit from a small pool of money."

Under Ned junior, Trappey operating costs ballooned as a series of ill-fated factory streamlining plans were approved and then dropped. These manufacturing improvement programs were poorly matched with existing Trappey plant architecture and could not be implemented without significant expenditures. Attempts to advertise and market Trappey products and to adopt profitable pricing tactics fell flat as well because Ned junior was unable to design a cohesive strategy for building the Trappey brand. The upshot: Trappey's losses widened each year McIlhenny owned it.

Despite this checkered track record, Ned senior inexplicably promoted his son to oversee manufacturing throughout McIlhenny Co. As one of his first acts, Ned junior hired a young college graduate, also without plant supervisory experience, to be an assistant plant manager. And in an inept effort to force an organizational structure where one wasn't needed, Ned junior told McIlhenny agricultural and shipping supervisors that they mustn't go to factory manager Ed Guidry anymore with problems or questions; instead, all issues should be directed to Ned junior's new assistant.

"That destroyed morale," a McIlhenny Co. manager said. "Until then, we dealt with problems as they came up by talking directly to each other and resolving them quickly most of the time. Suddenly, we had to go through a new chain of command, a bureaucracy made up of people who weren't particularly good at their jobs. Many of us began to ignore problems rather than try to resolve them."

As he watched the Trappey acquisition hemorrhage cash, Ned senior confronted yet another more distressing crisis, which struck directly at the heart of the fundamental business structure that had sustained McIlhenny Co. almost since its founding. In the early 1990s, the Internal Revenue Service determined that McIlhenny employees with homes on Avery Island were underreporting their wages. Living virtually for free in the company town, the workers were, in effect, compensated by McIlhenny Co. for the fair rental value of their housing, but they failed to declare this amount or pay taxes on it. The IRS told McIlhenny Co. to close this loophole.

There were creative ways to respond to this ruling without penalizing or alienating the workers. For example, some in the Tabasco business argued that Simmons could continue to subsidize rents in Tango Village and report this amount as other wages on the employees' W–2s. And if he wanted to be especially generous, Simmons could offset the higher income taxes that the workers would incur with small raises. Under this plan, McIlhenny Co. would be responsible for minimal additional outlays and the company town, which had already undergone a wave of departures when Walter McIlhenny was president, would be kept intact.

Simmons rejected these options and chose an approach that might have seemed the least costly in the short run but would prove to be extremely expensive over time. He eliminated the housing subsidy entirely, charging rents of as much as $100 a month on small cottages, up from $1.50 previously. People living in the larger homes were asked to pay above $500 a month.

Imposed without a commensurate increase in pay, the unexpected surcharge angered McIlhenny workers. Many Tango Village residents had already become disenchanted with the low wages and the limited privacy in the company town. Now, with McIlhenny benevolence a thing of the past, there was little left to hold them there. As soon as Simmons levied the rents, an exodus from Avery Island ensued that included employees of all stripes—managers and laborers—trimming the population of Tango Village by 75 percent, to only 100 residents.

"When we were leaving Avery Island, I felt like the blacks did when Abraham Lincoln freed the slaves," said Joseph Terrell, who started working for McIlhenny Co. in the late 1940s and rose to the position of chief accountant. After residing in Tango Village for forty years, he and his wife moved out to purchase their own home in New Iberia. "By the time I left, employees couldn't ride freely around the island. The McIlhennys put a clamp on those activities. Some members of the family were building homes on the island and they wanted their privacy. So what they were running was a gated family community, not a company town anymore. We got out just in time."

Simmons miscalculated, or didn't understand, how much the company town had meant to McIlhenny Co., notably to its cost structure. With fewer workers living on Avery Island, McIlhenny couldn't maintain below-market-average salaries. No longer beholden to the family for shelter, education and protection, many Tabasco employees sought better-paying jobs elsewhere, or they used that pretext as a threat to demand—and often receive—higher wages from the McIlhennys. Consequently, McIlhenny reluctantly raised the base pay for new hires, conceding that was the only way to attract a talented pool of applicants. Accordingly, in the period following the shrinking of Tango Village, the Tabasco business's overhead rose steadily, primarily due to increased compensation costs. And the company's envied profit margins gradually began to descend to a low of just over 20 percent today, still high for a food company but not what McIlhenny was accustomed to.

Ned Simmons couldn't avoid the fact that something was seriously wrong with the family business. By the mid-1990s, overall sales of Tabasco sauce had risen to over 75 million bottles a year, a 25 percent increase since Simmons took over the company in 1986. But profitability had ebbed as his personnel and strategic decisions backfired. And with annual dividends dropping, McIlhenny stakeholders were increasingly restless.

His struggles notwithstanding, Simmons maintained the backing of the board, which at the time was dominated by the heirs of his grandfather, Edward Avery McIlhenny. However, Simmons had lost confidence in himself and didn't believe that he could fix the ailing company. Worse yet, Simmons didn't feel that there were any family members who could do a better job than him. So, in desperation, he offered a radical proposal to the board: hire Vince Pierse to run the company.

Chapter 13
THE OUTSIDER

Vince Pierse had a lengthy resume in manufacturing and consumer products. In the 1970s, he was an operations executive at Morton-Norwich Products, a food, pharmaceutical and chemicals conglomerate later acquired by Procter & Gamble. Subsequently, he founded a management consulting firm, whose clients included International Packaging and Westinghouse. When Simmons decided to recommend that Vince Pierse replace him as head of the family business, Pierse was already a familiar face on Avery Island. For the prior ten years, he had been an adviser to the McIlhennys, primarily involved in the development of international business.

Simmons told the board that McIlhenny Co. needed an agile chief executive, a tactical thinker with sufficient experience to identify what it would take to turn around the company. None of the McIlhennys fit this profile, Simmons said. And if that was the case, the company would be foolish to turn a highly qualified candidate away simply because he wasn't a member of the family, Simmons argued.

It was a difficult message to swallow. For more than 125 years, the McIlhennys had run *their* Tabasco company. There was always an heir capable of guiding the family business to the next generation.

And it was assumed that only a McIlhenny would possess the DNA to instinctually understand the company's business model and be driven by blood to protect it. But now Simmons was telling the board such insularity may have, particularly recently, placed the company in jeopardy.

Numerous family businesses reach the same crossroads. Often by the third or fourth generation, family businesses have so many disparate shareholders that the company itself is not the focus anymore, just the dividends it generates. And with each succeeding branch on the family tree, the lessons and beliefs of the founder become more distant and muddled—and the business less inherently attractive to the descendants—so that having a family member as chief executive can actually be a disadvantage.

Frequently, companies try to sidestep the issue of bringing in an outsider chief executive until an internal crisis makes it impossible to ignore any longer. For example, the candymaker Mars Inc. has been managed for many years by second-generation chairman John Mars and his sister Jacqueline Mars Vogel. Both are aging, and although there are no obvious CEO candidates in sight among founder Forrest Mars's grandchildren, the company has been hesitant to establish a succession strategy.

The 220-year-old Canadian brewery Molson Canada, beermaker John Molson's brainchild, found itself in the same situation decades back when a tragedy forced the family to quickly find a solution. In 1966, third-generation president P.T. Molson committed suicide at the family's mountain retreat. With no Molson heir prepared to run the business, David Chenoweth, a thirteen-year Molson senior executive and a former head of Pepsi-Cola Canada, was named president. The company has been without a Molson at the top ever since.

The McIlhennys never thought they would have to face this dilemma. They prided themselves on the strength of their single-mindedness, which translated into a belief that the company and the family sustained each other. Having Avery Island as the heart of the Tabasco company, they felt, insulated the family and distilled the business, somewhat like the Vatican does for Catholicism. Thus, Ned Simmons's proposal—in effect, a call for a Protestant pope—came as a shock.

Despite strong reservations, though, the board supported Simmons and agreed to Pierse's appointment. However, a large minority of the board, led by Simmons's cousin Paul McIlhenny—like Ned, a great-grandson of the founder Edmund—was livid about the decision. Paul told the board that hiring Pierse, not the company's recent sluggish performance, was a certain sign that the family business was declining. Breaking with a commitment to the past by turning over the family business to a non-McIlhenny would hurry the day when the company would be wrested from the McIlhennys, Paul said. Perhaps that would be a good thing, he added, because after Pierse was through, more than likely the company would be unrecognizable to the family anyway.

A stirring argument, but even Paul's supporters knew that in making it he had an ulterior motive. "Paul believed that he should have been named president," said an elder McIlhenny family member. "He had been working there as a vice president since the late 1960s when he got out of college. It was his turn, he thought. Hiring Pierse was a slap in the face."

Vince Pierse, an irreverent Australian who seemed a bit too smooth and fast for the slow-motion swelter of Avery Island, wasted little time in putting his imprint on the Tabasco business. In his initial weeks on the job in the summer of 1996, Pierse removed two lingering ills from Ned Simmons's era: He fired Ned Simmons Jr. and set in motion plans to sell Trappey, although he knew he would have to do so at a loss. Then he formulated an aggressive marketing strategy, chiefly intended to expand McIlhenny revenue significantly. To the dismay of some family members, however, Pierse warned that it would take a period of time and considerable expense for this program to fully bear fruit.

"I heard grumbling, but I didn't care if the McIlhenny family liked it or not," Pierse said, speaking from his post-McIlhenny business address, a Colorado bed-and-breakfast. "My responsibility wasn't to provide a dividend determined by the family members. My job was to increase sales of the product, whatever it took. Tabasco has a huge gross margin; you can screw up royally and still make a nice profit. With a product like that, it's easier and smarter to increase profits by selling more bottles than by cutting costs and eviscerating the brand."

Pierse's strategy was two-pronged. First, attract new Tabasco consumers with eye-catching promotions and advertising, not discounts.

"They were trying to sell the product with coupons in some stores, but taking cents off of a brand like Tabasco never results in a new customer," Pierse said. "People who want the quality that Tabasco offers are willing to pay the price for it. The only consumers taking advantage of the coupons were existing customers ready for another bottle. So McIlhenny was subsidizing sales that they would have gotten anyway."

Second, convince Tabasco lovers to use it more.

"As the joke goes: You can tell how long a marriage has lasted by the amount of Tabasco sauce left in the bottle," Pierse chuckled. "We had loyal customers, but they didn't use the product enough. We needed a sustained campaign to build consumption. We had to persuade people that if you put it on eggs, you can also put it on pizza or chop suey."

The centerpiece of Pierse's marketing message was "Tabasco sauce is hot," an idea he arrived at after considering the appropriate way to counter rivals' contentions that Tabasco was both too spicy and not sufficiently spicy for the modern pepper sauce consumer. Under Ned Simmons, McIlhenny reacted to this branding straitjacket that its competitors had squeezed Tabasco sauce into by imprudently acquiring Trappey. Traditionally a reluctant advertiser, McIlhenny never considered a marketing effort to make its own assertions for Tabasco, preempting its opponents' attempts to define it. Instead, McIlhenny, as always, relied on word of mouth and its powerful brand name to sell its product. But while that approach had served the company well, by the mid-1990s conditions in the pepper sauce business had changed radically. Consumers had more information, more choices and more channels to buy these products. And silence in this noisy environment, as McIlhenny's falling market share demonstrated, was suicidal.

Striking back, Vince Pierse proposed a television advertising campaign that ignored competitors' claims entirely and made no overt statements about Tabasco sauce, either. Rather, it would depend in large part upon the viewer's subconscious perception of the familiar product to deliver the desired message; namely, that Tabasco sauce is, in fact, synonymous with heat, but it is a pleasing tartness that has attracted consumers for more than 100 years. A simple set of spots was envisioned: short, mimed vignettes with a single character using the peppery fire in Tabasco sauce to unusual, and ultimately comical, effect. Nothing but the bottle's presence would identify the product; no voice-overs would explicitly testify to its virtues.

Such so-called neural marketing is a gamble, arguably practiced most adeptly by Nike, whose swoosh is often the sole representation of its product in its distinctive ads. In this type of advertising, the viewer's mind is asked to fill in the missing information. The technique can only be successful in the rare instances when a brand is so ingrained in the public psyche that consumers instantly recognize it by its look, logo or packaging, and that their subliminal beliefs concerning the product match the characteristics the advertiser wants to promote.

Ned Simmons and Paul McIlhenny initially balked at Pierse's advertising plan, but they weren't objecting to the inherent risks. They were opposed to the way Tabasco sauce would be portrayed, preferring a cool and restrained image for the brand. Pierse's retort: Would Porsche concede that its cars are slow merely because they don't have the speed of a Lamborghini?

"The McIlhennys thought that saying Tabasco sauce is hot was a detriment to the product," said Tom Moudry, who handled the

McIlhenny account for DDB Needham Advertising in Dallas. "All of their advertising—and there wasn't much of it, mostly print ads in women's magazines—had focused on how well Tabasco sauce enhanced the flavor of food. They were determined not to appear too radical. But hot is a distinguishing feature of Tabasco sauce."

Pierse eventually won over the McIlhennys, who grudgingly accepted that he should be free to run the business as he saw fit. The result was one of the most admired commercials in advertising history—the "Mosquito" spot, a thirty-second plug that ran during the 1998 Super Bowl. In it, a man in his twenties, wearing shorts, is enjoying a slice of pizza on his ramshackle front porch, deep in what appears to be the Louisiana woods. The din of crickets, owls and other night creatures is the lone sound. Before each bite, the man pours a generous swath of Tabasco sauce onto the pizza. The camera pans down and shows two additional bottles of Tabasco sauce at his feet. A mosquito appears and the man watches quizzically as the bug lands on his thigh, bites him and flies off. A second later, the mosquito explodes in a mass of flames. Cut to the man chewing and smiling in triumph, a Tabasco bottle displayed on screen.

"It's a wonderful payoff at the end," said Moudry, currently creative director at Martin/Williams Advertising in Minneapolis. "It directly presented the core message of the product: it's hot enough to set a mosquito on fire, yet tasty enough to put on pizza. The spot is so simple and so brand focused."

Mosquito garnered a top prize at the Cannes International Advertising Festival, and the commercial is frequently used by marketing professors to illustrate near-perfect product promotion. Other memorable ads in this series followed, including a playfully unorthodox one depicting God as a Tabasco buff accidentally sprinkling blistering drops of pepper sauce on Earth, blowing up meadows, buildings, spacecraft and finally Stonehenge.

The TV ads and a separate print campaign that featured celebrities dishing about the foods that they put Tabasco sauce on—Dan Aykroyd freely drips it on "everything humans can consume," while George H.W. Bush and Kenny Rogers use Tabasco on pork rinds—

generated renewed buzz for the product. Tabasco sauce had shed its dowdy image and was suddenly hip, a distinction secured when the brand garnered an intriguing mention in *Maxim* magazine's ultimate road map for a man's world. In the section, "10 things we shouldn't have to tell you" was this item: eggs, corned-beef hash and Tabasco sauce is the breakfast of the gods.

The positive publicity slowly produced gains. Sales rose modestly in 1997 and the hemorrhaging of market share was stanched. But the McIlhenny family was hoping for more dramatic results, and Pierse had to continually remind the family that a successful marketing strategy required as much patience as creativity. It takes time to reinvigorate a tired product, Pierse told them. The McIlhennys, however, were unable to get used to the enormous financial outlays involved in national marketing. During Pierse's first year, the company's annual marketing budget rose to roughly $5 million, a fivefold increase from the year before. Then came NASCAR.

The favorable consumer response to the advertising campaign convinced Pierse that the Tabasco brand had been underdeveloped. It had become an international product with fervent customers in 120 countries in spite of the McIlhennys' distaste for marketing, he believed. Imagine the outcome, he thought, had the family actually put some effort into promoting its brand? So in mid-1997, Pierse choreographed the biggest splash yet for the product, placing Tabasco sauce next to Jack Daniel's, M&M's, Philip Morris, McDonald's and other marketing juggernauts on the NASCAR circuit.

Team Tabasco was a Pontiac Grand Prix driven by stock car racing superstar Todd Bodine. With the diamond-shaped Tabasco label on the hood and fiery yellow flames on an orange background, the aerodynamic vehicle looked fast standing still. Unfortunately, it didn't measure up to expectations. Team Tabasco failed to qualify in five of its first thirteen races. For the whole 1997–1998 season, its best finish was thirteenth.

But the disappointing on-track performance didn't diminish the value of McIlhenny's NASCAR sponsorship. Although McIlhenny enjoyed significant shelf space in supermarkets, without its own trucks and warehouses around the country, the family business struggled for prime exposure in individual stores—for instance, through floor displays or Tabasco-themed promotions. Such beneficial product placements—the specialty of companies like Frito-Lay or Gillette—are generally negotiated by the companies' local distribution operations, unique from region to region, and are not dictated by the grocery chain's corporate management. The NASCAR deal created a channel in which McIlhenny could overcome this disadvantage. In the days leading up to a race, Pierse would put replicas of Team Tabasco cars in front of supermarkets in the area and run a slew of advertisements to draw consumers to the stores; in exchange, the grocers would give Tabasco prominent display space inside.

"We would promote, promote, promote," said Pierse. "And in the first six months of our NASCAR deal, sales in the Southeast went up eighteen percent."

Back at Avery Island, though, Pierse was one of the few people enthusiastic about the $15 million a year NASCAR initiative. The price tag so exceeded McIlhenny's annual marketing budget prior to Pierse joining the company that the expenditure was difficult to rationalize. Many on McIlhenny's board—even supporters of Ned Simmons who largely endorsed Pierse's strategies—began to wonder if Pierse was too profligate for their family business.

For Paul McIlhenny, who never got over being denied the top spot at the family business in favor of an outsider, such internal misgivings apparently gave him the opportunity he had been waiting for. Publicly, he and Pierse had fashioned a truce, a separation of duties allowing them to work together at least semiharmoniously in the same executive suite. Paul handled much of the public McIlhenny activities, including press interviews and tasks always performed by McIlhenny family chief executives, like choosing the Tabasco pepper that would yield the seeds for the subsequent year's crop and approving the pepper mash before it was bottled. Pierse ran the company's day-to-day operations and made the strategic decisions. But privately, Paul chafed. And by the summer of 1998, he had accumulated additional leverage that could be used to exploit the board's growing dissatisfaction with Pierse.

A year earlier, John Stauffer McIlhenny had died at eighty-seven. The grandson of company founder Edmund, John was Walter McIlhenny's brother and John Avery McIlhenny's son. In published biographical notes describing the E. A. McIlhenny Natural History Collection that John established at Louisiana State University, he was portrayed as "trained as a research chemist, but freed by family fortunes to pursue his personal interests." A bachelor, John left his household goods and furnishings to the LSU Foundation, stipulating that the proceeds from their sale be used to maintain the McIlhenny collection. He also gave the school his stake in McIlhenny Co. Since the Tabasco business bylaws outlawed selling or leaving McIlhenny shares to anyone but family members or the company itself, this inheritance would have to be undone, a circumstance Paul McIlhenny swiftly turned to his benefit: he personally purchased most, if not all, of the LSU shares.

That afforded Paul a substantially larger stake in the family business than he had had when Vince Pierse was approved by the board over his objections. Moreover, a long-simmering feud between Ned Simmons and one of his nephews drove Simmons's nephew into Paul's camp, further weakening the group of shareholders led by Edward Avery McIlhenny's direct descendants, who Simmons had relied upon for support in appointing Pierse. As a result, Paul had effectively gained control of the McIlhenny board. And when he raised the possibility of firing Vince Pierse soon after the exorbitant NASCAR sponsorship began, few board members resisted. Simmons and his backers on the board realized they didn't have the numbers to overrule Paul anymore. Besides, scanning the budget data, they, too, had doubts about Pierse.

Pierse was abruptly fired as head of McIlhenny Co. in August 1998, and Paul McIlhenny finally got the job he had long sought. In retrospect Pierse believes his dismissal was in the offing for as many as twelve months, yet he was shocked when it happened. "Once Old John died, Ned Simmons's majority block of votes on the board was gone. Forty-nine percent doesn't make it, so I was on my way out," Pierse said. "If I had one more year—that is my only regret. We were just starting to see the results. It was strategis interruptis."

Chapter 14

THE FAMILY BUSINESS AT 140

Vince Pierse's departure did nothing to solve McIlhenny Co.'s fundamental problems. Since Paul McIlhenny became president, Tabasco sauce sales have increased sluggishly, approaching 150 million bottles in 2005 mostly on the wings of unyielding consumer interest in chili products. Profit margins remain stubbornly depressed at about 20 percent. Following a brief boost during Pierse's marketing blitz, Tabasco's market share has slowly begun to decline again. Meanwhile, dividends continue to lag, as McIlhenny shares are diluted by the growing number of people in the extended family. And worst of all, the doubled-edged attack from the chilihead hot sauces and the low-end, discount products rages on, unabated.

Pierse's firing did have one long-lasting—if unwelcome—effect, though: it exposed a precarious rift among the McIlhennys that had been advancing for several decades but had not yet surfaced. Some in the family's large and growing younger generation angrily attacked the company's board, made up primarily of family elders, for its shortsightedness in spurning Pierse. They argued that Pierse didn't deserve his fate: although an outsider, he respected the economy of the founder's uncomplicated business model, never attempting to replace it. If radical, they said, Pierse solely displayed it in his unconventional marketing strategies, which were essential in the current business environment.

With Pierse gone, these younger McIlhennys feared the company would adopt anew the parochial style of management that had already proven deficient in dealing with ebbing sales and profits. And in so doing, McIlhenny Co. might pass up a golden opportunity to become a major food company, a smaller version of Heinz and Campbell's, which at one time were family businesses with single products.

Paul McIlhenny by and large dismissed the concerns of these family critics. Rotund and ruddy-faced—he was fifty-four years old when he became president of the family business—Paul was certain only a McIlhenny could chart a course for the company that, importantly, preserved its traditions, one of them being a healthy skepticism of expensive, scattershot advertising campaigns. Indeed, immediately upon taking the reins of the company, Paul dispatched the Vince Pierse era by firing a handful of senior employees who had been close to the ousted president.

Gene Jefferies's termination was the most unexpected and memorable for its insensitivity. The company's chief of agriculture for twenty-two years and the originator of McIlhenny's Latin American network, which produced a consistent supply of inexpensive peppers, Jefferies enjoyed the ardor of many younger family members for saving the company when circumstances were dire. He was also a favorite of Pierse's, whom Jefferies impressed by his mastery of both the physiology of the Tabasco crop and the psyche of its growers.

Jefferies's close relationship with Pierse was his undoing, though Paul McIlhenny never revealed that publicly. Instead, McIlhenny seized upon a single uncharacteristic error by Jefferies to strip him of his job. In early 1999, a farmer in Brazil embezzled money from McIlhenny by overstating the size of his Tabasco harvest in monthly production reports. To do this, he took advantage of Jefferies' generous payment system, which compensated growers in advance of pepper mash delivery based exclusively on the farmers' word for the size of their crop. Not long after the bogus reports were submitted, Jefferies traveled to Brazil to count barrels and inspect the quality of the mash. The farmer showed him a few casks in a warehouse and said the rest were spread over numerous sites in other cities. Before Jefferies could get to the next location, the farmer trucked mash there that Jefferies had previously examined and presented it as new. Unknowingly, Jefferies approved the same casks over and over in venue upon venue. The grower kept up this charade for some months without discovery. But the scheme unraveled during a surprise visit by McIlhenny employees to a warehouse that the farmer had claimed contained dozens of barrels of mash; instead, it was empty.

Less than $200,000 was stolen, but Jefferies was chagrined. When he devised the payment plan decades earlier, it was controversial. No other company had initiated anything like it, chiefly due to a belief that the Latin American growers could not be trusted. Jefferies felt, though, if he treated the farmers with respect and gave them financial support, they would, in turn, be loyal to McIlhenny Co. and deliver a steady stream of peppers. During Jefferies's tenure, the Brazilian alone failed to live up to the tacit agreement.

Already distanced from Jefferies for his allegiance to Pierse, Paul told McIlhenny family members that Jefferies was too lenient and bighearted with the growers. The incident in Brazil, Paul said, was entirely Jefferies' fault. Maybe, Paul added, he's not the right guy for the job anymore; perhaps at sixty-three Jefferies is too old to handle the extensive travel and supervisory responsibilities.

Paul's concerns never reached Jefferies directly, though. In one meeting, Jefferies asked McIlhenny, "Am I going to lose my job over this?"

"Of course not, Gene," McIlhenny replied. "Don't even think about retiring."

Two weeks later, when Paul was out of town, McIlhenny Co.'s head of human resources called Jefferies into his office "to talk about the Brazil thing."

Jefferies gathered his notes and went in. The HR chief told Jefferies to put down the papers and then measuredly read aloud Jefferies' termination letter.

Upon returning, Paul hired Took Osborne, a young cousin raised in Connecticut with no farming experience, to be chief of agriculture. Subsequently, Paul shelved the prepayment program with the Latin American growers, a move that has exposed McIlhenny Co. for the first time in years to a potential shortage of Tabasco peppers.

The way Paul fired Jefferies stunned McIlhenny Co.'s employees. In the past, McIlhenny had always treated its factory and management workers with a great deal of regard. To get a pink slip, someone would have had to commit a crime or a serious blunder that cost the company millions of dollars. Indeed, many of the people still living on Avery Island in the depleted company town were old-timers who remained on the family's payroll doing odd jobs well beyond retirement. Nobody could remember the last time an employee as well liked and competent as Jefferies was let go.

But Paul McIlhenny has set a different tone for the business, in part because its employees have lost much of their individual value. When Tango Village was at its peak, maintaining a courteous, even familial, relationship with the workers—integrating their day-to-day existence with the thrum of life on the island—translated into low overhead. It was a business advantage for the McIlhennys. But with the company town a shambles, the employees were viewed in a harsher light: as a cost, not a savings. Rather than partners in the business, they were perceived as adversaries.

Hence, McIlhenny Co. has become a more austere place to work. Distinct from prior McIlhenny presidents, Paul can be frequently overbearing, his steely gaze inimical, and bouts of kindness are rare. He has driven a few secretaries to tears for infractions as trivial as lending the company car to an employee without approval. Worker turnover at all levels has increased markedly in the past decade.

In most other ways as well, the worst forebodings of family members who feared the company would become myopic again post-Pierse have proved true. Whenever possible, Paul has indeed surrounded himself with family members who lack experience in consumer goods, management, agriculture or manufacturing, and he has entrusted them with skilled executive jobs.

His growth strategy is equally unpromising. In recent years, Paul introduced a series of new flavors under the Tabasco brand name: habanero, garlic, chipotle, green pepper and sweet and spicy. These extensions to the company's product line are sold as premium products with a price tag of upwards of $3 (or more, in the case of habanero) for a five-ounce bottle. But being averse to advertising, Paul has been reluctant to create a marketing campaign that would effectively support these new items by, as some experts suggest, linking them to classic Tabasco sauce in quality and not just name. Predictably, these products have attracted scant notice and have had difficulty gaining a significant amount of space on supermarket shelves. Their percentage share of McIlhenny Co.'s revenues has been disappointing, below double digits, while the cost of producing them has further reduced the company's profit margins.

In truth, Paul can't make the same claims for McIlhenny's new lines that he could for Tabasco sauce. Unlike Tabasco, chipotle, habanero, and the other recent blends are not aged for three years, the peppers are not as painstakingly chosen and each batch is not examined for perfection and consistency. By placing the Tabasco name on items of inferior quality, McIlhenny may eventually diminish the value of its flagship product.

The McIlhennys are at a pivotal moment in their epic run. Having tried and then rejected a nonfamily member in the top position, the company's leadership has turned inward, where the talent pool is thin and fresh ideas are at a premium. Indeed, as early as 1986, then-president Ned Simmons recognized this acute scarcity of skills on Avery Island when he told a reporter, "We have gotten big enough that we cannot manage the company without outside talent."

Saddled by this handicap of their own devising, McIlhenny management has cocooned itself within the routine of maintaining smooth daily operations of the business, while sidestepping the critical issues that threaten the company's future. Among them: repositioning the beleaguered Tabasco brand to reclaim lost market share, as Vince Pierse did with his short-lived "Tabasco sauce is hot" campaign; launching a coherent public relations or marketing campaign to promote the new product lines, either under the Tabasco umbrella or distinct from it; controlling labor costs in the wake of the company town's demise; and exploring modernization techniques in manufacturing, distribution or sales to juice profit margins.

McIlhenny Co. is, in effect, handcuffed by its history. Edmund McIlhenny's descendants have interpreted the many years of success sprouting from the founder's unique business philosophy as a signal that the family business must be a confined, closed, immutable place. But sharply altered business and social conditions have made it arduous, if not impossible, to thrive that way anymore. The combination of globalization and technology are rewriting the well-worn Baedeker for product development, marketing and manufacturing.

Now anyone can create a recipe for pepper sauce in a kitchen in Boise, Berlin or New Delhi; manufacture it in an outsourcing plant in Vietnam; advertise it inexpensively on Google; sell it through a Web site; and distribute it from a clearinghouse in the Philippines—in all, competing against established brands instantly while never handling the finished product. There are other similar scenarios, branding realities in an era of universal communications, that ultimately call for equally global responses from category leaders like McIlhenny, whose market share and profit margins are suffering. But the McIlhennys, caught between tradition and modernity—indeed, between Avery Island and the new world—are so far without answers.

By apparently neglecting the company's challenges, Paul McIlhenny has further tempted the ire of the younger shareholders, who are increasingly impatient with the business's torpid pace of growth and the lack of imagination in the executive suite. Some are sufficiently frustrated to consider the unthinkable. "Look, if we can't maintain growth in a brand as powerful as Tabasco in a world begging for chili products, then maybe it's time for some other company that knows more about selling consumer goods to try," said a thirty-fve-year-old McIlhenny shareholder.

Fourth- and fifth-generation McIlhennys are far removed in time from the founding of the family business. Often, they live at long distances from Avery Island, barely ever visit and have no other connection to the company except their bloodline. Even they would admit that the degree of their activism is in an inverse ratio to the size of the profit-sharing checks.

Ironically, McIlhenny Co. faces this internal revolt as a result of its unusually inclusive shareholder structure, which in essence generously allots dividends to every McIlhenny heir, a group numbering nearly 200 now. Family businesses protect themselves from the oversight of dozens of distant relatives as the company matures by limiting the scope of the ownership class or the amount of money awarded to family members each year. Perhaps illogically—failing to address the possibility that the company would still exist in the year 2000, when his many great-great-grandchildren would be having children themselves—Edmund McIlhenny directed that the Tabasco business should be a private refuge for his descendants, all of them. Consequently, it is something of a conundrum for McIlhenny elders today that the shareholders with the least appreciation for the family business's remarkably unique character—specifically, its simple, georgic business model and its guarded resistance to unfettered innovation—may influence its future the most.

This disagreement among family members will have to be addressed squarely in the coming years. All of the obvious ways to mediate it, though, are either extremely difficult or undesirable. The McIlhennys could revise the company bylaws to concentrate power and ownership rights in a smaller group. But that would contradict the founder's wishes and, worse yet, require the approval of all shareholders. Equally daunting, the McIlhennys could cave in to the extended clan and draw up a plan to drive annual revenue well beyond the current $250 million; however, nobody currently within the company has any credible ideas to achieve that or the will to rewrite the business model in a way that would transform McIlhenny into a much larger operation, maybe with more products and manufacturing facilities and likely managed by non-McIlhennys.

If either of these—or something in between—is not realistic, the remaining choices, although plausible, are simply too disturbing for the McIlhennys to seriously broach: offering shares in the company to the public or selling the family business to one of the many giant corporations, like Heinz, Campbell's and Kraft, said to have standing $1 billion-plus offers on the table for the Tabasco brand. Currently, there is little support for giving up McIlhenny Co.'s treasured independence—especially among those on Avery Island and their closest kin—even if the money shared by the McIlhenny family would besubstantial. But if the growing klatch of restive shareholders is not pacified, it's not inconceivable that soon the votes to cash in, to part with all or most of the family business, will be in the majority.

Whatever the outcome, it's been a magnificent journey for the McIlhennys, distinguished by extraordinary business acumen and a family's ingenuity spooling seamlessly through epochs of slavery, war, invention, genius, myth, racial unease, half-truths and untruths.

The arc of the McIlhenny family defies the quotidian at every turn. What began with Edmund and Mary—the unlikely love affair of a wealthy Baltimore-bred banker and the much younger daughter of a Louisiana plantation boss—has produced one of the most recognizable brand names in the world. Tens of millions of people pour Tabasco sauce on their food or in their drinks every single day, many more than once. Hundreds of thousands of rabid fans trek each year to Tabasco's home on Avery Island, some just to take pictures of their families next to the giant Tabasco model in the bustling factory where 600,000 bottles are produced every twenty-four hours.

Despite the obstacles the McIlhennys face now as they attempt to balance their rich past with the unrelenting presence of the future, it's wise to remember that no one yet has gotten wealthy betting against the McIlhennys. They are a stunningly resilient family: on the cusp of the fifth generation, the McIlhennys have already defied all of the odds.

NOTES

In researching and writing this book, I spoke to former and current McIlhenny Co. executives, factory workers, household help and pepper pickers, as well as McIlhenny family members and friends, family business specialists, southern Louisiana historians and archivists, Iberia Parish and Avery Island community leaders and residents, and chili pepper experts. Some of the people I interviewed are quoted in the book; others asked that their names not be used because they did not want to anger the extremely guarded Avery Island McIlhennys, who formally declined to participate in the project. I also relied on a significant amount of archived material, particularly company documents from McIlhenny, Heinz, Kraft and Trappey; the Avery Family Papers in the Southern Historical Collection at the University of North Carolina and the E. A. McIlhenny Natural History Collection at Louisiana State University; local newspaper accounts; magazine articles; books; relevant Web sites; and unpublished dissertations. Only by blending together all of this—snippets of oral histories told in many short and long conversations and small or large slices of written information—could I produce the broader, untold narrative of the McIlhennys and their very famous product.

I've chosen to highlight below the material that I found to be most valuable and indispensable, sometimes for just one or two facts that I couldn't have found anyplace else and other times for a unique perspective, a small or large insight about the McIlhennys or Tabasco sauce. Also, I've elaborated on a few points in the book for which additional information was especially worth presenting.

Prologue: Tabasco Road

page 4 *Edmund McIlhenny told and retold this tall tale so often*: This Friend Gleason story, a similar one or discussions about it can be found in many articles or books that cover the history of Tabasco sauce. Among them: James Conaway, "On Avery Island, Tabasco Sauce Is the Spice of Life," *Smithsonian Magazine,* May 1984; McFadden Duffy, "Wetlands for Wildlife," *Louisiana Conservationist,* September–October 1976; Roger M. Grace, "Tabasco: A Hot Sauce with an Uncertain Background," *Metropolitan News-Enterprise* (Los Angeles), July 8, 2004; John McNulty, *The World of John McNulty* (Garden City, N.Y.: Doubleday, 1967), p. 219; Amal Naj, *Peppers: A Story of Hot Pursuits* (New York: Knopf, 1992), pp. 158, 163–167; Richard Schweid, *Hot Peppers: The Story of Cajuns and Capsicum* (Chapel Hill: University of North Carolina Press, 1999), pp. 44–45.

page 10 *This desire to sugarcoat the truth is a recurring motif in the story of McIlhenny Co.*: Former McIlhenny Co. president Ned Simmons had an interesting comment concerning the half-truths that so freely populate the McIlhenny family's history: "With any company like ours, myth, error and falsification gets woven into the story and gets repeated until it becomes fact." See Martha Carr, "Nutria Tales: The Rat's Out of the Bag; Tabasco Mogul Didn't Bring Rodents Here," *New Orleans Times-Picayune,* September 29, 2002.

Chapter 1: The Forebears

page 14 *On his wedding day, Edmund McIlhenny felt like an intruder on Petit Anse*: One of the few sources of written material about Edmund McIlhenny's early life is John Chase, "Partners in Progress," in *New Orleans: An Illustrated History by John R. Kemp* (Woodland Hills, Calif.: Windsor Publications, 1981).

page 15 *McIlhenny was hired on the spot*: For an in-depth account of the New Orleans financial services environment in which Edmund McIlhenny developed his business expertise, I am indebted to George D. Green, *Finance and Economic Development in the Old South: Louisiana Banking, 1804–1861* (Stanford, Calif.: Stanford University Press, 1972).

page 15 *But New Orleans wasn't like the rest of the South*: For a captivating museum exhibit about antebellum Louisiana, see *Two Centuries of Louisiana History: The Cabildo*, Louisiana State Museum, New Orleans (http://lsm.crt.state.la.us/cabildo/cabildo.htm).

page 20 *Elizabeth Triett was the first white settler to set foot on the island*: Background on the life of Elizabeth Triett and her son John Hayes can be found in James Conaway, "On Avery Island, Tabasco Sauce Is the Spice of Life," *Smithsonian Magazine*, May 1984; Gertrude C. Taylor, "The Saga of Petit Anse Island," *Attakapas Gazette*, Fall 1984.

page 20 *After months of wandering, they found shelter in Opelousas Post*: For a description of the Opelousas Post, see Glenn R. Conrad, "Friend or Foe? Religious Exiles at the Opelousas Post in the American Revolution," *Attakapas Gazette*, vol. 12, 1977, pp. 137–140.

page 21 *salvation came deep in the southland, at the Gulf of Mexico, in the form of a much-weakened Indian tribe known as the Attakapas*: A little-known tribe, the Attakapas nonetheless played a significant role in the history of south-central Louisiana. More information about the Attakapas is available in Jim Bradshaw, "Archaeologists Weigh Evidence of Man's Arrival in Acadiana," *Advertiser* (Lafayette, Louisiana), March 3, 2004; Alana Carmon, "Attakapas Tribe,"

http://ccet.louisiana.edu/03a_Cultural_Tourism_Files/01.02_The_
People/Native%20American%20Tribes/Attakapas.html, University
of Louisiana at Lafayette Center for Cultural and Eco-Tourism;
Taylor, "Saga of Petit Anse Island."

page 21 *the Attakapas had refused to set foot on this island's soil
or to speak in specific detail about it*: Historians believe that the
tribe had probably witnessed a massive tsunami-like flood, perhaps
accompanied by a tornado, which on an eight-square-mile island
like Avery Island could have in minutes swallowed up the shelters
they had built and trapped humans and animals in a tidal wave.

page 21 *Yet, despite Triett's role in founding the island, she is hardly
remembered*: Avery Island is so dominated by the McIlhennys now,
so intertwined with Tabasco sauce and the family business, that it is
as if the island didn't exist before Edmund McIlhenny moved in. At
the school on Avery Island, where the story of McIlhenny Co. and
its success is very much a part of the curriculum, Elizabeth Triett's
name never comes up. "To be honest, I don't even know who she
is," said Eleanor Dore, who was raised on Avery Island and has
taught at the school for thirty years.

page 22 *Merely the passage of a weak-kneed bill intended to eventually outlaw human bondage in New Jersey*: Before the 1804
Gradual Emancipation Act was approved, New Jersey was the sole
northern state not to have outlawed slavery or enacted legislation
to phase it out. More than 12,000 slaves, about 5 percent of the
state's population, resided there. And while there were rabid aboli-
tionist movements throughout the Northeast, particularly in Massachusetts, Connecticut and New York City, New Jersey was more
racist, dominated by large landowners who identified more with
their fellow farmers in the southern states than the industrialists
of the North. Under New Jersey's emancipation legislation, female
children of slaves born after 1804 were to be freed at twenty-one;
males would be freed at twenty-five.

page 23 *Unwilling to idly watch the value of his black workers decline, John Marsh decided to move them out of New Jersey*: John Marsh's journey from New Jersey to Louisiana is covered in the Avery Family Papers, Iberia Parish, Louisiana, Southern Historical Collection, Library of the University of North Carolina at Chapel Hill; Taylor, "Saga of Petit Anse Island."

page 24 *Marsh grudgingly accepted an invitation to meet Daniel Dudley Avery*: Sources for information about Daniel Avery's life include the Avery Family Papers, Iberia Parish, Louisiana, Southern Historical Collection, Library of the University of North Carolina at Chapel Hill; Ken Ringle, "Blowing the Lid off Tabasco; Cousin Ken's Spicy Tale of the Family Business," *Washington Post*, April 21, 1993.

Chapter 2: White Hot

page 30 *Some of this resignation is contained in a letter that Avery wrote in 1862 to his son Dudley*: This letter was read to me by a McIlhenny family member. Additional correspondence between the Averys can be found in the Avery Family Papers, Iberia Parish, Louisiana, Southern Historical Collection, Library of the University of North Carolina at Chapel Hill.

page 31 *No matter how far down the laborers descended and regardless of where they struck the gigantic block, there was only salt*: "A Little World," *Scribner's Magazine*, August 1881.

page 31 *In his memoirs, he wrote*: Major General Richard Taylor, *Destruction and Reconstruction* (D. Appleton, 1879).

page 37 *An orphan from Limerick, Ireland, White became a fixture in New Orleans society in the early 1800s*: Accounts of Maunsel White's life and his version of Tabasco sauce are available in Dave DeWitt and Nancy Gerlach, "Seas of Hot Sauces," *Chili Pepper,* May–June

1990; Dave DeWitt and Chuck Evans, *The Hot Sauce Bible* (Berkeley, Calif.: Crossing Press, 1996); Roger M. Grace, "Was Col. Maunsel White the True Originator of Tabasco Sauce?" *Metropolitan News-Enterprise* (Los Angeles), July 15, 2004; Roger M. Grace, "Is Tabasco Sauce Patterned after Col. White's 'Tobasco Extract'?" *Metropolitan News-Enterprise* (Los Angeles), July 22, 2004; Amal Naj, *Peppers: A Story of Hot Pursuits* (New York: Knopf, 1992), pp. 158–162.

page 38 *an amalgam of culinary styles that became known as Creole, Cajun or just plain Louisiana cuisine*: Carl Lindahl, Maida Owens, and C. Renée Harvison. *Swapping Stories: Folktales from Louisiana* (Jackson: University Press of Mississippi, 1997); Maida Owens, *Smithsonian Folklife Cookbook* (Washington, D.C.: Smithsonian Press, 1991).

page 45 *in the early 1900s, some years after her husband's death, Mary McIlhenny approached Maunsel White's widow*: Naj, *Peppers*, p. 167.

Chapter 3: E. McIlhenny's Tabasco Pepper Sauce

page 48 *Recently, archaeologists from the University of Alabama spent six weeks unearthing artifacts and ruins from the laboratory's site*: History Tent, Pepper Fest: McIlhenny Co. Web site (http://www.tabasco.com/tabasco_history/excavation_history.cfm).

page 49 *In 1870, with fewer than 2,000 bottles of E. McIlhenny's Tabasco sauce in circulation, McIlhenny patented his recipe*: Roger M. Grace, "McIlhennys Speak with Forked Tongues in Telling of Tabasco Origin," *Metropolitan News-Enterprise* (Los Angeles), October 14, 2004.

page 51 *McIlhenny was initially so desperate for national distribution of Tabasco sauce that he offered Hazard a 50 percent stake*: Roger M. Grace, "More Tabasco Sauce Lore Appears to Be Fiction" *Metropolitan News-Enterprise* (Los Angeles), July 29, 2004.

page 52 *excavated a Tabasco bottle from around 1870*: Scott Sonner, "Rebuilding History," Associated Press, July 2, 2002.

page 53 *a period of steadily falling fortunes for the Averys and the Petit Anse plantation*: For correspondence relating to the downfall of the Averys, see the Avery Family Papers, Iberia Parish, Louisiana, Southern Historical Collection, Library of the University of North Carolina at Chapel Hill.

Chapter 4: The Business Model

page 57 *Tabasco sauce debuted in the midst of the Industrial Revolution*: For a detailed description of the business environment during the Industrial Revolution, see the excellent book by Alfred D. Chandler Jr., *The Invisible Hand* (Cambridge, Mass.: Harvard University Press, 1977).

page 59 *H.J. Heinz provides more suitable contrast with McIlhenny Co.*: Ibid., pp. 253, 295, 296, 349, 414; Nancy F. Koehn, *Brand New: How Entrepreneurs Earned Consumers' Trust from Wedgwood to Dell* (Cambridge, Mass.: Harvard Business School Press, 2001), pp. 45–90.

page 60 *For farmers and factory owners, these were expensive purchases*: Ross Thomson, "From the Old to the New: The Social Basis of Innovation in the Antebellum United States," *Business and Economic History Online*, Fall 2004.

page 61 *they were deserting the fundamental attributes that fueled their commercial triumphs in the first place*: More than a hundred years later, McIlhenny's cautious business philosophy offers a road map that many of the best companies, consciously or not, still follow. An apt example is Southwest Airlines, whose return on equity between 1972 and 2002 outranked every publicly trading company. Jim Collins, the business management consultant who wrote the best sellers *Built to Last* and *Good to Great*, decided to see if he could determine why Southwest was so much better than other companies. "If you look at Southwest's operating model in the late 1970s, there are roughly ten points in it—to be the best low-cost, high-spirit airline, steadily increasing profit per fuselage, et cetera; that's what they built the business on," Collins said on *The Charlie Rose Show* (August 4, 2005). "Now, if you compare that operating model to 2005, nine of ten points are the same. But here's the point. If somebody were to say, who is going to most succeed in a world characterized by an immense amount of change; instability; discontinuous, radical events, you would say it's the ones that change the best. One of the things we're learning [from Southwest] is that there's some very, very deep wisdom about not changing."

page 65 *Avery Island, it should be noted, is a geological oddity*: Avery Island's origins are covered in these articles: Herman B. Deutsch, "The Bird That's Not on Nellie's Hat," *Saturday Evening Post*, October 14, 1939; David S. Oakes, "Isle of Spice," *Central Manufacturing District Magazine*, date unknown.

page 67 *the federal government commissioned an investigation into what could be done with the valuable salt mine on the island*: Avery Island commercial salt mining ventures and techniques are explored in "On the Rock-Salt Deposit of Petit Anse," American Bureau of Mines (1867); *Modern Marvels: Salt Mines*, video, A&E Television Networks, 1999; Jim Bradshaw, "Flickering Candles Illuminated Mine When Journalist Visited," *Advertiser* (Lafayette, Louisiana), April 21, 2004; Oakes, "Isle of Spice."

Chapter 5: Rough Rider

page 77 *One statistic about family businesses has remained unchanged since Edmund McIlhenny made Tabasco sauce*: I relied on numerous resources in researching the history, influence and significance of family businesses. Among the more valuable were Craig E. Aronoff, "Megatrends in Family Business," Family Firm Institute (www.ffi.org); Joseph H. Astrachan and Melissa Carey Shanker, "'Family Businesses' Contribution to the U.S. Economy: A Closer Look," Family Firm Institute (www.ffi.org); Cox Family Enterprise Center, Kennesaw State University (http://www.kennesaw.edu/fec/index.html); Family Business Consulting Group (http://www.efamilybusiness.com/fbcg_home.php); William T. O'Hara, *Centuries of Success: Lessons from the World's Most Enduring Businesses* (Avon, Mass.: Adams Media, 2004); Rothman Institute of Entrepreneurial Studies, Fairleigh Dickinson University (http://view.fdu.edu/default.aspx?id=932).

page 78 *a dozen or so brands were attempting to go head-to-head with Tabasco sauce*: Dave DeWitt and Chuck Evans, *The Hot Sauce Bible* (Berkeley, Calif.: Crossing Press, 1996).

page 79 *In the aftermath of McIlhenny's death, that task fell to Edmund and Mary's eldest son, John Avery* For brief but relatively comprehensive biographies of John Avery McIlhenny, see Shane K. Bernard, "Soldier, Patriot, Christian, Gentleman: A Biographical Sketch of John Avery McIlhenny," *Attakapas Gazette,* 1993; "2nd Lieutenant John Avery McIlhenny," Spanish American War Centennial Web site (http://www.spanamwar.com/rrmcilhenny.htm).

page 80 *"knew they would be willing to assist me with their advice"*: James Conaway, "On Avery Island, Tabasco Sauce Is the Spice of Life," *Smithsonian Magazine,* May 1984.

page 82 *John compounded the company's deepening problems by introducing two new products*: This ill-timed brand extension was viewed as such memorable folly that as recently as two decades ago, in a newspaper article, it was still recalled by McIlhenny executives as "a disastrous push into specialty food products in the early 1900s." Steven Prokesch, "McIlhenny Finally Bestirs Itself," *New York Times,* June 29, 1986.

page 84 *An auction of John's collected items was held*: Ruth Laney, "The Treasures of Tabasco: Collectors Swarm Estate of John S. McIlhenny," *Maine Antiques Digest*, 1998.

page 86 *The affair took place in February 1903*: Shane Bernard, "Alice in Mardi Gras Land," *New Orleans Times-Picayune*, February 6, 1994.

page 90 *He died in 1942 at the age of seventy-five*: "John A McIlhenny, Former Civil Service President, Will Be Buried Today," *Washington Post*, November 10, 1942.

Chapter 6: Great White Father

page 93 *Almost immediately, he booked passage as a naturalist on the relief expedition to the Greenland ice cap*: Reports of Edward Avery McIlhenny's life as a naturalist and outdoorsman can be found in Harris Dickson, "The Promotion of Bird City," *Saturday Evening Post*, February 10, 1934; Herman B. Deutsch, "The Bird That's Not on Nellie's Hat," *Saturday Evening Post*, October 14, 1939; E. A. McIlhenny Natural History Collection, Louisiana State University, Baton Rouge, Louisiana.

page 97 *"He kept the name"*: "Famed Louisiana Naturalist Dies," *New Orleans Times-Picayune*, August 9, 1949.

page 100 *The plan E.A. devised was elegant*: For detailed accounts of Edward Avery McIlhenny's manufacturing system, see Robert Buckman, "U.S. Fervor for Tabasco Hasn't Cooled," *Dallas Morning News*, February, 17, 1991; McFadden Duffy, "Wetlands for Wildlife," *Louisiana Conservationist*, September–October 1976; "Greenleaf Tabasco, a New Tobacco Etch Virus Resistant Tabasco Pepper Variety," Agricultural Experiment Station, Auburn University, December, 1970; Robert Lopez, "Factory Adds Spice to State's History," *Beaumont Enterprise*, February, 18, 2005; Profile: History of Tabasco Sauce, National Public Radio, November

29, 2002; Steven Prokesch, "McIlhenny Finally Bestirs Itself," *New York Times*, June 29, 1986.

Chapter 7: Fighting Words

page 106 *Almost from the moment Tabasco sauce was launched, Edmund McIlhenny was wary of competitors appropriating the name of his product*: In-depth chronicles of the McIlhenny family's long battle to keep other companies from using the word *Tabasco* in their products are offered in Roger M. Grace, "Early Court Decisions Deny Exclusive Use of 'Tabasco,'" *Metropolitan News-Enterprise* (Los Angeles), August 26, 2004; Roger M. Grace, "Louisiana High Court: McIlhenny Libeled Rival 'Tabasco' Maker," *Metropolitan News-Enterprise* (Los Angeles), September 2, 2004; Roger M. Grace, "U.S. Appeals Court Confers Victory on McIlhennys," *Metropolitan News-Enterprise* (Los Angeles), September 9, 2004; Roger M. Grace, "Facts, as Portrayed by McIlhennys, Accounted for Fifth Circuit Victory," *Metropolitan News-Enterprise* (Los Angeles), September 16, 2004; Roger M. Grace, "McIlhenny Wins Another Bout over Use of Word 'Tabasco'," *Metropolitan News-Enterprise* (Los Angeles), September 23, 2004; Roger M. Grace, "Rival Louisiana Hot Sauce Makers Engage in Heated Litigation," *Metropolitan News-Enterprise* (Los Angeles), September 30, 2004; Amal Naj, *Peppers: A Story of Hot Pursuits* (New York: Knopf, 1992), pp. 163, 169–171.

page 107 *Bernard F. Trappey, who was well acquainted with the McIlhennys, led the charge against this questionable trademark*: The saga of the Trappey family's ultimately futile attempts to win the right to call its pepper sauce Tabasco is examined in these sources: Dave DeWitt and Nancy Gerlach, "Seas of Hot Sauces," *Chili Pepper,* May–June, 1990; Naj, *Peppers,* pp. 155, 156, 159, 168, 171–174; Richard Schweid, *Hot Peppers: The Story of Cajuns and Capsicum* (Chapel Hill: University of North Carolina Press, 1999), pp. 34–37, 78, 93, 117–118.

page 115 *Bayer had conspired in making the name generic, the court said*: Bayer Co. v. United Drug Co., 272 F. 505 (S.D.N.Y. 1921), http://cyber.law.harvard.edu/metaschool/fisher/domain/tmcases/bayer.htm.

page 115 *while DuPont held the sole claim to Dacron*: Commenting on DuPont's strategy, Steve Weinberg, one of the nation's foremost brand-management attorneys, said, "To protect a trademark a company should give potential competitors room to operate in the marketplace without infringing on its brand by establishing and promoting a generic name that the product could be called as well. And a company must enforce that trademark any time anyone tries to adopt it in any way." Weinberg successfully led one of the more intriguing trademark battles in recent memory, pitting client Play-Doh against its modeling-clay rival, Fun Dough. In what is now called the famous mark doctrine, Weinberg argued that Fun Dough was in violation of Play-Doh's trademark because it attempted to piggyback on the success of a widely recognizable brand by introducing a product with a similar name. Concurring with Weinberg, the courts ruled that well-known brands are entitled to a broader scope of protection from trademark infringement, a notion that the McIlhennys have had at the heart of their trademark protection strategy for more than a century.

page 116 *The extent of McIlhenny's legal activities was evident in the in-house attorney's office*: Steven Prokesch, "McIlhenny Finally Bestirs Itself," *New York Times*, June 29, 1986.

page 116 *But by far the most bizarre trademark infringement brouhaha*: Naj, *Peppers*, pp. 175–176.

Chapter 8: Tango

page 122 *E. A. McIlhenny broke ground for the new Tabasco company village*: Architectural drawings of some of the houses and buildings in Tango and Salt Village can be seen in *Built in America*:

Historic American Buildings Survey/Historic American Engineering Record, 1933–Present, U.S. Library of Congress, Washington, D.C. (http://memory.loc.gov/ammem/collections/habs_haer).

page 124 *It would indeed be ironic if the name* Tango Village: *ToTango: A History of Argentine Tango* (http://www.totango.net/sergio.html).

page 125 *in 1933, E.A. published a book of African slave songs*: E. A. McIlhenny, *Befo' 'de War Spirituals* (Boston: Christopher Publishing, 1933).

page 125 *"by these two old darkies"*: E. A. McIlhenny Natural History Collection, Louisiana State University, Baton Rouge, Louisiana.

page 125 *What's now known as the New Iberia incident occurred*: For an excellent and detailed recounting of this racial episode and a book worth reading cover to cover, see Adam Fairclough, *Race and Democracy: The Civil Rights Struggle in Louisiana, 1915–1972* (Athens: University of Georgia Press, 1995), pp. 84–98, 186, 406, 418–419, 498.

page 126 *taken to Sheriff Gilbert Ozenne's office*: In a strange bit of historical coincidence, Sheriff Ozenne turns out to be the great-uncle of Louisiana governor Kathleen Blanco. Blanco, who has Cajun roots, grew up on a sugarcane farm in Grand Coteau, a tiny village within earshot of New Iberia, whose only landmark is the Our Lady of Prompt Succor Church. During a visit to her hometown, Blanco had proudly spoken about her great-uncle, although she had not known about the New Iberia incident and his role in violently evicting black professionals from the community. "He was a great guy, with sparkly blue eyes," she said. Adam Nossiter, "Blanco's Acadian Heritage: Cautious, Deliberate, Insular," Associated Press, December 21, 2003.

page 127 *but neglects to say that these men—all of them physicians—were forcibly expelled*: Glenn Conrad, *New Iberia* (Lafayette: Center for Louisiana Studies at the University of Southwestern Louisiana, 1986).

page 127 *The McIlhennys chose to publicly keep mum*: In fact, this episode was so well concealed that Susan Dorsey didn't find out that her grandfather, E.L., had been terrorized by white police into leaving New Iberia until she was in her mid-twenties and graduated from Southern University Law Center in Baton Rouge. At Southern University, Dorsey had two roommates who, by coincidence, were from New Iberia, a city she knew only by name as the place that her father and grandfather were from. During a school break, Dorsey traveled to New Iberia for the first time with her roommates. "As soon as my roommates' families heard about my background, they said, 'I know who you are,'" Dorsey said. "But I couldn't get them to say any more. They clammed up." A few years later, Dorsey passed the Louisiana bar and decided to move to St. Mary Parish, adjacent to Iberia Parish, to practice law. When she was introduced at state court for the first time, Fifth Circuit judge John Duhé shook her hand and asked where she was from. "I said my grandfather was the first black physician in New Iberia, and he said, 'Oh, you're that Dorsey,' but nothing else," Dorsey related. "I called my father; I had to know what was going on. And he finally told me the whole story. I wasn't shocked or mad. For me, it was validation in a sense: considering what my grandfather went through, I knew that this was the right place for me to practice law."

page 128 *Doc Russell, E.A.'s black childhood playmate, was buried there*: John McNulty, *The World of John McNulty* (Garden City, New York: Doubleday, 1967), p. 218.

Chapter 9: Nirvana

page 135 *his passion for nature produced a backdrop of wild landscapes*: Edward Avery McIlhenny's remarkable recasting of Avery

Island's landscape is captured in detail in Herman B. Deutsch, "The Bird That's Not on Nellie's Hat," *Saturday Evening Post*, October 14, 1939; Harris Dickson, "The Promotion of Bird City," *Saturday Evening Post*, February 10, 1934; E. A. McIlhenny Natural History Collection, Louisiana State University, Baton Rouge, Louisiana; David S. Oakes, "Isle of Spice," *Central Manufacturing District Magazine*, date unknown.

page 140 *the environment McIlhenny designed was a stunning tableau*: For the most unexpected and artful homage to McIlhenny's botanical efforts, read the eerie short story "Avery Island," written by Costa Rican writer Victoria Urbano. She tells a phantasmagorical tale of being held captive in its giant bamboo thickets and valleys of live oaks and forced to face taboo truths about her sexuality and lovers. Victoria Urbano, ed., *Five Women Writers of Costa Rica* (Beaumont, Tex.: Asociacion de Literatura Femenina Hispanica, 1978).

page 143 *it would seem E.A. would have been hard-pressed to find time to protect a dying species* Accounts of the development of Bird City on Avery Island are available in Dickson, "Promotion of Bird City"; Oakes, "Isle of Spice."

page 148 *the nutria fur frenzy in the United States took flight*: "Avery Island the Enduring Star of 1948 Film, 'Louisiana Story,'" *New Orleans Times-Picayune*, March 25, 2001; Martha Carr, "Nutria Tales: The Rat's Out of the Bag; Tabasco Mogul Didn't Bring Rodents Here," *New Orleans Times-Picayune*, September 29, 2002; Sam Smith, "Fur Trappers Are Taking On the Scourge of the Marshlands," *New York Times*, May 28, 2002.

page 150 *stained by a nickel-and-dime incident*: "Education Boards End McIlhenny's Landscape Work," *New Orleans Times-Picayune*, April 17, 1940; "Leche, McIlhenny Charges in L.S.U. Garden Contract," *New Orleans Times-Picayune*, September 28,

1940; "Naturalist Puts Up Bond of $5,000 on Fraud Charge," *New Orleans Times-Picayune*, October 1, 1940.

page 152 *He died on August 8, 1949, at the age of seventy-seven*: "Famed Louisiana Naturalist Dies," *New Orleans Times-Picayune*, August 9, 1949; "Edward A. M'Ilhenny, Explorer and Writer," *Washington Post*, August 9, 1949.

Chapter 10: Sic Semper Fidelis

page 156 *"I could have been a typical rich man's brat"*: Eric Morgenthaler, "Walter S. McIlhenny Makes Tabasco Sauce in Milieu of Old South," *Wall Street Journal*, January 10, 1975.

page 157 *Walter came back to Avery Island a military legend*: James Conaway, "On Avery Island, Tabasco Sauce Is the Spice of Life," *Smithsonian Magazine*, May 1984; "Brigadier General Walter S. McIlhenny USMCR (Deceased)," www.sec.state.la.us/archives/Marines/marine-mcilhenny.htm.

page 158 *At precisely 11:00 every morning, Walter arrived at the Tabasco factory*: Conaway, "On Avery Island, Tabasco Sauce Is the Spice of Life"; Phyllis C. Richman, "Pepper Sauce with a Pedigree," *Washington Post*, June 8, 1983.

page 159 *under Walter, it was a more starchy, anachronistic affair*: Marion Burros, "The Heat Is On; Hot Sauces Are Burning Their Way across America," *New York Times*, March 18, 1998; Conaway, "On Avery Island, Tabasco Sauce Is the Spice of Life"; John McNulty, *The World of John McNulty* (Garden City, New York: Doubleday, 1967), pp. 218–220.

page164 *The possibility of expanding international sales, though, was an attractive alternative*: Morgenthaler, "Walter S. McIlhenny Makes Tabasco Sauce in Milieu of Old South."

Chapter 11: New Iberia Connection

page 180 *plying literary guests like Henry Miller, Gertrude Stein and Sherwood Anderson with plenty of brandy*: Henry Miller traveled to New Iberia in the early 1940s and was instantly charmed by the region's unorthodoxy. An iconoclast himself who had left what he perceived as the amoral materialism of the United States to seek a more pristine existence in France, Miller believed that something beyond the blending of cultures was responsible for New Iberia's singularity. In his view, the remoteness of the area——buried deep in the nation, disconnected from the mainstream of intellectual and cultural currents——produced an atypical American. "Here there are more eccentric, bizarre characters, I imagine, than any other part of the United States," Miller wrote about the South in an essay on New Iberia in *The Air-Conditioned Nightmare*. "The South breeds character, not sterile intellectualism. With certain individuals the fact that they are shut off from the world tends to bring about a forced bloom . . . They live a rich, quiet life of their own, in harmony with their environment and free of the petty ambitions and rivalries of the man of the world." Henry Miller, *The Air-Conditioned Nightmare* (New York: New Directions, 1945), p. 108.

page 181 *he convinced a town priest to bury jazz cornetist Bunk Johnson:* Jonathan Williams, *The Magpie's Bagpipe: Selected Essays of Jonathan Williams* (New York: North Point Press, 1982).

Chapter 12: Hot Enough for You?

page 185 *Walter McIlhenny died on June 22, 1985*: "Tabasco King Dies at 74," *New Orleans Times-Picayune,* June 23, 1985; Wolfgang Saxon, "W. M'Ilhenny Dies; Maker of Tabasco," *New York Times,* June 24, 1985; "Louisiana's Walter S. McIlhenny Dies; Tabasco Sauce Scion Felled by Stroke," *Los Angeles Times,* June 26, 1985.

page 187 *had suddenly seized the fancy of the mainstream public*: Marion Burros, "The Heat Is On; Hot Sauces Are Burning Their Way across America," *New York Times,* March 18, 1998; Kathleen

Deveny, "Rival Hot Sauces Are Breathing Fire at Market Leader Tabasco," *Wall Street Journal,* January 7, 1993; Dave DeWitt, "Why Chiles Conquered America," http://www.fiery-foods.com/dave/hot_us.asp; Dave Hirschkop, "Some Like It Really Hot," *San Francisco Chronicle,* January 10, 2003; Sharon Huntington, "A Brief History of Hot Stuff," *Christian Science Monitor,* February 3, 2004.

page 189 *Wilbur Lincoln Scoville is not the sort of person*: Amal Naj, *Peppers: A Story of Hot Pursuits* (New York: Knopf, 1992), pp. 10, 25–28.

page 189 *Scoville wrote in a report to the* Journal of the American Pharmaceutical Association: Ibid., p. 25.

page 193 *At a Fiery Foods show in Albuquerque, New Mexico*: Larry W. Greenly, "Extreme Hot & Spicy: Today's Hot Sauces Unlike Those of Yesteryear," www.fiery-foods.com/zine-industry/showtime.asp; Sue Anne Pressley, "At Fiery Foods Show, Check Tongue at Door; Aficionados Heat Up a $2 Billion Annual Industry," *Washington Post,* August 24, 1997.

Chapter 13: The Outsider

page 206 *But now Simmons was telling the board such insularity may have, particularly recently, placed the company in jeopardy*: Simmons seemed to acknowledge this handicap some years earlier when he told a reporter in 1986, "We have gotten big enough that we cannot manage the company without outside talent." Steven Prokesch, "McIlhenny Finally Bestirs Itself," *New York Times,* June 29, 1986.

ACKNOWLEDGMENTS

My heartfelt thanks to my agent, John Ware. Pondering a bottle of Tabasco sauce while sipping his Virgin Mary, John had the sudden inspiration that this world-class product made in little-known Avery Island by an even lesser-known family surely would be a perfect topic for a wonderful story. It was my good fortune that John decided to share his inspiration with me. On his suggestion, I did some research into the McIlhennys and their curious operation in deepest Louisiana. Not surprisingly, John's instincts were right. Tabasco sauce—and everything that has gone into making it for 140 years—was a wonderful subject. But John was more than merely an ideas man on this project. His help during the crafting of the proposal and his editing in the early stages of the manuscript were invaluable.

This book has been blessed with an extraordinary amount of support at Collins, more than I could have hoped for. Thanks to Marion Maneker, Collins publisher, who backed the book from the moment he read the proposal; he visualized the unusual arc in the story line immediately. Leah Nathans Spiro, my first editor (well, actually, my second editor—but that's a long tale), also deserves my deep gratitude. A colleague from an earlier time in our careers, we met again at Collins, and Leah's support and encouragement, as well as her advice to let the narrative unwind, one step at a time, was the perfect guidance at just the right time.

Special thanks, above all, to the book's last editor, Genoveva Llosa. Arriving at the end of the project, after a first draft had already been written, Genoveva nonetheless gave it unwavering attention. Her effort and commitment showed in her dedication to making certain that the language, tone and structure of the book was consistent throughout and together struck the right chord. To my good fortune, Genoveva is an editor with a great amount of skill and a great deal of energy. In many ways, the book is a testament to her hard work.

During my research I met many wonderful people in New Iberia and Avery Island who patiently spent hours and hours with me sharing old and new recollections about the McIlhennys, Iberia Parish and the mores of the Deep South. Too many to mention, but some stand out: Gene Jefferies, Ed and Pal Terrell, Joseph DuBois, Simon and Linda Freyou, Danny Bullaird, Edward Greenleaf, Dorothy Spencer, James and Susan Edmunds, Michael Bell, Joe Lopez, W.J. Trappey, Raleigh Rogers and Susan Dorsey.

Thanks also to my friends who had to put up with Tabasco stories for many years and, probably without knowing, encouraged me by their apparent interest and, since most of them are excellent writers, good advice. I'm grateful to Jim and Gina Vescovi, Will and Karen Balliett, Felix Kessler, Jill Larson and Michael Eskin.

And a most special thanks to Claudia Weinstein and my good buddy, her daughter Noa; you need love when you're obsessing about one topic for more than three years. They gave it.

INDEX

Louisiana cuisine, 38, 39–43
Lunsford, J. Rodgers, 114
Lunsford, Julius, 114
Lutes, Dave, 195

Manufacturing process, 58–59
Marine Military Academy, 158
Marketing
  current, 220
  Vince Pierse and, 207–211
  Edmund McIlhenny and, 18–20
  Edward Avery McIlhenny and, 95–
    96, 153
  premarketing campaign, 51
Marsh, George, 25
Marsh, John Craig, 22–25
Mars Inc., 206
Mars, John, 206
Mass production technologies, 58
Maunsel White's Concentrated Es-
  sence of Tabasco Peppers, 42,
  109
McCormick reaper, 50
McIlhenny, Ann (nee Newcomer),
  14
McIlhenny, Edmund, 1
  on automation, 61–63
  Avery Island as company town and,
    8–9, 69–73
  birth and childhood, 14
  chile experimentation, 3
  death of, 75
  early banking career, 15, 17–18
  entrepreneurial nature, 37, 44–45
  father-in-law's feelings toward, 2,
    26–27
  marketing "fable," 2–4
  marriage to Mary Eliza Avery, 13–
    14
  Maunsel White and, 44–45
  in New Orleans, 15–20, 35–36
  Petit Anse ownership and, 54
  plantation life and, 63–64
  recipe development, 47–48
  red pepper plant discovery, 2–3
  sales and marketing skills of, 18–20
  salt mining and, 69–72

Southern Pacific railway line and, 178
Tabasco sauce invention, 196
McIlhenny, Edmund (great-great
  grandson), 116
McIlhenny, Edward Avery ("Mr.
  Ned"), 7, 85, 91–104
  appearance and personality, 96–97,
    98
  black workers and, 125–129
  business growth under, 99, 153–
    154
  childhood, 91–93
  construction of Baptist church for
    black workers, 129–130
  death of and preceding stroke, 152–
    153
  gardens of, 142–143
  "healing" skills of, 139–140
  Leche and LSU landscaping inci-
    dent, 151–152
  management style, 104
  manufacturing system designed by,
    100–103
  marriage of, 121
  as naturalist, 93–94, 143–148
  nutria fur commercial project, 148–
    149
  plant selection for seed generation,
    103–104
  sales strategies, 95–96, 153
  spiritual world view, 142
  Tango Village and, 120–124, 136–
    137, 140–141
  trademarking issues, 110–111
  work habits, 135–136
McIlhenny, Jack, 88
McIlhenny, John, 14
McIlhenny, John Avery, 7, 79–85,
  147
  death of, 90
  mass marketing efforts, 81–82
  as politician and world traveler, 84
  product extension efforts, 82–83
  in Roosevelt administration, 90
  as Rough Rider, 84
  salt mine "ball," 86–87
  trademarking efforts, 107, 110–114

ABOUT THE AUTHOR

A former *BusinessWeek* editor and national editor at Bloomberg News, Jeffrey Rothfeder has written for publications from the *New York Times* to the *Washington Post*, has spoken at congressional hearings, and has appeared on numerous national television and radio programs, including *20/20*, *Nightline*, *Nova*, *Today*, *Good Morning America*, *The Oprah Winfrey Show*, and *All Things Considered*. His articles have also appeared in *Playboy*, *Popular Science*, *Chief Executive*, *Forbes*, *Consumer Reports*, and *Strategy+Business*.